RICHARD M. NIXON
1913 –

Chronology - Documents - Bibliographical Aids

Edited by
HOWARD F. BREMER

Series Editor
HOWARD F. BREMER

Oceana Publications, Inc.
Dobbs Ferry, New York 10522
1975

Library of Congress Cataloging in Publication Data

Nixon, Richard Milhous, 1913-
    Richard M. Nixon, 1913.

    Bibliography: p.
    Includes index.
    SUMMARY: A chronology of the life of former
president Richard M. Nixon, a compilation of twenty-
four of his speeches, and a bibliography of books,
articles, and documents by and about him.
    1. United States--Politics and government--1969-
1974--Sources. 2. Nixon, Richard Milhous,
1913- -- Chronology. [1. United States--Politics
and government--1969-1974--Sources.
    2. Nixon, Richard Milhous, 1913- --Chronology.
I. United States. President, 1969-1974 (Nixon)
II. Bremer, Howard F.
E838.5.N57   973.924'092'4   75-23324
ISBN 0-379-12083-6

Manufactured in the United States of America

CONTENTS   163087

EDITOR'S FOREWORD.   v

CHRONOLOGY
    Early Life (1913-1947)   1
    Congressman and Senator (1947-1953).   3
    Vice President (1953-1961)   5
    Lawyer and Politician (1961-1969).   10
    First Term (1969-1973)   16
    Second Term (1973-1974).   61
    Retirement (1974).   79

DOCUMENTS
    My Side of the Story, September 23, 1952   85
    Principles of U.S. Government, December 9, 1963.   95
    Inaugural Address, January 20, 1969.   96
    Campus Revolutionaries, June 3, 1969   101
    America's Role in the World, June 4, 1969.   107
    President's State of the Union Message,
       January 22, 1970   113
    Cambodia, April 31, 1970   122
    State of the Union Message, January 22, 1971   128
    United States -- Peoples Republic of China,
       July 15, 1971.   138
    A New Economic Policy, August 15, 1971   140
    The Economic Plan, October 7, 1971   146
    State of the Union Message, January 20, 1972   151
    A Trip for World Peace, February 28, 1972.   160
    Address to the People of the Soviet Union,
       May 28, 1972   163
    The Moscow Summit, June 1, 1972.   168
    The Republican Candidate for President,
       August 23, 1972.   175
    Second Inaugural Address, January 20, 1973   184
    Ending the War and Restoring Peace,
       January 23, 1973   188
    The Indochina Conflict, March 29, 1973   191
    The Watergate Affair, April 30, 1973   197
    The Watergate Charges, August 15, 1973   203
    State of the Union Address, January 30, 1974   211
    Presidential Tapes and Materials, April 29, 1974   222
    Presidential Resignation, August 8, 1974   232

BIBLIOGRAPHY
    Nixon's Writings   237
    Nixon: Biographies, Campaigns, Domestic Policies, Foreign
       Policies   238
    Periodicals.   242
    Watergate.   242

NAME INDEX   247

EDITOR'S FOREWORD

In this Chronology every attempt has been made to cite the most accurate dates. The problem in modern times is a different one. The amount of information available is so voluminous, the decisions and appointments so complex and numerous, that the major problem is one of selection of the more important ones. This involves a subjective judgment on the part of the editor, but it is hoped it is a reasoned judgment based on a long experience in dealing with historical events.

The events of Watergate have, of course, complicated the task. Future revelations and developments will undoubtedly add new information. At the moment, Watergate has been the tragedy in the administration of Richard M. Nixon and has seriously affected our judgment of his presidency. But every attempt has been made to present a balanced account of his entire period in office, his triumphs as well as his failures.

This is a research tool compiled primarily for the student. It is hoped that the presentation of the more significant events and documents, plus a critical bibliography, will stimulate the budding scholar to undertake additional research for background and the resolution of contradictory evidence.

Many thanks are due to a host of librarians, whose patient aid is much appreciated. A special note of gratitude is owed to my typist and proofreader, my daughter Wendy Ciliberti.

Howard F. Bremer
Professor Emeritus of History
Briarcliff College

CHRONOLOGY

1913   January 9. Born, Yorba Linda, California. Father, Frank; Mother, Hannah. The Quaker family soon moved to Whittier, California, a Quaker community where the father ran a general store.

1918-1926   Attended Whittier Grammar School.

1927-1928   Attended Buena Park High School in Fullerton, California, winning an oratorical contest and starring at debating.

1928-1930   Transferred to Whittier High School for his last two years. Still starred at oratory and debating.

1930-1934   Attended Whittier College, a local Quaker institution, majoring in history. Tried out for football without much success. But did excel in campus politics, being elected president of the student body.

1934   May 19. Awarded scholarship of $250 for Duke University Law School.

June. Graduated from Whittier College, second in class.

1934-1937   Attended Duke University Law School. Was graduated in June, 1937, third in class.

1937   November 9. Sworn in as member of San Francisco bar. Returned to Whittier to join the law firm of Wengert and Bewley.

1938   Met future wife "Pat" at a Little Theater group. Pat, a teacher of commercial subjects at Whittier High School, had been graduated from the University of Southern California in 1937 and prior to that had played bit parts in movies.

June 15. Registered in Whittier as a Republican.

1940   June 21. Married Thelma Catherine "Pat" Ryan at Mission Inn, Riverside.

1942   January 9. Began work in the tire rationing
                    section of the Office of Price Administration
                    in Washington, D.C.

                    March. Applied for Navy Commission.

                    September 2. Began training as a Navy Lieu-
                    tenant, junior grade, at Quonset, Rhode Is-
                    land. Shortly after assumed first post at
                    a naval air base at Ottumwa, Iowa.

1943   May. Sent to the South Pacific to set up
                    temporary bases for the Air Transport Com-
                    mand. Won popularity for "Nixon's Snack
                    Shack," a free hamburger shack for transient
                    flight crews. Was also known as a poker
                    player "who never lost a cent."

1944   Fall. Returned to San Francisco and subse-
                    quently to Washington as a lieutenant com-
                    mander on the Navy's legal staff.

1945   August. Republicans in California's Twelfth
                    Congressional District formed a candidate-
                    finding "Committee of One Hundred" to unseat
                    ten-year Representative Jerry Voorhis.

                    September 29. While in Baltimore, still in
                    the Navy and handling contract terminations
                    received expense check to fly to California
                    where he was offered the candidacy at a meet-
                    ing of the Committee of One Hundred at the
                    William Penn Hotel, Whittier.

1946   January. Retired from the Navy and returned
                    to California, setting up an office in Whit-
                    tier.

                    February 12. Announced candidacy for the
                    House of Representatives. Began campaign un-
                    der the tutelage of Murray Chotiner, Los An-
                    geles lawyer and campaign adviser to William
                    Knowland. Unfriendly biographers charge that
                    Nixon learned "dirty tricks" from Chotiner
                    and used them to discredit Voorhis.

                    February 21. Daughter, Patricia, born.

                    March 19. Filed in both the Democratic and
                    Republican primaries.

                    November 5. Nixon elected 64,784 to Voorhis'

49,431, to the Eightieth Congress, Republican dominated and made famous by President Truman's name for it as the "Do-Nothing Congress."

CONGRESSMAN AND SENATOR
1947-1953

1947   January 3. Sworn in as member of Congress. Was named to the Labor Committee, where he helped draft the Taft-Hartley Labor Law, and to the Un-American Activities Committee.

February 18. Delivered maiden speech in House, speaking for a contempt citation against Communist Gerhart Eisler.

August-October. Was appointed a member of a foreign aid study committee under the chairmanship of Christian Herter. His travel through Europe marked his first experience in foreign policy.

1948   May 14. Sponsored with Karl Mundt a Mundt-Nixon Communist Control bill requiring the registration of Communist and Communist-control groups. Passed in the House but was defeated in the Senate.

July 5. Daughter, Julie, born.

August 3. Whittaker Chambers, appearing before the House Committee on Un-American Activities testified that he had known Alger Hiss as a Communist in the Thirties. Hiss, a former State Department official who had been at Yalta with President Roosevelt, was now President of the Carnegie Endowment.

August 5. Alger Hiss denied knowing a man by the name of Chambers, and that he had ever been a Communist. President Truman called the case "a red herring."

August 10. Nixon visited Chambers at his Maryland farm and came away convinced of Hiss's guilt. He proceeded to fight the case against Hiss.

November 2. Re-elected to Congress, the eighty-first, winning by three thousand votes over Stephen Zetterberg, his Democratic opponent.

December 15. Alger Hiss indicted for perjury after denying he passed secret documents to Whittaker Chambers.

1949   November 3. Announced his candidacy for the Senate in a dinner speech at Los Angeles, running against Congresswoman Helen Gahagan Douglas, the actress.

1950   January 21. After an earlier trial had ended in a hung jury, 8 to 4 for conviction, a second trial found Hiss guilty of two counts of perjury. Hiss was sentenced to five years, served three years and eight months of his sentence, with time off for good behavior. The Hiss case made the young Nixon a national celebrity.

August 30. A "Pink Sheet" was issued which indicated the nature of the campaign, an attempt to link the voting records of Mrs. Douglas with that of the "notorious Communist party-liner," Vito Marcantonio, Congressman from New York.

October 10. Senator Joseph McCarthy spoke on Nixon's behalf over a regional network from Los Angeles, crying treason in the Truman Administration and calling for the resignation of Dean Acheson.

October 26. At a Los Angeles round table, called for the repudiation of the Yalta Pact.

November 7. Elected to the Senate over Helen G. Douglas 2,183,454 to 1,502,507.

1951   May. Attended conference of the World Health Organization at Geneva. Visited General Eisenhower in Paris.

April 11. President Truman's dismissal of General MacArthur led Nixon to propose a resolution demanding his reinstatement.

1952   May-June. Played a discreet back-of-the-scenes role in the Eisenhower-Taft-Warren presidential nomination struggle.

1952 July 11. Republican National Convention at Chicago, Illinois, nominated Nixon as the running mate to Dwight David Eisenhower.

  July 7-12. Meeting at Chicago, the Democrats nominated Governor Adlai Erving Stevenson of Illinois for President and Senator John Jackson Sparkman of Alabama for Vice President.

  September 18, Existence of a secret fund, contributed by Californians with various business interests, to help Nixon help pay political expenses, was disclosed in the press.

  September 19. The nation's press, two to one, called for Nixon's withdrawal. So did Harold Stassen, former governor of Minnesota, and a Republican leader.

  September 20. Eisenhower, campaigning in St. Louis, said he was taking his time, but that "Nixon has got to be clean as a hound's tooth." Tom Dewey advised a television appearance.

  September 23. Broadcast "Checkers" speech from Los Angeles over radio and television. The speech was obviously a "corny soap opera" but a political triumph. General Eisenhower "embraced" Nixon the next day.

  November 4. Eisenhower and Nixon were elected, receiving 442 electoral votes to their opponents' 89. The popular vote was 33,936,252 to 27,314,992.

VICE PRESIDENT
1953-1961

1953 January 20. Inaugurated, at 40, the second youngest Vice President in American history.

  August 13. Appointed Chairman of the President's committee on government contracts.

  October 6-December 14. Traveled extensively throughout Asia, in Australia and in New Zealand on good will tour.

1954   April 16. In off-the-record remarks before
            the American Society of Newspaper Editors,
            used the occasion for a "trial balloon" on
            the reaction to sending American troops to
            Vietnam.

            March-May. Attempted to mediate in the Mc-
            Carthy-Army feud, but without success. His
            early support for McCarthy disappeared after
            the Wisconsin Senator attacked President Ei-
            senhower and seemed to be splitting the Re-
            publican party.

1955   February 6-March 5. Traveled throughout Cen-
            tral America and the Caribbeans on a good
            will tour.

            September 24. President Eisenhower suffered
            heart attack at Denver, Colorado. He was
            hospitalized there, and returned to Washing-
            ton November 11. Vice President Nixon pre-
            sided over the cabinet meetings, but in no
            way became an "acting-president."

1956   February 12. Speaking at a Lincoln's Day
            dinner in New York City, boasted about Re-
            publican advances in the field of civil rights,
            especially "a great Republican Chief Justice,
            Earl Warren." Politicians and editors se-
            verely rebuked Nixon for bringing partisan-
            ship into the Supreme Court.

            February 29. President Eisenhower announced
            his availability for a second term. He had
            suggested to Nixon that the Vice President
            might be better off in a cabinet post.

            March 7. At a press conference President
            Eisenhower stated he had advised Nixon to
            "chart your own course." A Harold Stassen
            "dump Nixon movement" was in the works.

            April 26. Announced candidacy for second
            term as Vice President.

            June 8. President Eisenhower hospitalized
            to undergo an ileitis operation.

            August 22. Supported by Stassen's choice,
            Christian Herter, and by President Eisenhower,
            Nixon was easily renominated.

September 13. First visit to Eisenhower's
Gettysburg home.

November 6. Elected for second term as Vice
President. Eisenhower-Nixon received 457
electoral votes to Stevenson-Sparkman's 73.
The popular vote was 35,585,316 to 26,031,322.

1956   December 18-24. Traveled to Austria and Germany to inspect the Hungarian Refugee situation.

1957   January 3. During one of his infrequent uses
of his constitutional role as presiding of-
ficer of the Senate, incurred the wrath of
Senate conservatives in an antifilibuster
ruling.

February 28-March 21. Traveled in Africa
and Italy. On return reported on need for
aid for African states.

September 3. President Eisenhower sent Nixon
a memorandum which for the first time in history assigned a Vice President a major role
in foreign policy.

November 25. President Eisenhower suffered
a mild cerebral stroke. Fortunately, he recovered quickly, but the implications led to
an arrangement with Nixon which he made public the following February.

1958   February 26. President Eisenhower stated
that he had a clear understanding with Vice
President Nixon on what should be done if
he were incapacitated. The twenty-fifth a-
mendment later put this into the constitution.

April 27. Took off with Pat for an eighteen-
day tour of eight South American countries.
In many cities they were met by rioting,
stone-throwing crowds.

May 13. Violent mobs in Caracas, Venezuela
throwing objects at the Vice President's ca-
valcade, injured members of his staff and
seemed to threaten Nixon's life. President
Eisenhower ordered a rescue mission readied
(code name "Operation Poor Richard"). Authorities in Caracas were able to get things

under control.

May 15. Arrived back in Washington to receive a hero's welcome from President Eisenhower and other dignitaries.

November 24-29. Went to England for the dedication ceremonies of the American chapel at
St. Paul's.

September-November. The Vice President campaigned for Republicans up for election,
covering 33,000 miles in 32 states.

October 16. President Eisenhower warned Nixon against making foreign policy a partisan
issue in the election.

November 4. Nixon's efforts were in vain.
The Democrats gained fifteen Senate seats and
forty-six in the House.

1959   January 31. President Eisenhower named Nixon
chairman of a permanent cabinet committee on
price stability for economic growth.

July 22, Traveled to Moscow to open the
United States exhibition.

July 24. Carried on his famous "kitchen debate" with Khrushchev.

August 1. Spoke to the Russian people over
television.

August 2. Received a warm reception from
the Polish people on a stop off in Warsaw on
the way back to Washington.

August 5. Returned to Washington.

1960   March 16. President Eisenhower endorsed
Nixon as his successor.

July 13. Democratic National Convention in
Los Angeles, California, nominated John Fitz-
gerald Kennedy for President, and Lyndon
Baines Johnson for Vice President.

July 22. Met with Nelson Rockefeller in New
York City who refused to run for the Vice
Presidency. They then tried to reconcile

their differences in what has been termed
"The Treaty of Fifth Avenue" with debatable
success.

July 25-28. Republican National Convention
at Chicago, Illinois nominated Nixon for
President, with Henry Cabot Lodge as Vice
President.

August 3. Opened campaign in Hawaii.

August 24. President Eisenhower, at a press
conference, when asked "to give us an example
of a major idea of his (Nixon's) that you a-
dopted," replied, "If you give me a week I
might think of one."

September 26. First of a series of four
television debates with Kennedy broadcast
from Chicago, Illinois.

October 7. Kennedy challenged United States
involvement in the Formosa Strait and for a
time the debate raged around retreat from
Quemoy and Matsu.

October 19. After President Eisenhower proclaimed an embargo on Cuban trade, the debate turned to the correct stand toward Cas-
tro.

November. In retrospect, the election seemed
to be determined by the candidates' image,
rather than ideas. The youthful, handsome
Kennedy projected "vigor" compared with the
somber, jowly Nixon.

November 8. Narrowly lost election to Kennedy who received 303 electoral votes to his
219. The popular vote was Kennedy-Johnson
34,227,096 to Nixon-Lodge 34,108,546. Harry
F. Byrd (D., Va.) received 15 electoral
votes.

November 14. Met in conference with President - elect Kennedy at Key Biscayne, Florida.

December. Joined law firm of Adams, Duque,
and Hazeltine. Earl Adams of Los Angeles
had been one of the original Nixon supporters
in 1945. The Nixons bought a house in Bel
Air. His income approached $200,000 a year

and he began to move in the upper circles.

LAWYER AND POLITICIAN
1961-1969

1961   Wrote Six Crises - to be published in March,
            1962.

1962   June. Easily defeated Joseph Shell for the
            Republican nominee for governorship of Cali-
            fornia to run against Governor Edmund G.
            "Pat" Brown.

            Summer-Fall. During the campaign, his cam-
            paign manager was H. R. (Bob) Haldeman.
            Others involved were John D. Ehrlichman,
            Robert H. Finch, Murray Chotiner, Ronald L.
            Ziegler and Congressman Patrick J. Hillings,
            who had succeeded to Nixon's old seat. Also,
            Herbert G. Klein became his chief press ad-
            visor and spokesman. Rose Mary Woods, his
            personal secretary for over ten years, was a
            key member of his staff.

            October 7-10. Ex-President Eisenhower toured
            ten states campaiging for GOP candidates, in-
            cluding Nixon's gubernatorial campaign in
            California.

            October. A last minute campaign issue was
            made by the Democrats of a loan to Nixon's
            brother Don, by the Hughes Tool Company.

            November 7. Lost California governor's race
            to Brown by 300,000 votes. In his concession
            speech, Nixon shocked the press and the po-
            litical world by a bitter speech against the
            press, "You won't have Nixon to kick around
            any more...."

            November 11. A massive 80,000 telegrams and
            letters poured into ABC protesting a televi-
            sion special by Howard K. Smith called "The
            Political Obituary of Richard M. Nixon."
            Alger Hiss appeared briefly on the show.

1963   April. Attacked Kennedy's "concessions" on
            Castro during the Cuban Missile crisis the
            year before.

            June 1. Moved to New York and joined the

old established law firm of Mudge, Stern, Baldwin and Todd. He bought an expensive apartment in mid-town Manhattan. Nixon's name soon headed the firm.

Summer. Began series of overseas trips to meet leading personalities.

November 22. President Kennedy was assass-inated by Lee Harvey Oswald, a supporter of left-wing causes, in Dallas, Texas. Nixon had been in Dallas for a meeting the day be-fore, but back in New York, was dazed by the shocking news. He attended Kennedy's funeral in Washington.

December. Senator William Proxmire (D., Wis-consin), had inserted into the Congressional Record Nixon's answer to the requirement for winning admission to the bar in New York State, a statement on the principles under-lying our form of government. Proxmire re-ferred to it as a "classic description."

1964   July 13. Republican Convention met in San Francisco and nominated Senator Barry M. Goldwater (Ariz.) for President and Congress-man William E. Miller (N. Y.) for Vice Presi-dent. Nixon had been an earlier favorite by a small margin, although claiming he was not a candidate.

July-August. Nixon's attempts to unify the conservative and liberal factions in the Re-publican party were not aided by Goldwater's statement in his acceptance speech: "Ex-tremism in the defense of liberty is no vice ...moderation in the pursuit of justice is no virtue."

August 24. Democratic Convention met at At-lantic City, New Jersey and nominated Lyndon B. Johnson for President and Hubert H. Hum-phrey (Minn.) for Vice President.

September 30. Began a thirty-three day, thirty-six state speaking tour in support of the Goldwater-Miller ticket.

November 3. Johnson scored a landslide vic-tory over Goldwater, 486 electoral votes to 52.

December 9. Met with former President Eisenhower and Senator Barry Goldwater in New York
City for a private conference on the Republican party's position.

1965   October 24. While usually trying to picture
himself as a moderate, he aroused many liberals by his claim that the anti-war Rutgers
professor, Eugene D. Genovese, should be
fired for saying he would welcome a Viet Cong
victory.

1966   January. Hired political writer Patrick J.
Buchanan, the first outward signal of running
in '68. He spent the year mixing politics,
law and social activities.

Fall. Worked hard for Republican candidates
for Congress, trying to turn the election
into a referendum on LBJ.

October 23-25. President Johnson held an
Asian summit meeting in Manila where he made
an offer of a mutual withdrawal of forces
from South Vietnam. Nixon sharply criticized
it as a surrender, and this brought a sarcas-
tic, brutal, personal attack on Nixon from
LBJ.

November 5. Former President Eisenhower defended Nixon against charges of President
Johnson that Nixon was confusing the Allied
position in regard to the United States' pledge
to withdraw its troops from Vietnam if North
Vietnam did the same. Eisenhower called
Nixon "the best informed, most capable, and
most industrious Vice President in the history of the United States."

November 8. The Republicans made sweeping
gains in the elections, 47 in the House, 3
in the Senate, 8 governors. Nixon had created many debts for his efforts from the Republican party and was the likely candidate
for '68 even though behind George Romney in
the polls.

1967   January 1. John Newton Mitchell joined the
Nixon law firm. He and Nixon were old friends.

Toured in Europe with Representative Robert
Ellsworth (R., Kan.), and in South America

with old friend Bebe Rebozo.

August. Governor George Romney of Michigan
had been campaigning hard all year for the
Republican nomination. But he seriously hurt
his image by stating he had been "brainwashed"
while on his Vietnam tour in 1965.

November 30. Senator Eugene J. McCarthy of
Minnesota announced that he was a candidate
for the Democratic nomination, in other words,
an effort to dump Johnson and end the war.

Announced the engagement of his younger daughter, Julie, 19, to David Eisenhower, 19, the
former president's grandson.

1968   February 1. Formally announced his candidacy
for the presidency by filing for the New
Hampshire primary.

February 24. Governor Nelson Rockefeller of
New York still claimed he was not a candidate
and was backing Romney, though conceding he
might be drafted.

February 28. Romney withdrew his candidacy
after polls showed him running far behind in
New Hampshire.

March 12. Senator Eugene McCarthy (Minn.)
showed surprising strength in the New Hampshire Democratic primary. Nixon, as expected, won the Republican by a landslide.

March 16. Senator Robert Kennedy (N. Y.)
announced his candidacy for the Democratic
presidential nomination.

March 31. President Johnson announced that
he would neither seek nor accept another term.

April 2. Nixon easily won the Wisconsin primary, receiving 79.4% of the Republican vote.
Governor Reagan, who had not himself campaigned, received 11%. McCarthy was the
Democratic leader.

April 4. The Reverend Martin Luther King,
Jr., civil rights leader, was killed by a
sniper's bullet in Memphis, Tennessee. Most
of the candidates, Nixon among them, attended his funeral in Atlanta, Georgia.

April 27. Vice President Humphrey announced
his candidacy for the Democratic presidential nomination.

April 30. Governor Nelson Rockefeller (N.
Y.) announced his candidacy for the Republican presidential primary.

May. Nixon won primaries in Indiana, Nebras-
ka, and Oregon.

June 1. Met Senator Strom Thurmond (R., S.
C.) and cemented his "Southern strategy" by
winning over the defense-minded Senator by
assurances of a start on an Antiballistic
Missile system.

June 4. Senator Robert Kennedy was assass-
inated in Los Angeles the night he was winning the California Democratic presidential
primary. The assassin was a Palestinian Arab,
Sirhan B. Sirhan. The Nixons attended funeral services at St. Patrick's Cathedral in
New York City.

July 18. Former President Eisenhower, from
the Walter Reed Army Medical Center where he
was recuperating from a fifth heart attack,
endorsed Nixon for president.

August 8, With Governor Reagan entering the
race at the last minute, and the rival Gallup and Harris polls differing between Rockefeller and Nixon's strength, Nixon won the
nomination at Miami Beach, Florida on the
first ballot. The surprising choice for
Vice President was Governor Spiro T. Agnew
of Maryland, who had made Nixon's nominating
speech.

August 28. Vice President Humphrey won the
Democratic presidential nomination. On the
next day, Senator Edmund S. Muskie of Maine
was nominated for Vice President. The Chicago convention was marked by serious confron-
tations between agitators and police.

September-October. The Nixon campaign was
run like a well-oiled machine, staffed by
veteran supporters like Ehrlichman and Haldeman, plus press aides Klein and Ziegler.
The chief obstacle was Spiro Agnew's habit

of "putting his foot in his mouth."

October 3. George Wallace, American Inde-
pendant Party presidential nominee, named
retired air force general Curtis E. Le May
as his vice presidential running mate. Le
May's atom bomb threats probably ended any
chance Wallace might have had of throwing
the final vote to Congress.

October 7. The Supreme Court opened its
1968-69 term. Chief Justice Earl Warren pre-
sided, postponing his resignation until the
end of the term when President Johnson's
choice to succeed him, Associate Justice Abe
Fortas, met strong opposition in the Senate.

November 5. Elected to first term as President of the United States. Received 43% of
the popular vote. Nixon 31,785,480 (301
electoral votes), Humphrey 31,275,166 (191
electoral votes), Wallace 9,906,473 (46 electoral votes).

November 9. Announced that Vice President
Agnew would be given added policy-making re-
sponsibilities, with an office in the White
House.

November 11. Visited the White House for
briefings from President Johnson and his
aides.

November 14. Stated that President Johnson
had agreed not to make any major foreign
policy decisions without Nixon's approval.
The next day Johnson clarified the announcement by saying only he would make decisions
until Inauguration Day.

December 4. Was warned by President Johnson
that to try to end inflation too sharply
would risk a recession.

December 11. Presented his newly appointed
cabinet over nation wide television: Secretary of State William P. Rogers, Secretary
of the Treasury David Matthew Kennedy, Secretary of Defense Melvin R. Laird, Attorney
General John Newton Mitchell, Postmaster General Winton Malcolm Blount, Secretary of the
Interior Walter Joseph Hickel, Secretary of

Agriculture Clifford Morris Hardin, Secretary
of Commerce Maurice Hubert Stans, Secretary
of Labor George Pratt Shultz, Secretary of
Health, Education, and Welfare Robert Hutchinson Finch, Secretary of Housing and Urban
Development George Wilcken Romney, Secretary
of Transportation John Anthony Volpe.

December 14. Met with Israeli Defense Minister Moshe Dayan in New York City.

December 19. Purchased two houses in Key
Biscayne. Eventual expense to government of
$575,000 met much criticism.

December. Younger daughter Julie was married
to David Eisenhower, grandson of ex-president
Dwight D. Eisenhower.

December 28. Ordered his foreign policy advisors to consider the options which might
be open to the United States in Vietnam.

1969   January 3. The Ninety-first Congress convened. Nixon began his term facing a Congress controlled by the opposition party,
the first president since Zachary Taylor in
1849 to do so.

January 5. Named Henry Cabot Lodge to replace W. Averell Harriman as chief United
States negotiator at the Paris peace talks
on Vietnam.

FIRST TERM

January 20. Took the oath of office, admin-
istered by Chief Justice Earl Warren, and
thus inaugurated as the 37th President of
the United States. Spiro T. Agnew became
the 39th Vice President.

Other key appointments: Henry A. Kissinger,
principal advisor on foreign policy; H. R.
Haldeman, White House Chief of Staff; John
D. Ehrlichman, Counsel to the President;
Dwight L. Chapin, Special Assistant to the
President as appointments secretary; Hugh W.
Sloan, Jr., Staff Assistant to the President;
Herbert G. Klein, newly created position of
Director of Communications for the executive

branch; Egil Krogh and Edward L. Morgan, deputy counsels, reporting to Ehrlichman.

January 23. All cabinet appointees confirmed
with the Senate's approval of Walter J. Hickel as secretary of the interior.

January 30. Told Defense Department to develop a plan to end the draft and rely on a
volunteer army.

February 5. Announced the end of political
patronage in the U.S. postal service. Asked
for prompt ratification of the treaty to
halt the spread of nuclear weapons.

February 14. Announced appointment of John
W. Dean, III as associate deputy attorney
general and chief aide to Kleindienst. Appointed Vice President Agnew to head a White
House Office of Intergovernmental Relations.

February 15. Willie Mae Rogers resigned as
the President's consultant on consumer affairs after serving five days.

February 19. Announced decision to transfer
all programs in Head Start and the Job Corps
from the Office of Economic Opportunity to
the established departments.

February 20. Requested legislation from Congress to revise the presidential election
procedure.

Named John Eisenhower, the former President's
son, to be ambassador to Belgium. Confirmed
by Senate March 13.

February 23. Arrived in Brussels to begin
an eight day European tour. He was accompanied by Henry Kissinger, the trip's chief
planner.

March 2. Returned to Washington after European tour.

March 4. Warned that the U.S. would take appropriate action against a new Viet Cong offensive.

March 10. Received report from Secretary of

Defense Melvin R. Laird on the completion of
a fact-finding visit to South Vietnam.

March 11. Appointed John N. Irwin as a special envoy to attempt a solution of differences between the U.S. and Peru.

March 13. The Senate approved the international agreement to prevent the spread of nuclear weapons, 83 to 15.

March 14. Asked Congress to approve a modified Sentinal antiballistic missile program.

Stated that there was no prospect of a reduction of United States forces in Vietnam.

March 22. Said that the problem of handling
student protests should be dealt with by college authorities.

March 26. Asked Congress to extend the 10%
income tax surcharge for one year.

March 27. Date written on deed of pre-Presidential papers, valued at $576,000 to the Na-
tional Archives. The deed was actually made
on April 10, 1970, but back dated to permit
its use as a charitable deduction on his 1969
tax return. The Tax Reform Act of 1969 which
went through Congress late in the year and
which the President signed on December 30,
made such deductions invalid if made after
July 25, 1969. Edward L. Morgan, on John D.
Ehrlichman's staff, was later (December 19,
1974) sentenced to four months in prison for
his part in the illegal act.

March 28. Dwight David Eisenhower, 34th president of the United States, died in Washington, D. C.

April 1. Conferred separately with 12 world
leaders who were in Washington to attend the
funeral of President Eisenhower.

April 4. Announced some relaxation of controls over United States lending and invest-
ments in foreign countries.

April 7. Signed a bill increasing the National debt ceiling from $358 billion to $365 bil-

lion. Permitted additional temporary increase
of $12 billion through June 30, 1970.

April 8. Announced that $200 million was a-
vailable for reconstruction in 20 cities suffering riot damage.

Held talks with King Hussein of Jordan at the
White House.

April 9. Appointed Virginia Harrington Wright
Knauer to succeed Betty Furness as special
assistant for consumer affairs.

April 11. Announced a severe reduction of
the Job Corps program.

April 12. Announced a $4 billion reduction
in the federal budget for the fiscal year
1970.

April 14. Outlined ten programs in domestic
areas which he planned to submit to Congress.

April 17. Sirhan Sirhan convicted of first
degree murder in the killing of Senator Robert
F. Kennedy.

April 18. Ordered the resumption of United
States reconnaissance flights off North Korea,
claiming that the attack on a United States
plane on April 15 was a calculated act of aggression.

April 21. Sent message to Congress asking
for a 50% reduction in the 10% income tax
surcharge, effective January, 1970 and a repeal of the 7% investment credit.

April 22. His advisors began discussions of
tax reform proposals with Congressional leaders.

April 23. Proposed a new attack on organized
crime by the federal government.

April 30. Asked Congress for authority to
consolidate all federal aid programs to states
and cities.

May. Wiretaps to disclose leaks to newspapers were initiated this month at the request

of Henry Kissinger to J. Edgar Hoover.

May 6. Navy Secretary John H. Chafee said
that there would be no disciplinary action
taken against the crew of the "Pueblo."

May 9. Secretary of State Rogers announced
that the South Vietnamese and the United
States were agreed that elements of the peace
plan offered by the National Liberation Front
could be a basis for discussion.

Disclosure in New York Times of secret United
States bombing of Cambodia led to F.B.I. wire-
taps placed on suspected sources of leaks.
Involved in requesting the taps were Henry A.
Kissinger, his deputy, General Alexander M.
Haig, and, according to Kissinger, Nixon him-
self. J. Edgar Hoover, F.B.I. head, agreed.

No agreement was reached at the conclusion
of the second stage of talks between the
United States and Peru.

May 11-19. New York Governor Nelson A. Rockefeller left for Central America, beginning
the first of four fact-finding missions at
the request of the President.

May 13. Proposed legislation to revise the
military draft system.

May 14. Proposed a peace plan which, in part,
would provide for the mutual withdrawal of
United States and North Vietnamese troops from
South Vietnam.

May 15. Associate Justice Abe Fortas resigned
from the Supreme Court following charges of
unethical financial conduct. Thus, Nixon had
an opportunity to appoint another conservative to the Court besides a Chief Justice to
replace resigning Earl Warren.

May 21. Nominated Warren E. Burger, a judge
of the United States Court of Appeals for the
District of Columbia, to become Chief Justice
of the Supreme Court.

May 23. Peru canceled the proposed visit of
Governor Rockefeller after the United States
halted sales of military equipment in retalia-

tion for Peruvian seizures of United States
tuna fishing boats.

May 27. Governor Rockefeller arrived in Bo-
gotá, Columbia, to begin his second fact-
finding tour of Latin America.

President Nixon asked Congress to convert
the Post Office Department into a public corporation.

May 28. Asked for $2.6 billion in foreign
aid, the smallest amount in the history of
the program.

May 31. Governor Rockefeller forced to cut
short his visit to Bolivia in face of threats
of massive protests.

June 1. Governor Rockefeller was requested
by President Rafael Caldera of Venezuela to
postpone his visit to that country.

June 3. Speaking on a college campus in Madison, South Dakota, President Nixon spoke
out against violence by college students.

June 4. Speaking at the Air Force Academy
in Colorado Springs, President Nixon criticized those whose attacks were aimed at the
military-industrial complex.

June 5. The United States has become a
"bloody-minded people in both action and re-
action," was the finding of a study group
of the National Commission of the Causes and
Prevention of Violence.

June 8. Meeting with South Vietnamese President Nguyen Van Thieu on Midway Island,
Nixon announced that 25,000 United States
troops would be withdrawn from South Vietnam
by August 31, 1969.

June 9. The Senate confirmed Nixon's appointment of Warren E. Burger as Chief Justice by a vote of 74 to 3.

Reporting on the Midway Conference, South
Vietnamese President Thieu continued his refusal to accept a coalition government.

June 16. Governor Rockefeller arrived in
Brazil to begin the third of his four trips
to Latin America.

June 19. Stated that former Defense Secretary Clifford's timetable for withdrawing
troops from South Vietnam could be improved.
Also said that the United States might offer
a moratorium on MIRV tests in an arms control agreement with the Soviet Union.

June 20. The 1953 defense agreement with
Spain was extended until September 26, 1970.

June 23. Warren E. Burger received the oath
of office from retiring Earl Warren to become the 15th Chief Justice of the United
States.

June 25. The Senate approved a resolution
which would bar the executive branch from
committing troops or financial resources to
foreign countries, without the express approval of Congress.

June 26. Nixon's administration stated that
it opposed an extension of the 1965 Voting
Rights Act and offered alternatives.

June 27. Secretary of Health, Education,
and Welfare Finch gave up his attempt to
have the controversial John H. Knowles appointed assistant secretary.

June 28. Plans for President Nixon to visit
five Asian countries and Rumania in late
July and early August were announced by the
White House. Henry Kissinger would accompany the President.

July 3. White House announced that it would
meet the September, 1969 deadline for compliance with the 1964 school desegregation
order, except for "bona fide" problems.

July 6. Governor Rockefeller completed his
Latin American tours.

July 8. First contingent of United States
troops to be withdrawn from South Vietnam
were flown to the United States.

July 9. Ordered a 10% reduction of military
and civilian governmental personnel in foreign countries.

July 10. A secret "military contingency"
agreement with Thailand in 1965 was admitted
by the State Department.

July 15. Purchased home at San Clemente,
California. Again, much criticism later developed because of the $701,000 spent by the
government for its protection and maintenance.

July 16. Apollo 11 spacecraft launched from
Cape Kennedy.

July 19. Mary Jo Kopechne killed when a car
driven by Senator Edward M. Kennedy (D., Mass.)
plunged off a bridge near Chappaquiddick,
Massachusetts.

July 20. Apollo 11 lunar module, "Eagle",
landed on the moon. Astronauts Neil Armstrong and Edwin Aldrin, Jr. left craft for
walk on moon's surface. Astronaut Michael
Collins remained in the orbiting command
module, "Columbia." As millions watched on
television, Armstrong, at his first step on
the moon proclaimed: "That's one small step
for man, one giant leap for mankind."

July 22. Ordered a $3.5 billion cut in Fed-
eral spending.

July 24. Arrived at the U.S.S. Hornet, the
recovery carrier stationed off Pago Pago in
the Pacific Ocean, and greeted the returning
Apollo 11 astronauts.

July 25. From the island of Guam, stated
that peace in Asia was the responsibility of
Asians, although the United States would continue its role.

July 26. Arrived in Manila, the Philippines,
the first stop in his Asian tour.

July 30. Briefly stopped off in South Vietnam on an unannounced visit.

August 2. Received enthusiastic welcome upon
arrival in Bucharest, Rumania.

August 3.   Returned to Washington.

August 6.   The Senate approved by one vote the Safeguard ABM system.

August 7.   Signed bill which continued the 10% income tax surcharge through December, 1969.

August 8.   Revealed plans for welfare reform, including a "family assistance plan."

Announced in joint communique with Chancellor Kiesinger of West Germany the establishment of a "hot lines" system between Washington and Bonn.

August 10.   C. G. (Bebe) Rebozo accused by Representative Wright Patman (D., Tex.) and chairman of the House Banking and Currency Committee, of being given "special favors" by the Small Business Administration.

August 13.   In a special message to Congress proposed plan for sharing federal revenues with state and local government.

August 18.   Nominated Clement F. Haynsworth, Jr., of South Carolina, Chief judge of the United States Fourth Judicial Circuit, to fill the United States Supreme Court seat left vacant by the resignation of Abe Fortas.

August 21.   Secretary of Defense Laird released plans for cutting defense spending in 1970.

September 4.   President Ho Chi Minh of North Vietnam died.

September 16.   Announced the withdrawal of an additional 35,000 troops from South Vietnam.

Vice President Agnew, addressing a Southern governors' conference in Williamsburg, Virginia, stated his opposition to busing school children to achieve racial balance.

September 18.   Addressing the General Assembly, asked for UN help in bringing peace to Vietnam.

The House of Representatives approved a proposed constitutional amendment which would abolish the electoral college and provide for the direct popular election of the president.

September 19. Announced that there would be a 50,000 man reduction in the military draft for the rest of 1969.

President Thieu of South Vietnam stated his opposition to a cease-fire without a political settlement.

September 23. Announced decision to continue plans for a supersonic airliner.

Secretary of Labor Shultz ordered that contractors put into effect the so-called Philadelphia Plan, setting goals for hiring on federally assisted projects.

September 24. Senator Hugh Scott of Pennsylvania was elected minority leader by Republican senators. Robert P. Griffin of Michigan was named as whip. The death of Senator Everett M. Dirksen, long-time Republican leader from Illinois, on September 7, brought about the change.

September 25. Asked Congress to increase social security benefits by 10% and provide future increases based on cost-of-living.

Senator Charles E. Goodell (R., N.Y.) proposed legislation which would require the withdrawal of all United States troops from Vietnam by the end of 1970. Governor Rockefeller, who had appointed Goodell to fill Bobby Kennedy's seat, rebuked the Senator for his position.

September 27. President Thieu of South Vietnam stated that United States troop withdrawal would take "years and years" because his country had "no ambition" to take over the fighting.

October 7. A joint draft treaty to ban all nuclear weapons from the ocean floor was submitted by the United States and the U.S.S.R. to the Geneva disarmament conference.

October 10. Relieved Lt. General Lewis B.
Hershey of his position as director of the
Selective Service System, effective February
16, 1970. Hershey had held the post for 28
years.

October 13. Said that street demonstrations
would not deter him from making a major speech
on Vietnam policy next month.

October 14. Hanoi radio praised the efforts
of antiwar protestors in the United States.

October 15. Antiwar Moratorium gatherings
throughout the United States drew massive
support.

October 17. Named Arthur F. Burns as chairman of the Federal Reserve Board to succeed
William McChesney Martin.

Asked that all parts of the United States
economy use restraint in the battle against
inflation.

October 19. Vice President Agnew, speaking
to a Republican gathering in New Orleans,
Louisiana, said that the Vietnam Moratorium
was "encouraged by an effete corps of impu-
dent snobs who characterize themselves as
intellectuals."

October 20. Defended his selection of Judge
Haynsworth for the Supreme Court, claiming
that the judge's attackers were guilty of
vicious character assassination.

Proposed that penalties for the use and pos-
session of narcotics be reduced.

October 28. Warned Congress that unless it
speeded action on appropriation bills he
would be unable to submit a budget in January, 1970.

October 29. The Supreme Court, in an unanimous decision, ordered school districts to
end racial segregation at once and to operate
"now and hereafter only unitary schools."
The decision was a blow to the Nixon administration.

October 31. Said that social and economic progress in Latin America must come about through their own initiative.

November 3. Announced that North Vietnam had rejected secret peace offers and submitted a plan for the withdrawal of United States troops on a gradual, but secret basis.

November 4. Republicans won governorships in New Jersey and Virginia. President Nixon had campaigned in both states. Democrats, however, won 5 of 7 elections to fill seats in the United States House of Representatives.

John Ehrlichman became assistant to the President for domestic affairs.

Charles W. Colson named legal counsel to the President, reporting to Haldeman.

Daniel Patrick Moynihan, Nixon's advisor on urban affairs, was elevated to the rank of counselor with cabinet rank.

November 6. President Nixon's disclosure of secret peace talks was branded by North Vietnamese delegate Xuan Thuy at the Paris peace talks as "a betrayal of a promise" and a "perfidious trick."

November 10. Released the report by Governor Rockefeller on his Latin American visits.

November 13. Signed bill to increase spending for food stamps from $340 million to $610 million for fiscal 1970.

Vice President Agnew claimed that the 3 television networks were not providing responsible news coverage, being often biased, noting their hostility to Nixon's November 3 speech on Vietnam.

November 14-15. A second Vietnam Moratorium in Washington was held by some 250,000 people. A "March Against Death" past the White House was ignored by the President.

November 16. First reports published of what came to be known as the My Lai massacre,

in which United States troops killed some
500 South Vietnamese civilians.

November 17. United States and U.S.S.R. began strategic arms limitation talks in Helsinki, Finland.

November 19. Signed a $20.7 billion Military
Procurement Authorization which included beginning work on the Safeguard antiballistic
missile system and a simplified fighter plane.

November 20. Announced the resignation of
Henry Cabot Lodge as chief United States ne-
gotiator at the Paris peace talks, effective
December 8.

Ordered that the use of DDT in residential
areas be ended within 30 days.

Vice President Agnew added the United States
press to the TV networks, charging poor coverage, particularly singling out the New York
Times and the Washington Post.

November 21. The Senate, by a vote of 55 to
45, refused to confirm the nomination of
Clement Haynsworth to the Supreme Court. He
was charged with ethical "insensitivity" and
with holding anti-labor and anti-civil rights
views.

Met with Japanese Prime Minister Eisaku Sato
in Washington, D. C. and agreed to return
Okinawa and the other Ryukyu Islands to Japan
in 1972.

November 24. Signed the Nuclear Nonproliferation Treaty which would attempt to prevent non-nuclear nations from obtaining nuclear weapons. The Senate had approved it
on March 13. U.S.S.R. President Nikolai
Podgorny also signed the Treaty in similar
ceremonies in Moscow.

November 25. Ordered the destruction of all
United States stocks for waging germ warfare.

November 26. Signed a Selective Service Reform bill which would permit selection of
draftees by a lottery system. A drawing was

held on December 1.

December 1. The Army reported that 60,000 United States troops had left South Vietnam.

December 2. The House of Representatives endorsed President Nixon's "just peace" in Vietnam.

December 10. Asked that the appropriation for the National Foundation of the Arts and the Humanities be almost doubled, from the $40 million for fiscal 1971.

December 15. Announced further reductions in United States forces in Vietnam.

December 17. Called on Congress for restraint in spending and cutting taxes at the same time.

December 22. Strategic arms talks ended in Helsinki, to be renewed in Vienna in April, 1970 and later returning to Helsinki.

December 26. Vice President Agnew left Washington, D. C. for a 23 day tour of 11 Asian countries, including South Vietnam.

December 30. Signed the Tax Reform Act of 1969. Its major provisions were an extension of the income tax surcharge at 5% through June 30, 1970, by 1973 an increase in personal exemption to $750, and a repeal of the 7% investment credit.

Signed the Defense Appropriation Act of 1970 providing $69.6 billion for military expenditures, $5.6 billion lower than he had requested.

Signed the Coal Mine Health and Safety Act of 1969, tightening various safety requirements and providing disability benefits for coal miners.

December 31. Signed the Economic Opportunity Act of 1969, extending that office until June 30, 1971.

Signed a Foreign Aid Authorization providing $1.97 billion in foreign aid for 1970.

1970   January 1. Vice President Agnew visited
            South Vietnam on his Asian tour.

            January 2. Robert H. Finch, Secretary of
            Health, Education, and Welfare, announced
            the ending of its controversial blacklisting
            of some scientists.

            January 3. Gallop poll ranked Nixon as the
            man most admired by Americans. The Reverend
            Billy Graham was second, and Vice President
            Agnew third.

            January 9. South Vietnamese President Thieu
            stated that it was impossible and impracti-
            cal to withdraw all United States combat for-
            ces from South Vietnam in 1970.

            January 13. Named Murray M. Chotiner, one
            of his earliest political advisors, as spe-
            cial counsel to the President reporting to
            Haldeman.

            January 14. The Supreme Court ruled that
            six states in the Deep South must integrate
            their schools by February 1, 1970.

            January 15. White House reported agreement
            with Florida to bar construction of an inter-
            national jetport near the Everglades.

            January 19. Nominated Judge G. Harrold Cars-
            well of the United States Court of Appeals
            to the Supreme Court to fill the seat left
            facant by Abe Fortas.

            91st Congress convened for its second session,
            controlled by Democrats.

            Vice President Agnew returned to Washington
            after his Asian tour.

            January 20. United States and China resumed
            formal talks on the ambassadorial level in
            Warsaw.

            January 22. State of the Union Message to
            Congress stressed the problem of pollution.

            January 26. Announced his veto of the $19.7
            billion appropriation for the Department of
            Health, Education, and Welfare before a na-

tionwide television audience as inflationary.

January 27. Began two days of talks with
Prime Minister Harold Wilson of Great Britain.

January 28. The House failed to override
the President's veto of the two appropriation bills.

January 30. Economic report to Congress
dealt with need for an economic slowdown to
curb inflation.

In a press conference, discussed foreign policy in Vietnam and the Middle East.

January 31. Arthur F. Burns succeeded William McChesney Martin, Jr., as chairman of
the Federal Reserve Board. He acted as a
counselor to the President with full cabinet
rank.

February 2. Submitted a federal budget for
fiscal 1971 to Congress. It showed a surplus
of $1.3 billion in a budget just over $200
billion.

February 3. Sent to Congress a proposal for
changing the system of farm price supports.

February 4. Replying to a letter from Soviet Premier Kosygin, the President asked
for the adoption of his three point program
for Middle Eastern peace.

February 5. Met with ten big city Mayors at
a session of his Counsel for Urban Affairs
held in Indianapolis, Indiana.

February 7. Secretary of State Rogers began a ten nation tour of Africa.

February 10. Sent to Congress a special
message on pollution control.

February 11. Secretary of Defense Laird began three-day visit to South Vietnam.

February 18. Senate voted to curb de facto
school segregation.

Sent Congress a "new strategy for peace,"
describing it as the first presidential
"state of the world" message.

February 21. Presidential commission headed
by Thomas Gates, former Secretary of Defense,
suggested that the armed forces be made
largly volunteer.

February 23. President Georges Pompidou and
Mme. Pompidou of France began an eight-day
state visit.

February 25. United States military expansion in Laos criticized in the Senate.

February 26. Stated need to eliminate or
revise 57 federal programs for a saving of
$2 billion a year.

Defense Secretary Laird denied presence of
United States troops in Laos.

February 27. Asked Congress for legislation
to deal with transportation strikes.

March 2. After demonstrations against French
Middle East policy in several cities, President Pompidou accused authorities in Chicago of being accomplices. President Nixon
substituted for Vice President Agnew at a
dinner in New York City honoring the French
President.

March 4. Signed special legislation passed
to halt a nationwide railroad strike.

March 5. Nuclear nonproliferation treaty
went into effect when the United States and
the U.S.S.R. deposited their instruments of
ratification.

March 6. Announced that he had asked for
aid from the Soviet Union and Great Britain
to restore the 1962 Geneva agreement on Laos.

March 13. Nominated Curtis W. Tarr, assistant Secretary of the Air Force, to be director of the Selective Service System to
replace General Lewis B. Hershey. Confirmed
by the Senate on March 20.

March 17. Major General Sammuel W. Koster,

superintendent of the Military Academy at
West Point, and thirteen other officers, accused by the Army of suppressing information
on the alleged My Lai massacre.

March 18.   Prince Norodom Sihanouk over-
thrown in coup in Cambodia.   General Lon
Nol became Premier.

Strike of New York City postal workers began.   The action, protesting failure of Congress to act on pay increases, crippled mail
service for eight days.

March 23.   Declared a state of national emergency and ordered federal troops into New
York City to help handle the mail.

March 24.   Announced that his administration
would continue to eliminate de jure segregation.

March 25.   Federal air traffic controllers
crippled flights in United States by insti-
tuting "sick-outs."

April 1.   Nineteenth decennial census conducted.   Total United States population in
1970 was 204,765,770, a 13% increase over
1960.

April 2.   Governor Francis W. Sargent of
Massachusetts signed bill providing that
men from that state would not be required
to fight in an undeclared war.

April 3.   Signed the Water Quality Improvement Act of 1970, liabilities for cleaning
up oil spills and establishing controls on
acid mine drainage.

April 8.   The Senate rejected the nomination
of G. Harrold Carswell to the Supreme Court.
It was claimed he was racially biased and
had a "mediocre record" on the bench.   President Nixon claimed that the Senate was
guilty of regional discrimination.

April 9.   Senate asked President Nixon to
propose to the U.S.S.R. a mutual suspension
of the deployment of nuclear strategic weapons to take place immediately.

April 14.   Nominated United States Court of
Appeals Judge Harry A. Blackmun to the Supreme Court.

Appointed Admiral Thomas H. Moorer as chairman of the Joint Chiefs of Staff to succeed
General Earle G. Wheeler.

April 15.   Gerald R. Ford, Republican leader of the House of Representatives, asked
for an investigation of Justice William O.
Douglas, charging unethical conduct.   Douglas
was the court's most liberal member.

April 20.   Pledged to withdraw 150,000 more
United States troops from Vietnam in the
next year.

Received appeal from Cambodian Premier General Lon Nol for extensive military aid.

April 23.   Issued an executive order ending
occupational and parental deferments for
the draft.

April 29.   Ordered an investigation into Israeli reports that pilots from the Soviet
Union were flying combat support missions
for the United Arab Republic.

April 30.   Announced that United States was
sending combat troops into Cambodia to attack enemy Vietnamese sanctuaries.

May 1.   Egyptian President Abd-Al Nasser
launched a new diplomatic offensive in a
"final appeal" to President Nixon, warning
that any increased attempt to secure military superiority for Israel would affect
United States-Arab relations for decades or
even centuries.

May 4.   National Guardsmen fired on antiwar
demonstrators at Kent State University, Ohio,
killing four students.

May 6.   Secretary of the Interior Hickel
sent letter to President Nixon in which he
stated that attacks on young people's motives would only intensify their hostility.

May 7.   Assured university presidents that

verbal attacks on students by members of his
administration would be halted.

May 8. Discussed United States involvement
in Cambodia at a nationwide television news
conference.

Democratic Senator George McGovern led formation of a Committee to End the War by re-
pealing the Tonkin Gulf Resolution, barring
funds for support of United States forces
in Cambodia, and withdrawing all United
States troops from Vietnam in a year.

Construction workers, so-called "hard hats,"
disrupted antiwar demonstrators on Wall
Street in New York City.

May 9. Paid unannounced visit to antiwar
demonstrators at the Lincoln Memorial.

May 11. Met with Forty-five state and ter-
ritorial governors to discuss policies in
Southeast Asia and student protests. It was
reported that 448 colleges and universities
were closed or on strike.

May 12. Senate confirmed Judge Blackmun to
the Supreme Court by a unanimous vote.

May 20. Large crowd of workers demonstrated
at City Hall in New York City in support of
President Nixon's Southeast Asia policy.

May 26. President Suharto of Indonesia received by President Nixon at the White House.

June 1. Seventy-three Senators signed a letter to Secretary of State Rogers urging that
the United States provide Israel with the
aircraft needed for its defense.

June 3. Announced the incursion into Cambodia as most successful.

June 5. Meeting secretly in the Oval Office
of the White House with F.B.I. and C.I.A.
leaders, President Nixon set up an interagency committee for stepped-up domestic intelligence.

June 6. Nominated Elliot L. Richardson, Un-

dersecretary of State, to become Secretary
of Health, Education and Welfare to succeed
Robert H. Finch who was named counselor to
the President.

June 10. Named Secretary of Labor Shultz as
director of the new Office of Management and
Budget; Casper W. Weinberger named deputy
director; Undersecretary of Labor James D.
Hodgson nominated as Shultz's successor; John
D. Ehrlichman was named the executive director of a new Domestic Council.

James E. Allen, Jr., United States commissioner of education, removed from office by
President Nixon. Allen had been critical of
administration policies.

June 13. Named a nine-member Commission on
Campus Unrest, to be chaired by former Pennsylvania Governor William Scranton to investigate causes and recommend solutions.

June 15. The Supreme Court ruled that draft
exemptions as conscientious objectors could
be given to those who objected to war for
moral or ethical reasons.

June 17. Addressed nation on television,
asking for wage and price restraint but ruling out mandatory controls.

June 22. Signed into law a measure lowering
the voting age to eighteen in federal elections.

June 25. Secretary of State Rogers launched
a new peace offensive for the Middle East,
to become known as the Rogers plan and accepted in principle by the Arabs and the Soviet Union.

June 29. Last United States ground troops
withdrawn from Cambodia.

June 30. Congress overrode President Nixon's
veto of the Hill-Burton bill providing $2.7
billion for hospital construction.

Announced that there would be "no advisors
with Cambodian units."

July 1.   Named David K. E. Bruce as the chief
United States delegate at the Paris peace
talks.

Told TV audience that the American incursion
into Cambodia had given that country an "in-
finitely better" chance of survival.

July 7.   Used his emergency powers to stop
a strike involving three railroads.

July 8.   Issued a Republican policy paper on
the American Indian repudiating the termination policy of the Eisenhower era and promising self-determination without the threat
of termination.

July 9.   Proposed a reorganization of Federal
Agencies dealing with problems concerning the
environment.

Named John W. Dean, III counsel to the President on the recommendation of Haldeman.

July 14.   Met with twelve governors in Louis-
ville, Kentucky to discuss domestic problems.

July 16.   Received Prince Charles and Princess Anne of Great Britain at the White House.
The royal pair were making an informal visit
to the United States.

July 18.   Warned Congress about its spending.

July 20.   At a news conference stated that a
coalition government in Vietnam, if chosen
in an open election, would be acceptable to
the United States.

July 23.   Approved the plan drawn up for the
Interagency Committee on domestic intelligence by White House aide Tom Charles Huston,
even though its activities were clearly illegal.

U.A.R. President Nasser accepted the United
States proposal for a three-month cease-fire.

July 24.   Signed the Emergency Home Finance
Act of 1970, providing additional funds for
mortgages and hoping to lower interest rates
for home buyers.

July 28. F.B.I. Director J. Edgar Hoover
protested the Huston plan and President Nixon rescinded his approval.

Presidential commission, headed by Gilbert
W. Fitzhugh, chairman of the board of the
Metropolitan Life Insurance Company, called
for radical reorganization of the Department
of Defense.

July 29. Signed the District of Columbia
Criminal Justice Act providing "no-Knock"
provisions in cases where a suspect might
destroy evidence.

August 3. Caused considerable difficulty
in the trial of Charles Manson for the murder of Sharon Tate and six others by stating
in Denver, Colorado his belief in Manson's
guilt. The trial was still in progress.

August 5. Agreement with Spain extended
United States use of bases for five years.

August 10. Signed legislation extending unemployment insurance coverage.

August 11. Rejected, even prior to its release, the report of the Commission on Obscenity and Pornography. The Commission,
appointed by President Lyndon Johnson in
1968, was chaired by William B. Lockhart.

August 12. Signed the Postal Reorganization
Act, establishing an independent United
States Postal Service. Granted eight per-
cent pay raise to postal employees.

August 17. Signed a bill extending the Defense Production Act, although objecting to
the provision giving him authority to freeze
wages, prices, and rents.

August 18. The Senate overrode the President's veto of a $4.4 billion aid to educa-
tion bill and the bill became law. The
House had voted on August 13 to override the
veto. An attempt to override his veto of a
housing aid bill failed.

August 19. Requested the Senate ratify the
1925 Geneva protocal barring the use of bio-

logical and chemical weapons in warfare.

August 20-21. Met with President Diaz Ordaz
of Mexico at Puerto Vallarta to discuss boun-
dary disputes.

August 22. Vice President Agnew began tour
of Asia to insure leaders in South Korea,
Thailand, South Vietnam, and Nationalist
China of continued United States support.

September 1. Amendment proposed by Senator
McGovern and Senator Mark Hatfield (R., Ore.)
to withdraw all United States troops from
Vietnam by the end of 1971 defeated in the
Senate.

September 10. Vice President Agnew coined
the term "radic-libs," short for "radical-
liberals" to describe, apparently, anyone
to the left of President Nixon who was running for Senate seats. Most Democrats were
included and one Republican, Charles Goodell
of New York.

September 11. Ordered federal arms guards
on United States airlines' overseas flights,
when a rash of hijackings by Arab Commandos
broke out.

September 16. Called for responsible university leadership.

September 18. Israeli Premier Golda Meir
met with President Nixon at the White House
to discuss Mideast problems.

September 21. Appointed retired Air Force
Lt. General Benjamin O. Davis, Jr., to head
a newly created position of heading civil
aviation security in the Department of Transportation.

September 22. Named Sidney P. Marland, Jr.,
of New York to be commissioner of education.
Former commissioner James E. Allen, Jr., had
been dismissed in June.

September 26. Presidential Commission on
Campus Unrest issued report calling on the
President to use his moral influence to heal
discord.

September 27. Arrived in Rome to begin a
five-nation European tour.

September 28. President Nasser of the U.A.R.
died of a heart attack.

September 30. Presidential Commission on
Obscenity and Pornography found no harmful
effects in obscenity and recommended the eli-
mination of restrictive laws for adults.
President Nixon rejected the report and said
he would prefer to strengthen the laws and
later (October 24) called it "morally bank-
rupt."

October 4. Met in Ireland with the United
States delegation to the Paris peace talks
after visiting Yugoslavia, Spain, and Great
Britain.

October 7. In a television address, proposed
a five-point peace plan for Indochina including a "cease-fire in place" and a negotiated
withdrawal of United States troops.

October 12. Announced that 40,000 United
States troops would be withdrawn from South
Vietnam by Christmas, 1970.

Vetoed law which would restrict campaign
spending on radio and television.

October 15. Signed the Organized Crime Control Act permitting wider use of wiretaps in
organized crime cases, and the Urban Mass
Transportation Act authorizing the expendi-
ture of $3.1 billion over six years for mass
transit systems.

Anwar Al-Sadat elected President of United
Arab Republic.

October 22. Held lengthy conference with
Soviet Foreign Minister Andrei Gromyko at
the White House.

October 23. Addressed the UN General Assembly, calling for "peaceful competition" among
nations.

October 24. Met with Japanese Prime Minister Sato at White House to discuss problems

in textile trade.

October 26. Signed a Foreign Bank Account
and Transaction Act to check on foreign bank
transactions made to avoid United States
taxes; a Credit Reporting bill restricting
credit agencies from providing information
about individuals, and the Legislative Reform Act of 1970 requiring publication of
roll call votes in the House of Representatives.

October 27. Signed the Comprehensive Drug
Abuse Prevention and Control Act easing penalties for using marihuana and providing
more programs to deal with drug abuse.

October 29. During campaign rally in San
Jose, California, was target of a barrage
of thrown objects and heckling.

October 30. Signed the Railroad Passenger
and Service Act of 1970 establishing a semi-
public corporation to run passenger service.

October 31. In campaign speech in Phoenix,
Arizona, called for an end to the appease-
ment of "thugs and hoodlums."

November 3. Elections gave Republicans
small gain in the Senate but losses in the
House. The Administration was especially
pleased with the defeat of some of its targets, Charles E. Goodell in New York (defeated by James L. Buckley, Conservative),
Albert A. Gore (D., Tenn.). and Joseph D.
Tydings (D., Md.).

November 16. Congress began first lame duck
session in 20 years.

November 20. The Senate Finance Committee
rejected President Nixon's proposed Family
Assistance Plan.

November 21. United States aircraft resumed
bombing of military targets in North Vietnam, Laos, and Cambodia.

November 23. The Senate failed to override
President Nixon's veto of the bill to limit
campaign spending on radio and television.

November 25. Announced the dismissal of
Secretary of the Interior Walter Hickel, who
had been critical of the Administration's
handling of young people. Rogers Morton,
Republican national chairman, was named as
Hickel's successor.

November 27. Daniel Moynihan, presidential
advisor, turned down the position of chief
United States representative to the UN, deciding to return to Harvard.

November 30. Signed Agricultural Act of
1970 establishing a three-year program of
price supports and limiting payments to farmers to $55,000 per crop.

December 10. Held first news conference in
four months discussing Middle East and Far
East policies as well as economic policy and
campus unrest.

December 11. Named Representative George
Bush, Texas Democrat, to succeed Charles W.
Yost as United States delegate to the United
Nations.

December 14. Named former Texas Governor
John B. Connally to replace David M. Kennedy
as Secretary of the Treasury. Sworn in February 11, 1971. Kennedy remained on White
House Staff as advisor.

December 15. Signed bill granting the Taos
Pueblo Indians title to 48,000 acres in New
Mexico, including the tribe's sacred Blue
Lake.

Subcommittee of the House Judiciary Committee
reported that it found no grounds for the
impeachment of Justice William O. Douglas.

December 16. Vetoed bill which would extend
manpower training programs rather than re-
organizing them as he had requested.

December 21. Supreme Court upheld vote for
eighteen-year-olds in federal elections, but
ruled that the law did not apply in state or
local elections.

December 26. Signed several minor bills in-

cluding one to provide federal birth control
information, but "pocket-vetoed" one to finance special training of more family doctors.

December 29. Signed the Occupational Health
and Safety Act of 1970 authorizing the Secretary of Labor to set safety standards for
United States jobs.

December 31. Signed a Clean Air bill requiring car manufacturers to achieve a 90% reduction of certain pollutants by 1975.

1971   January 2. Ninety-first Congress adjourned
its lame duck session.

January 4. Told ABC news commentator Howard
K. Smith, "I am now a Keynesian."

January 11. Announced tax aids to business
for 1971.

January 12. Reverend Philip F. Berrigan and
five others were indicted on charges of plot-
ting to kidnap Henry Kissinger and bomb the
heating systems of federal buildings in Washington, D. C.

January 13. Named Postmaster General Winton
M. Blount to head the newly created Postal
Service.

January 15. Senator Robert J. Dole of Kansas
succeeded Representative Rogers Morton as
chairman of the Republican National Committee.
Morton had been named Secretary of the Interior.

January 18. Senator George McGovern of South
Dakota announced his candidacy for the Democratic Presidential nomination in 1972.

January 19. Halted construction of Cross-
Florida Barge Canal to prevent environmental
damage.

January 21. Ninety-second Congress opened
its first session with Representative Carl
Albert (D., Okla.) as the new Speaker of the
House and Senator Mike Mansfield (D., Mon.)
reelected Senate majority leader.

January 22. Delivered State of the Union

Message.

January 28. Requested Congress grant pay
hikes and increased benefits for servicemen
to aid in creating an all-volunteer army.

February. Voice-activated tape recorders
installed in the Oval Office of the White
House, as well as in other key locations
used by the President.

February 1. Annual economic message to Congress asked for help in reducing unemployment and inflation.

February 17. Held news conference where he
ruled out the use of tactical nuclear weapons in Indochina.

February 23. Suspended regulations which
called for the payment of union wages on
federally assisted projects.

February 25. Delivered a second "state of
the world" message to Congress, declaring
the need to draw China into a constructive
relationship with the world community.

March 11. Rejected Japan's offer to limit
textile exports, stating he would prefer
United States import quotas.

March 17. Signed bill increasing the temporary ceiling on the national debt to $430
billion and providing a 10% increase in social security benefits.

March 29. Signed executive order placing
restraints on wages in the construction industry and reestablishing federal support
of union wages.

April 5. Representative Hale Boggs (D.,
La.), House Majority Leader, called for the
resignation of F.B.I. director Hoover because of the tapping of phones of members
of Congress, including his.

April 6. President Nixon was accused of
compromising the judicial process by his
interference in the trial of Lt. William
L. Calley, Jr., found guilty in the My Lai

Massacre trial on March 29.

April 7. Announced an additional reduction of 100,000 United States troops in Vietnam by December 1.

April 14. Announced relaxation of trade restrictions with China.

April 23-24. About 200,000 antiwar protestors rallied in Washington, D. C., with Vietnam veterans hurling their medals toward the Capitol.

May 1. At a news conference stated he would ask for a tax cut if needed to get the economy moving.

The newly created National Railroad Passenger Corporation, called Amtrak, took over most of the railroads in the United States.

May 3. Attempts by antiwar protestors to shut down government operations in the nation's capitol failed. 7,000 were arrested.

May 5. 1,200 antiwar demonstrators arrested by police in Washington, D.C. President Nixon praised the action and denied that constitutional rights were violated. However, a suit by the American Civil Liberties Union brought a jury award of $12 million on January 16, 1975.

May 8. The Reverend Carl McIntire led a "pathetic" demonstration at the Washington Monument, calling for a military victory in Vietnam. The rally was to have featured South Vietnamese Vice President Ky, but the Nixon Administration blocked his visit, fearing a riot.

May 18. Signed a Wage-Price Controls bill, extending to April 30, 1972 the president's authority to place controls on wages, prices, salaries, and rents.

June 1. Promised to undertake a national offensive against drug addiction.

June 5. Dedicated at Catoosa, Oklahoma, the Arkansas River Navigation System, completed

at a cost of $1.2 billion and linking Okla-
homa with the Mississippi River.

June 10. Lifted the twenty-one-year embargo
on sending nonstrategic goods to China and
permitting issuance of licenses for imports.

June 11. Issued statement saying that he
supported bans on racial discrimination in
housing.

June 12. Patricia (Tricia) Nixon, 25, elder
daughter of the President, married Edward
Finch Cox, 24, in the White House Rose Garden.

June 13. New York Times began publication
of the Pentagon Papers, leading to White
House anxiety about leaks of classified information and within a week the creation of
a special unit, later known as the "Plumbers"
to stop the leaks. Daniel Ellsberg, Defense
Department official in Johnson years, later
admitted the leak.

June 15. West German Chancellor Willy Brandt
met with President Nixon at the White House.

June 17. Secretary of State Rogers signed
treaty returning Okinawa to Japan.

Named Jerome H. Jaffe of Illinois to head a
special Action Office for Drug Abuse Prevention.

June 27. Vice President Agnew began a thirty-
two day goodwill tour of ten Asian, African,
and European countries.

June 30. The Supreme Court ruled, 6 to 3,
that the New York Times and the Washington
Post were free to publish the Pentagon Papers
since the Government had not proved the national security was endangered.

Twenty-sixth Amendment to the Constitution
ratified by Ohio, the necessary thirty-
eighth state, and eighteen-year-olds received the vote in all elections.

July 6. Former C.I.A. agent E. Howard Hunt
was hired as a $100 a day consultant to

Charles Colson, counsel to the President.

July 9.   Paul Norton McCloskey, Jr., (R., Calif.), who had been elected to Congress after an upset primary victory over Shirley Temple Black, announced he would seek the Republican presidential nomination. McCloskey was a critic of President Nixon's Vietnam policy.

July 9-11. Henry Kissinger secretly traveled to China, met with Chou En-Lai in Peking, and arranged for President Nixon's visit.

July 12. Signed an Emergency Employment Act authorizing $2.25 billion to provide public service jobs at the state and local levels.

July 15. Announced that he planned to visit China before May, 1972.

July 17. John D. Ehrlichman, President Nixon' chief domestic advisor, who had been appointed to supervise the "plumbers" recruited David Young and Egil Krogh, Jr., for the unit. Krogh then hired former F.B.I. agent G. Gordon Liddy. Colson also assigned Hunt to join the group.

Vice President Agnew, at an African news conference, said that blacks in the United States could learn from African leaders. The statement drew much criticism from the black community in this country.

July 28. William J. Porter named to replace David K. E. Bruce as chief United States delegate to the Paris peace talks.

August 5. Signed a $4 billion Antipoverty Act extending aid to Appalachia.

August 9. Signed bill providing a $250 million federal loan guarantee for the Lockheed Aircraft Corporation.

August 11. Ehrlichman approved a "covert operation" proposed by "plumbers" Krogh and Young to obtain a profile on Ellsberg from his psychiatrist, Dr. Lewis Fielding.

White House warned that federal officials

were in danger of losing their jobs if they
tried to use excessive busing to desegregate
school systems.

August 15. Announced drastic economic moves
including a ninety day freeze on wages and
prices. Came to be known as Phase One of
the President's program.

August 31. Claiming executive privilege, refused to give the Senate Foreign Relations
Committee military information.

September. Committee for the Re-election of
the President (C.R.P.) employees began campaign to discredit various Democratic candidates by printing false or scurrilous materials and infiltrating their campaigns. Former Treasury Department attorney Donald H.
Segretti headed the "dirty tricks" activities.

September 3. "Plumbers," directed by Hunt
and Liddy, burglarized the Los Angeles office
of Ellsberg's psychiatrist.

September 9. Announced a modified system of
economic controls would go into effect on
November 13 and become known as Phase Two.

September 16. In a news conference stated
that the United States would vote to seat
China on the UN Security Council.

September 25. The death of Hugo L. Black
gave President Nixon a second appointment
opportunity for the Supreme Court. John M.
Harlan had retired on September 23. Black
had actually retired on September 17.

September 26. Met Japanese Emperor Hirohito
and Empress Nagako in Anchorage, Alaska. Hirohito was on his way to visit various European countries, marking the first time a Japanese emperor had left his country during
his reign.

September 28. Signed bill extending the
draft for two years, providing a $2.4 billion
pay increase for the military, and requiring
him to set a certain date for troop withdrawal
if North Vietnam released American prisoners
of war.

October 1. James W. McCord, Jr., former
C.I.A. agent, began working part-time for
the Committee for the Re-election of the
President (C.R.P.).

October 7. Phase Two of President Nixon's
economic plan revealed.

October 12. Announced that he would meet
Soviet leaders in Moscow in May, 1972.

October 16. Vice President Agnew began an
official visit to Greece. Agnew, the son
of a Greek immigrant, later charged United
States liberals with making the Greek military regime their "favorite whipping boy."

October 20. Henry Kissinger arrived in Peking to arrange for President Nixon's forthcoming visit.

October 21. Nominated Lewis F. Powell, Jr.,
of Virginia and Assistant Attorney General
William H. Rehnquist as associate justices
of the Supreme Court.

October 22. Appointed George H. Boldt chairman of the Pay Board and C. Jackson Grayson,
Jr., chairman of the Price Commission.

October 28. Greeted Marshal Tito on the
Yugoslavian President's first state visit to
the United States. President Nixon called
Tito "a world statesman of the first rank."

November 11. Nominated Earl L. Butz, Purdue
Dean, as Secretary of Agriculture to succeed
Clifford M. Hardin, who had resigned.

November 14. Phase Two of the Nixon economic
program went into effect. Secretary of the
Treasury John B. Connally acted as its co-
ordinator and became chairman of the Cost
of Living Council.

November 19. Met a cool reception at an
AFL-CIO convention in Bal Harbour, Florida.
Organized labor demanded pay raises under
existing contracts and was refusing to participate on the Pay Board. Thus, the President's Phase Two was in danger.

December 2. Senate confirmed Earl L. Butz

as Secretary of Agriculture 51-44 after a
heated debate where he was charged of ties
with "big agriculture."

December 6. Senate confirmed the nomination
of Lewis F. Powell, Jr., to the Supreme
Court.

December 9. Vetoed legislation designed to
create a national system of day-care centers.

December 10. Senate confirmed the nomination
of William H. Rehnquist to the Supreme Court.

Signed the Revenue Act of 1971 granting a
7% tax credit for investment, increased personal exemption to $750, and repealing the
auto excise tax. A rider permitted each taxpayer to credit $1 for financing presidential
campaigns, beginning in 1976.

December 14. Met with French President Pompidou in the Azores.

December 18. Signed Alaska Claims bill granting native Eskimos, Indians, and Aleuts full
title to 40 million acres and $962.5 million
in settlement of their land claims.

Held news conference with Great Britain's
Chancellor of the Exchequer Anthony Barber
and West Germany's Finance Minister Karl
Schiller to announce the devaluation of the
dollar.

December 20. Met in Bermuda with Prime Minister Edward Heath of Great Britain and announced the termination of the United States
10% import surcharge.

December 22. Signed an Economic Stabilization Act Extension, approving a second one-
year presidential authority to stabilize the
economy.

December 23. Signed the Cancer Act of 1971
authorizing $1.59 billion for cancer research.

December 28. Signed bill requiring able-
bodied welfare recipients to register for
jobs or job training.

December 29. Concluded two-day meeting in

Key Biscayne, Florida with West German Chancellor Brandt.

December 30. Daniel Ellsberg was indicted by a Los Angeles federal grand jury of having illegally appropriated the Pentagon Papers.

1972   January 2. Mrs. Nixon began a week's goodwill tour of Africa.

January 4. Senator Edmund S. Muskie (D., Me.) announced his candidacy for the presidency.

January 5. Ordered the National Aeronautics and Space Administration (NASA) to start work on a manned space shuttle.

January 6-7. Met with Japanese Prime Minister Sato at San Clemente, California and made final plans for the return of Okinawa to Japan on May 15.

January 7. Announced that he was a candidate for reelection.

January 13. Announced a further withdrawal of 70,000 troops from Vietnam in the next three months, leaving 69,000 by May 1.

January 18. Second session of the ninety-second Congress convened.

January 20. Delivered State of the Union message to Congress.

January 24. Projected a budget deficit of $25.5 billion for fiscal 1973. A deficit of $38.8 billion for 1972 was estimated.

January 25. Revealed in a television address that unsuccessful secret negotiations with the North Vietnamese had been held in October, 1971.

January 27. Nominated White House assistant Peter G. Peterson to succeed Secretary of Commerce Maurice H. Stans, who had announced his resignation and would become chairman of the Finance Committee to Re-elect the President.

February 7. Signed a bill limiting campaign

spending for federal offices and a foreign
aid bill authorizing $2.75 billion for 1972.

February 9. In a "State of the World" message to Congress, stated that the end of a
bi-polar world required building a peace
through many nations.

February 15. Named Richard G. Kleindienst,
Deputy Attorney General, to succeed John
Mitchell as attorney general. Mitchell had
resigned to head Nixon's reelection campaign.

February 21. President and Mrs. Nixon ar-
rived in China and were greeted by Premier
Chou En-Lai and Communist Party Chairman Mao
Tse-Tung in Peking.

February 27. After a week of talks, banquets,
and sight-seeing a joint communique was released in Shanghai stating agreement on wi-
dening United States-Chinese contacts and a
gradual United States withdrawal from Taiwan.

February 28. Presidential party returned to
Washington. Addressed nation on television.

February 29. Columnist Jack Anderson disclosed that the International Telephone and
Telegraph Corporation had pledged $400,000
to help fund the Republican National Convention. The IT&T was involved in a Justice
department antitrust suit, so Mitchell and
Kleindienst, and possibly the White House,
were implicated.

March 7. In New Hampshire presidential primary President Nixon easily won the Republican vote, while Muskie topped McGovern in the
Democratic.

March 9. Ordered tighter security measures
for airlines following extortion plot against
TWA.

March 14. Governor George C. Wallace of Alabama, stressing the busing issue, won the
Democratic presidential primary in Florida.

March 16. Spoke out against large-scale
busing to achieve racial integration and
asked for legislation to deny court-ordered

busing.

March 22. AFL-CIO head George Meany and
other labor members quit the fifteen member
Pay Board claiming it was unfair. President
Nixon, the next day, reconstituted it as a
seven member public board.

April 3. Signed legislation devaluing the
dollar.

April 4. Senator McGovern won the Wisconsin
Democratic presidential primary. President
Nixon received 97% of the Republican vote.

April 10. Robert L. Vesco, under investigation for fraud, gave Stans a $200,000 cash
donation for the Nixon campaign.

April 14. Addressed Canadian parliament in
Ottawa during two-day visit.

April 15. Signed joint agreement with Prime
Minister Pierre Trudeau of Canada to control
pollution on the Great Lakes.

April 18. At the President's suggestion,
Chou En-Lai welcomed Congressional leaders
to China, Senators Mike Mansfield and Hugh
Scott from April 18 to May 3, and Representatives Hale Boggs and Gerald Ford from June
26 to July 5.

April 25. Revealed that Henry Kissinger had
just returned from a secret trip to Moscow.

Senator McGovern won the Massachusetts Democratic primary. Senator Humphrey won in
Pennsylvania.

April 26. Delivered address on troop removal
from Vietnam.

April 27. Senate Judiciary Committee finally
voted to approve Richard Kleindienst as attorney general after investigation of his
role in the IT&T case. Full Senate confirmation came on June 8, 64 - 19.

Senator Muskie discontinued campaigning in
presidential primaries.

May 2. F.B.I. director J. Edgar Hoover died

at 77 after heading the agency since 1924.

May 3. Named Assistant Attorney General L.
Patrick Gray, III acting director of the
F.B.I. to succeed Hoover.

May 8. Announced on television that he had
ordered the mining of North Vietnamese ports
as well as bombing military targets in the
north.

May 15. Governor Wallace was seriously wounded by an assassin's bullet while campaigning
in Laurel, Maryland.

May 16. Governor Wallace won the Maryland
and Michigan Democratic primaries.

May 22. Arrived in Moscow for summit meetings with Soviet leaders. First visit to
the U.S.S.R. by a United States president;
Nixon's 1959 trip was as Vice President.
Signed several agreements, notably on limiting weapons, with Chairman Leonid Brezhnev.

May 26-28. After several attempts, wiretaps
were placed in the Democratic National Committee headquarters in the Watergate Hotel
in Washington, D. C. Hunt, Liddy, and McCord
led the operation.

May 28. Addressed Russian people on television, stressing his desire for peace.

June 1. Reported to Congress on his trip to
the U.S.S.R.

June 6. Senator McGovern defeated Senator
Humphrey in California's winner-take-all primary. He also won in New Jersey, New Mexico,
and South Dakota.

June 9. Henry Kissinger arrived in Tokyo
for talks with Japanese leaders. Announced
at press conference that President Nixon had
invited Emperor Hirohito to visit the United
States.

June 17. Police in Washington, D. C. seized
James McCord, Frank Sturgis, and three Cubans
inside the Democratic Watergate headquarters,
and confiscated their cameras, wiretapping
equipment, and $2,300 in cash. Hunt and

Liddy, who were in the building, escaped,
but were later linked to the break-in attempt.

June 18.   Mitchell, Ehrlichman, Haldeman,
Dean, Colson and other members of the White
House Staff met in different groupings to
discuss Watergate.   There were attempts to
protect the President's direct knowledge or
involvement.

June 20.   Senator McGovern won the New York
primary and was almost assured of the Democratic presidential nomination.

On this date there was an eighteen and one
half minute period in the White House tapes
which had only a buzzing sound.   The time
was during a Nixon-Haldeman conversation.

June 22.   Held first press conference in
three months, opposing court-ordered busing
in Detroit.

June 23.   The White House tapes reveal that
on this date President Nixon might be said
to have instituted the "Watergate cover-up."
He ordered Haldeman to tell the F.B.I.,
"Don't go further into this case, period!"
He made clear that the reasons were political, but the pretext would be national security.

June 28.   Named General Frederick C. Weyand
to succeed General Creighton Abrams as commander of United States forces in Vietnam.
Abrams became Army Chief of Staff.

June 29.   Stans gave Herbert W. Kalmbach,
President Nixon's personal attorney, $75,000,
after Kalmbach said he was on a mission from
the White House.   First request for hush
money for Watergate conspirators.

July 1.   Signed bill raising Social Security
benefits 20% and providing automatic increases beginning in 1975 based on cost of
living.

John Mitchell resigned as President Nixon's
campaign manager after his wife, Martha, issued an ultimatum, give up politics or her.
Asked about Watergate, Martha had responded,

"politics is a dirty business." Clark Mac-
Gregor replaced Mitchell.

July 7-September 19. Anthony T. Ulasewicz,
former New York City police detective, at
Kalmbach's instructions, made cash drop-offs
of $187,500 to the Watergate defendants.

July 8. Announced trade agreement with the
Soviet Union in which that country would pur-
chase $750 million worth of grain over a
three-year period. It was later charged that
the deal had given a windfall profit to ex-
porters at the expense of United States farmers, consumers, and taxpayers.

July 12. Senator McGovern won the Democratic
presidential nomination at Miami Beach, Florida.

July 14. Senator Thomas Eagleton of Missouri
selected as the Democratic vice presidential
nominee, only to be dropped two weeks later
after disclosure that he had undergone psychiatric treatment. Sargent Shriver, first
head of the Peace Corps and a Kennedy brother-
in-law replaced Eagleton on the ticket.

July 19. Presidential advisor Kissinger conferred with Le Duc Tho of North Vietnam in
private meeting in Paris.

July 27. UN Secretary General Kurt Waldheim
charged that the United States had intentionally bombed the dikes in North Vietnam and
President Nixon claimed that the Secretary
General had been "taken in" by North Vietnamese propaganda.

August 12. Last United States combat troops
left South Vietnam.

August 16. Vetoed an appropriation bill of
$30.5 billion for the Department of Health,
Education, and Welfare charging it was inflationary.

August 22. Signed legislation requiring the
Secretary of State to submit to Congress within sixty days the text of any agreement, other
than a treaty, with another nation.

August 23. Accepted the Republican renomination at Miami Beach. Vice President Agnew was also renominated.

August 28. Stated that he would end the draft by July, 1973 if Congress passed a military pay bill by then.

August 29. During a news conference President Nixon remarked about Watergate that it would really hurt if one tried to cover it up, and that Dean had conducted a complete Watergate investigation. The President then said, "I can state categorically that his investigation indicates that no one in the White House Staff, no one in this Administration, presently employed, was involved in this very bizarre incident."

August 31. Began two days of talks with the new Japanese Premier, Kaknei Tanaka, in Hawaii.

September 9. Secretary of Agriculture Butz denied the charge that administration leaks about the Soviet wheat deal had led to windfall profits by grain speculators.

September 14. Dr. Kissinger, meeting in Moscow with Soviet officials, reported "significant progress" in trade agreements.

September 15. A federal grand jury brought indictments against the five men arrested in the Watergate break-in, plus Liddy and Hunt.

September 25. Speaking at the International Monetary Fund's annual meeting, announced United States support for reform of the international monetary system.

September 30. Signed a congressional resolution which amended a United States-U.S.S.R. agreement to freeze nuclear weapons for five years by insisting on numerical missile equality in a permanent treaty.

October 16. Representative Hale Boggs (D., La.), House majority leader, died in airplane crash in Alaska.

October 17. Vetoed a water pollution bill,

authorizing grants to states of $24.7 billion
over three years to build sewage disposal
plants. Congress easily overrode the veto
the next day. Nixon, however, impounded about
half the funds.

October 20. Signed a bill for revenue sharing with the states, providing $30.2 billion
for state and local governments over five
years.

October 21. Signed a bill giving the Environmental Protection Agency broad powers regula-
ting the sale and use of pesticides.

October 26. Henry Kissinger in Washington
confirmed reports from Hanoi that a peace
plan had been arrived at saying, "peace is
at hand," Kissinger had spent many days in
both Paris and Saigon.

Campaign manager Clark MacGregor admitted the
existence of a special Republican campaign
fund controlled by top administration officials, but denied its use for espionage.

October 27. Pocket vetoed nine bills which
would have spent more money than he requested.
Congress had adjourned October 18. President
Nixon did sign a bill creating a five-man
consumer product safety commission.

October 30. Signed sixty bills including
one providing $5.3 billion in increased bene-
fits for the aged, blind, and disabled, but
also raising Social Security taxes. The
bill, known as HR1, was one of the longest
pieces of legislation in history, and it had
been rumored that President Nixon would veto
it.

November 2. During a political address on
nationwide television stated there would be
a cease-fire in Vietnam only "when the agreement is right," South Vietnamese President
Thieu having called the proposal a surrender
of the South Vietnamese to the Communists.

November 7. Won reelection in a landslide,
520 electoral votes to McGovern's 17, Nixon
carrying every state except Massachusetts
and the District of Columbia. The popular

vote was 47,168,963 to 29,169,615. Republicans, however, failed to make in-roads into Democratic control of Congress.

November 8. Called for the resignation of all federal department heads, agency directors, and other presidential appointees, announcing his intention of making sweeping changes.

November 27. Secretary of Housing and Urban Development George Romney and Secretary of Defense Melvin Laird resigned.

November 28. Nominated Elliot L. Richardson as Secretary of Defense, Caspar W. Weinberger to succeed him as Secretary of Health, Education and Welfare. Roy L. Ash was named to succeed Weinberger as director of the office of Management and Budget.

November 29. Nominated New York City union leader Peter J. Brennan Secretary of Labor to succeed James D. Hodgson.

December 1. Announced that George Shultz would continue as Secretary of the Treasury and also become a presidential assistant.

December 4. Henry Kissinger and Le Duc Tho resumed peace talks in Paris.

December 5. Nominated Undersecretary of Commerce James T. Lynn as Secretary of Housing and Urban Development and announced that Rogers C. B. Morton would continue as the Secretary of the Interior.

December 6. Nominated Frederick B. Dent, a South Carolina textile manufacturer, as Secretary of Commerce to replace Peter G. Peterson who was sent on a foreign trade mission. Announced that Earl Butz would continue as Secretary of Agriculture.

December 7. Nominated Claude S. Brinegar, California oil executive, to replace John A. Volpe who was appointed Ambassador to Italy.

December 8. Announced that Attorney General Kleindienst would remain in office.

Dorothy Hunt, wife of E. Howard Hunt, Jr.,

indicted Watergate conspirator, killed in
plane crash. Her pocketbook, containing
$10,000 in $100 bills, was recovered.

December 16. Presidential advisor Henry Kissinger announced at a news conference that
peace negotiations had broken down because
the North Vietnamese had reneged on earlier
agreements.

December 17. The White House announced that
the heavy bombing of North Vietnam the past
few days had been personally ordered by President Nixon, and would continue until a settlement was reached.

December 24. North Vietnamese announced that
they would not resume peace talks until bombing of North ceased.

December 30. Announced halting of bombing
of North Vietnam and resumption of Paris
peace talks on January 8.

1973   January 3. First session of ninety-third
            Congress convened.

            January 8. In a conversation with Charles W.
            Colson, agreed to devise a public relations
            scheme to justify granting clemency to E.
            Howard Hunt, Jr.

            Henry Kissinger and Le Duc Tho resumed their
            secret negotiations in Paris.

            January 11. Announced Phase Three of his
            economic stabilization program ending manda-
            tory wage and price controls except in the
            food, health care, and construction fields
            and asking for "voluntary cooperation."

            E. Howard Hunt, Jr., pleaded guilty in the
            Watergate trial before Judge John J. Sirica.
            Four other defendants followed suit four
            days later. On January 30, Liddy and McCord
            were convicted. Judge John J. Sirica set
            sentencing for March 23.

            January 17. Removed most restrictions on
            the importation of oil with shortages becom-
            ing acute.

SECOND TERM

January 20. President Nixon and Vice President Agnew inaugurated for their second term.

January 22. Lyndon B. Johnson, thirty-sixth president, died at sixty-four following a heart attack at his Texas ranch.

January 23. Announced that Kissinger and Tho had initiated an agreement in Paris.

January 27. Secretary of State Rogers and Foreign Minister Nguyen Duy Trinh signed formal cease-fire agreement in Paris.

January 29. Submitted a budget of $268.7 billion for fiscal 1974 with cuts called for in many antipoverty and aid-to-education programs.

January 30. Presented Economic Report to Congress predicting a strongly expanding economy in 1973.

February 2. Sent message to Congress announcing his determination to "draw the line" on spending.

February 8. Former chairman of the Atomic Energy Commission James R. Schlesinger became director of the C.I.A., replacing Richard M. Helms.

Senator Sam J. Ervin, Jr., (D., N.C.) was named chairman of a Select Senate committee to investigate the Watergate case.

February 10. Received report from Vice President Agnew on the latter's tour of Southeast Asia.

February 12. Secretary of the Treasury Shultz announced a 10% devaluation of the dollar.

February 14. Addressed the nation on radio on natural resources and the environment prior to transmitting his second in a series of "State of the Union" messages to Congress.

February 17. Nominated L. Patrick Gray, III,

acting director of the F.B.I., to be its permanent head. Also named G. Bradford Cook to
be chairman of the Securities and Exchange
Commission.

February 23. After Henry Kissinger's five-
day visit to Peking it was announced that
liason offices would be established in each
country's capital. David K. E. Bruce named
on March 15 as the United States representative.

Met with Hafez Ismail, Egypt's foreign minister, in Washington.

February 24. Delivered address on Human Resources over nationwide radio prior to transmitting the message to Congress.

March 2. President Nixon stated that the investigation by John Dean indicated that no
one on the White House staff in July or August, 1972, was "involved in or had knowledge of the Watergate matter."

March 4. Delivered another "State of the
Union" message, on Community Development,
over nationwide radio prior to transmitting
it to Congress.

March 9. Warned Congress that he would veto,
or if his veto was overridden, impound funds
for several bills spending too much money.

March 10. Delivered another "State of the
Union" message over nationwide radio, this
one on law enforcement and drug abuse prevention.

March 15. Told newsmen that he had expressed
"concern" to Hanoi about military moves into
South Vietnam. Also said he was still opposed
to price controls for raw farm products.

March 20. Met privately with Republican minority leader of the Senate, Hugh Scott, and
told him he had nothing to hide, nor did the
White House staff. Later that day the tapes
revealed that he admitted to Haldeman that
they had plenty to hide, and the cover-up
story must be allowed to "come out."

March 21. President Nixon said later that

on this date in a conversation with John
Dean he first learned of the scope of the
Watergate cover-up. Mr. Dean told Mr. Nixon
that there was a "cancer growing in the Presidency." The White House tapes revealed considerable knowledge and activity on President
Nixon's part much earlier.

March 22. Asked Congress to completely re-
vamp the United States criminal code to make
the death penalty mandatory for certain
crimes and to abolish the insanity plea except in extreme cases.

March 23. Judge Sirica disclosed letter
from McCord charging perjury, because of
"political pressure," by the defendants in
the Watergate trial. Sirica deferred final
sentencing to all except Liddy, who received
six years, eight months to twenty years.

March 27. Vetoed a $2.6 billion vocational
rehabilitation bill, the first of the fifteen he had warned he would veto.

March 29. Announced a price ceiling on beef,
pork, and lamb.

Last prisoners of war released in Hanoi and
last United States troops were withdrawn
from South Vietnam.

Spoke to the American people over radio on
the need for maintaining a strong defensive
posture, even though peace in Indochina had
been achieved. The President promised American compliance with the Vietnam accord, but
warned of "consequences" if the North Vietnamese violated the terms.

April 2. At the San Clemente White House
began two-day meetings with South Vietnamese
President Thieu.

In St. Louis, Missouri, the United States
Court of Appeals ruled that President Nixon's
impounding of highway funds appropriated by
Congress was illegal.

April 3. The Senate failed to override the
President's March 27 veto.

April 5. Announced his withdrawal of the
Gray nomination to head the F.B.I., after
much criticism of Gray's actions in the Watergate investigation.

April 14. Told aides he would give "full
pardons" to the various Watergate participants before he left the White House.

April 15. Met with Attorney General Kleindienst and Assistant Attorney General Peterson who told him that high officials at the
White House were involved in a Watergate
cover-up.

April 17. Announced that "major developments" in the Watergate case had led him to
start his own investigation, and that White
House aides could testify before the Senate
committee under certain conditions. White
House Press Secretary Ronald L. Ziegler told
newsmen that previous statements concerning
White House involvement were "inoperative."

April 19. John Dean issued statement saying
he would not become a scapegoat in the Watergate case.

April 25. A taped transcript with Haldeman
revealed President Nixon's anxiety about ex-
posure of his conversation with Dean on
March 21. The tapes revealed that he told
Haldeman: "You, Ehrlichman, and I have to
put the wagons up around the President on
this particular conversation. I just wonder
if the s.o.b. had a recorder on him."

April 26. Jeb Stuart Magruder, who had been
deputy director of the reelection committee
resigned as policy development director in
the Department of Commerce.

April 27. Acting director of the F.B.I.
Gray resigned after disclosure that he had
burned sensitive papers taken from the White
House safe of E. Howard Hunt at the urging
of Dean and Ehrlichman.

William Ruckelshaus, administrator of the
Environmental Protection Agency, was named
temporary F.B.I. head. The President assured
Ruckelshaus that he was not involved in the

Watergate cover-up at all. After the new
F.B.I. director was assured and departed,
President Nixon phoned Henry Petersen of the
Justice Department and several others to try
to find out if John Dean had said anything
incriminating the President.

Judge W. Matt Byrne, Jr., judge in the Ellsberg case in Los Angeles, California, disclosed that Hunt and Liddy had been involved
in a burglary of Ellsberg's psychiatrist's
office in September, 1971. It was later disclosed that this was a "plumbers" operation
under the supervision of Ehrlichman and Egil
Krogh, Jr.

April 30. In a nationwide television address
the President accepted responsibility for the
Watergate affair, but denied prior knowledge
of it. The dismissal of Dean and the resignations of Haldeman, Ehrlichman and Attorney
General Kleindienst were announced. Defense
Secretary Richardson was named the new attorney general and Nixon said that Richardson
would have the authority to name a special
prosecutor to take over Watergate.

Signed bill which gave him authority to impose wage and price controls for one year.

May 2. After two days of talks with West
German Chancellor Brandt, issued a joint communiqué calling for "a comprehensive Atlan-
tic partnership among equals."

May 4. General Alexander Meigs Haig, Jr.
was appointed as White House chief of staff
to succeed Haldeman.

May 10. Mitchell and Stans were indicted
with Robert Vesco on charges stemming from
Vesco's secret contribution to Nixon's campaign fund.

May 11. Judge Byrne dismissed charges against
Ellsberg on the grounds of "improper government conduct."

May 17. The Senate Select Committee began
its televised hearings on Watergate.

May 18. Archibald Cox, a Harvard law pro-

fessor and former solicitor general under
Presidents Kennedy and Johnson, was named by
Richardson as special Watergate prosecutor.
Richardson's own nomination as attorney gen-
eral was confirmed by the Senate on May 23.

May 22. Again publicly declared his own innocence on Watergate, claiming his limiting
of investigation into the matter was because
of "national security" and that his aides
had exceeded his instructions.

May 24. F.B.I. head Hoover's 1970 opposition
to White House plans for massive domestic espionage was revealed by the New York Times.

June 1. Concluded two days of talks with
French President Pompidou in Reykjavik, Ice-
land, with inconclusive results on valuation
of the dollar.

June 5. Announced resignation of Communications Director Herbert Klein, replaced the
next day by Press Secretary Ronald L. Ziegler.

June 6. Named former Secretary of Defense
Melvin R. Laird as chief domestic advisor
on the White House staff, replacing Ehrlichman.

June 7. Nominated Clarence M. Kelley, po-
lice chief of Kansas City, Missouri, as
F.B.I. director. Confirmed by the Senate on
July 9.

June 13. Ordered a freeze on all prices except raw agricultural products and rents for
up to sixty days.

June 18. Welcomed U.S.S.R. Party Chairman
Brezhnev at the White House. The Chairman,
on a nine-day visit to the United States,
signed several agreements on détente along
with President Nixon.

June 25. John Dean began testimony before
the Senate Watergate Committee implicating
the President and his top aides in the cover-
up. Mitchell, Haldeman, and Ehrlichman denied that the President was involved.

June 29. Told Congress that United States

military involvement in Cambodia would end
by August 15.

Named Governor John A. Love, (R., Colo.),
director of the newly created Energy Policy
Office.

July 6. American Airlines chairman George
A. Spater revealed that his company had been
pressured to give an illegal corporate contribution to the 1972 Nixon campaign fund.

July 12. President Nixon was hospitalized
for one week with viral pneumonia. Former
Attorney General Mitchell, testifying before
the Senate Watergate committee, denied he
had authorized the break-in and stated that
he had tried to shield President Nixon from
knowledge of "White House Horrors."

July 16. White House aide Alexander Butterfield revealed to the Senate Watergate committee that virtually all presidential meetings and telephone conversations had been
recorded secretly since 1971.

Secretary of Defense Schlesinger admitted
secret B-52 bombings of Cambodia in 1969 and
1970.

July 18. Outlined Phase 4 of his economic
program to begin August 12. Would lift the
freeze on foods (except beef) and health-
care products.

July 23. Refused to relinquish presidential
tapes to the Ervin Committee on grounds of
"executive privilege."

July 24-27. Conferred in Washington with
Mohammad Pahlavi, the Shah of Iran.

July 30. Former chairman of the Joint Chiefs
of Staff General Earle G. Wheeler said that
President Nixon had personally ordered that
the bombing of Cambodia in 1969 and 1970 be
kept secret.

Australian Prime Minister (Edward) Gough
Whitlam met with President Nixon at the White
House.

July 31. Met with Japanese Premier Tanaka
at the White House. Announcement made next
day about a planned visit to the United
States by Emperor Hirohito.

Representative Robert F. Drinan (D., Mass.)
introduced an impeachment resolution against
President Nixon.

August 3. Warned Congress that a bombing
halt in Cambodia could have "dangerous potential consequences."

August 4. The Supreme Court ruled against
an injunction to immediately end bombing in
Cambodia.

August 6. The White House reported that $10
million had been spent for security on the
President's various homes.

August 7. Vice President Agnew announced
that he was "under investigation for possible violations of the criminal statutes."
The charges involved accepting "campaign contributions" while holding public office in
Maryland from individuals who later received
government contracts.

August 8. Before a nationally televised
press conference Agnew called the charges
against him "damned lies."

August 10. Signed a farm bill establishing
for four years a new method of subsidizing
wheat, feed grains, and cotton.

August 13. Signed a bill which for the first
time would permit the use of the Federal
Highway Trust Fund for mass transit purposes.

August 15. In televised address denied any
guilt in the Watergate cover-up.

August 20. Defended the secret bombing of
Cambodia in 1969 while speaking before a
Veterans of Foreign Wars convention in New
Orleans, Louisiana. The Secret Service can-
celed a motorcade when a possible plot to
assassinate the President was discovered.

August 22. Announced the resignation of

William Rogers and the nomination of Henry
Kissinger as Secretary of State. Dr. Kissen-
ger kept his old position as assistant to the
President for national office, and assumed
his new title on September 22.

August 29. Judge Sirica ordered President
Nixon to release the White House tapes for
his inspection, to determine whether useful
for the grand jury. The President announced
the next day that he would appeal the decision.

September 4. Ehrlichman, Krogh, Liddy, and
David R. Young indicted by a Los Angeles
grand jury for the burglary of Ellsberg's
psychiatrist's office.

September 10. In message to Congress urged
passage of more than fifty bills he had proposed.

September 13. United States Court of Appeals
urged an out-of-court settlement of the White
House tapes dispute, recommending their review by Cox.

September 25. Vice President Agnew asked
Speaker Albert to have the House investigate
charges against him since he claimed it would
be unconstitutional to have criminal charges
brought against an incumbent Vice President.
Albert refused.

September 27. Prosecutors in Baltimore,
Maryland, began presentation of evidence a-
gainst Vice President Agnew to a grand jury.

October 10. Vice President Agnew resigned,
pleading "no contest" to the charges against
him. Actually, the "plea bargaining" had
resulted in only one charge - evading income
tax in 1967. He was fined $10,000 and placed
on three years probation.

October 12. Nominated Gerald Ford, House
Republican leader, to become Vice President.

United States Circuit Court of Appeals ruled
5-2 that President Nixon must release tapes
to Judge Sirica.

October 16. Secretary of State Kissinger
and North Vietnamese negotiator Tho were a-
warded the Nobel Peace Price.

October 17-20. Arab oil embargoes drastically cut oil shipments to the United States
and raised prices.

October 19. President Nixon offered compromise plan on tapes by making available sum-
maries, to be verified by Senator John Stennis (D., Miss.). Part of the plan was that
Cox was to stop trying to get the tapes
through the courts.

October 20. Special Prosecutor Cox, refusing to agree to President Nixon's proposal,
also refused to resign saying he could only
by fired by the Attorney General. Richardson resigned rather than obey the President's
order to fire Cox. Deputy Attorney General
Ruckelshaus also refused and was himself
fired. Finally, Cox was fired by Solicitor
General Robert Bork, whom Nixon named as
acting Attorney General. The episode came
to be known as the "Saturday Night Massacre."

October 23. The events of October 20 brought
an outburst of criticism from Congress and
the public and President Nixon retreated,
promising to turn over the tapes to Judge
Sirica.

October 24. Vetoed a war-making powers bill
which would have limited a president's ability to wage an undeclared war without Congressional approval. Congress passed over
his veto on November 7.

October 25. Ordered an alert of all United
States forces because of developments in
the Middle East.

October 31. The White House announced that
two of the subpoenaed tapes were missing,
and claimed they were never made.

November 1. Nominated Senator William B.
Saxbe (R., Ohio) as attorney general. Leon
Jaworski, a Texas lawyer, was named as spe-
cial Watergate prosecutor.

November 5. Donald H. Segretti was senten-

ced by Judge Gerhard A. Gesell to six months
in prison for his activities in disrupting
the Democratic primary election in Florida
in 1972.

November 7. Addressed the nation over television on the energy crisis, asking their
cooperation and action from Congress to deal
with the oil shortage. Closed with an appeal for the American people's trust, saying
he would not walk away from the job he was
elected to do.

Congress, after many attempts to limit the
President's war-making power, finally passed
such a bill over President Nixon's veto of
October 24.

Secretary of State Kissinger and President
Sadat, meeting in Cairo, Egypt, announced
the resumption of diplomatic relations after
six years.

November 9. Judge Sirica sentenced six of
the defendants in the Watergate case. E.
Howard Hunt, Jr. received the greatest sentence - two and a half to eight years in
jail and a $10,000 fine.

November 9-15. After Gallup Polls showed
public confidence in his leadership was at
its lowest rating, 27%, began a series of
meetings with Republican leaders in an attempt to counteract the decline.

November 13. Oil company executives admitted making illegal contributions of $100,000
apiece with corporate funds to President
Nixon's 1972 campaign. Other similiar con-
fessions of wrong doing were made to the Senate Watergate Committee the next few days,
the executives claiming pressure from Commerce Secretary Stans.

November 14. The White House disclosed an
eighteen and a half minute gap in a tape of
a Haldeman-Nixon meeting in June, 1972.
Rose Mary Woods, the President's personal
secretary, said, on November 26, she might
have accidentally erased part of the missing
portion.

November 16. Signed bill authorizing construction of a trans-Alaskan oil pipeline
after it had been blocked by months of legal
bickerings.

November 17. In a televised appearance before newspaper editors in Orlando, Florida,
President Nixon said, "People have got to
know whether or not their President is a
crook. Well, I'm not a crook."

December 4. Named Deputy Secretary of the
Treasury William E. Simon to be director of
the newly created Federal Energy Office after
the resignation of John A. Love.

December 6. Gerald R. Ford was sworn in as
the fortieth Vice President after confirmation by Congress. Ford became the first person to be nominated and approved under the
provisions of the twenty-fifth amendment,
ratified in 1967.

December 8. Made public his personal finances. He had become a millionaire during his
term in office and paid less than $1,000 in
taxes in both 1970 and 1971.

December 11. Nelson A. Rockefeller (R.) announced his resignation as governor of New
York.

December 15. Signed a year-round daylight
savings bill.

December 24. Signed a bill providing home
rule for the District of Columbia.

December 31. Signed bill increasing Social
Security benefits 7%, effective March 1,
1974 and a further 4%, effective June, 1974.

1974   January 2. The Internal Revenue Service announced that it would examine President Nixon's tax returns "because of questions raised
by the press."

January 3. After being confirmed as President Nixon's fourth attorney general and
just before being sworn in, William Saxbe
called the Senate Watergate Committee's subpoena of some 500 White House tapes "a fish-

ing expedition."

January 4. The President refused to comply
with a subpoena from the Senate Watergate
Committee for more than 500 tapes, claiming
it would destroy the necessary confidentiality of presidential communications.

January 8. Issued two papers denying that
he had granted favors to the milk industry
or to IT&T in return for campaign contributions in 1971.

January 15. A panel of technical experts
appointed by Judge Sirica determined that
the eighteen and one half minute gap in the
June 20 tape was the result of five separate
manual erasures.

January 21. The Ninety-third Congress convened for its second session.

January 23. In a message to Congress on energy, proposed higher taxes on foreign profits of oil companies and a two year delay
on stricter emissions standards for autos.

January 29. Herbert L. Porter, staff member of the Committee for the Re-election of
the President, was found guilty of lying to
the F.B.I. in the early stages of the Watergate investigation. His fifteen month sentence (on April 15) was cut to thirty days.

January 30. In State of the Union message
called for an end to Watergate investigations and said he had no intention of resigning.

February 1. His annual Economic message to
Congress predicted severe inflation.

February 2. In letter to Cambodian President
Lon Nol promised that the United States would
continue the maximum possible assistance to
his government.

February 4. Sent $304.4 billion budget to
Congress for fiscal 1975.

February 6. The House of Representatives
voted 410 to 4 to proceed with its impeach-

ment probe and gave its Judiciary Committee
broad subpoena powers.

February 19. With long lines and waits at
the nation's gasoline pumps and mounting criticism about the government's handling of
the problem, Energy Administrator Simon ordered emergency allocations to twenty states.

February 25. Informed a Federal grand jury
that he would not testify on Watergate and
told a news conference he did not expect to
be impeached.

February 28. The President's position on
his impeachment was presented by his lawyers.
The report stated that it must be for "indictable crimes" of "a very serious nature"
and "committed in one's governmental capacity."

March 1. The Federal grand jury indicted
seven key former Presidential aides - Mitchell, Haldeman, Ehrlichman, Strachan, Mardian,
Parkinson, and Colson - for conspiring to
cover up the Watergate burglary.

March 6. Vetoed an emergency energy bill
which would have authorized gasoline rationing and a price rollback.

March 8. Presented a plan to reform campaign
contributions, among other things limiting
cash gifts to $50. He opposed public finan-
cing of campaigns.

March 19. Senator James Buckley of New York
called on President Nixon to resign, the
first conservative to do so.

March 26. Judge Sirica released to the House
Judiciary Committee the grand jury's report
concerning the President's involvement in
Watergate.

March 28. Secretary of State Kissinger returned to the United States following three
days of talks with Soviet officials. President Nixon's planned visit to Moscow in
June remained unchanged.

April 3. President Nixon paid $432,787 in

back taxes plus $33,000 interest after no-
tification by the I.R.S. The assessment was
largely based on the illegal donation of his
pre-presidential papers, made after the date
such contributions were prohibited.

April 5. Dwight L. Chapin, former appointments secretary to President Nixon, was
found guilty of lying about his relationships
with Donald Segretti and the "dirty tricks"
in the 1972 campaign.

April 8. Signed bill raising the minimum
wage to $2 by May 1 and providing future in-
creases and additional workers covered.

April 17. Named Energy Czar William E. Simon
to replace George P. Shultz as secretary of
the treasury. Shultz had resigned on March
14.

April 28. Mitchell and Stans were acquitted
of all charges against them in the Vesco
case.

April 29. Over nationwide television announced he would give the House Judiciary
Committee and make public edited transcripts
of the White House conversations which would
show the entire story. Chairman Rodino said
that the impeachment proceedings needed the
entire tapes.

April 30. The White House released over
1200 pages of edited transcripts of President Nixon's Watergate conversations revealing, as Republican Minority Leader Senator
Hugh Scott put it, a "deplorable, shabby,
disgusting and immoral performance" by all
those involved.

May 7. Signed bill creating a Federal Energy Administration with powers to fix gasoline allotments, ban prohibitive profits,
and develop export-import policies.

The President's lawyer, James D. St. Clair,
said that no further tapes would be turned
over to Jaworski, or to the House Judiciary
Committee.

May 9. The House Judiciary Committee began

hearings on the possible impeachment of President Nixon.

May 13. House Minority Leader Ford said that he had read the transcripts and that "the overwhelming weight of the evidence" proves the President "innocent of any of the charges."

The White House tapes reveal that President Nixon held a long talk with Rabbi Baruch Korff, who was to become one of his strongest supporters. Still proclaiming his innocence, he claimed that Watergate had been overblown by the press, but that he would survive.

May 16. Former Attorney General Kleindienst pleaded guilty to a criminal offense, giving false testimony before the Senate confirmation hearing.

May 21. Jeb Stuart Magruder was sentenced to a prison term of ten months to four years by Judge Sirica for his part in the break-in and cover-up.

May 23. Gerald Ford urged President Nixon to give the House Judiciary Committee all relevant evidence, "the quicker the better." The President, however, stated he would reject the subpoenas for Watergate related tapes issued by the House Judiciary Committee. Chairman Rodino called Nixon's refusal a "very grave matter" and might be grounds for impeachment.

May 24. Special Watergate prosecutor Jaworski appealed directly to the Supreme Court to rule on his subpoena for additional tapes.

June 7. Former Attorney General Kleindienst was given a light and suspended sentence by Judge George L. Hart, who described Kleindienst as a man of "highest integrity" but with "a heart that is too loyal."

June 11. Henry Kissinger, at a Salzburg, Austria news conference, threatened to resign unless he was cleared of charges that he participated in illegal wiretaps.

June 12-19. On a five-nation visit to the Middle East, made important declarations of friendship, with Egypt in particular.

June 17. Herbert W. Kalmbach, President Nixon's former presonal lawyer, was sentenced
to six to eight months in prison and fined
$10,000. He had been allowed to plead guilty
on February 25 to a lesser charge in exchange
for his cooperation on the Watergate Case.

June 21. Charles Colson, former White House
aide, said that President Nixon had urged
him to commit the acts for which he was about
to be imprisoned. Colson was sentenced to
one to three years and fined $5,000.

June 24. Rumors about the President's health
were confirmed by a White House announcement
that he had suffered from phlebitis before
and during his Middle East trip.

June 28. Meeting with Soviet leader Brezhnev in Moscow, agreed to a further limitation
of defensive anti-ballistic missiles in their
two countries.

July 2. In Moscow, addressed the Soviet people on television.

July 3. Back in the United States reported
to the American people on his summit meetings in the U.S.S.R.

July 9. Earl Warren, retired Chief Justice
of the Supreme Court, died at eighty-three.

July 12. Signed bill which curbed his power
to impound appropriated funds by requiring
agreement by Congress.

Ehrlichman, Liddy, Barker and Martinez were
found guilty in the "plumbers trial" of the
break-in at Ellsberg's psychiatrist's office.
Ehrlichman was also found guilty of perjury.

July 16. During an interview, called Watergate "the broadest but thinnest scandal in
American history."

July 24. The Supreme Court ruled 8-0 that
President Nixon must turn over sixty-four
tapes of Watergate discussions. Among the
tapes was the revealing June 23, 1972 con-

versation with Haldeman. The President's
lawyer, James St. Clair, announced that President Nixon would comply.

July 27-30. The House Judiciary Committee,
conducting its hearings before nationwide
television, voted three articles of impeachment against President Nixon - obstruction
of justice, abuse of power, and unconstitu-
tionally defying its subpoenas.

July 29. Former Secretary of the Treasury
John B. Connally was indicted on five counts
by the Watergate grand jury.

July 31. Ehrlichman was sentenced to twenty
months to five years for his part in the
Fielding burglary.

August 2. Dean was sentenced to one to four
years for his part in the cover-up.

August 5. Released three new transcripts of
conversations he had with Haldeman on June
23, 1972, six days after the Watergate break-
in. The tapes showed that the President had
personally ordered a cover-up. He released
a statement with the transcripts' release
admitting he had kept this evidence from his
own lawyers and his supporters on the Judiciary Committee.

August 6. Told his cabinet he did not intend to resign and would let the constitutional process run its course. Calls for
his resignation had been coming from even
his staunchest supporters in Congress.

August 7. President Nixon met with Senators
Scott and Goldwater, and Representative John
Rhodes who told him he would have only ten
supporters in the House and fifteen in the
Senate in an impeachment trial.

August 8. During the day met with Kissinger,
Ford and a few Congressional leaders and
stated his decision to resign. That night,
on nationwide television, announced his resignation effective at noon the next day.

August 9. After a brief farewell speech to
his staff, left the White House to board Air

Force One to fly to California. At 11:35
A.M., while he was still airborne, his letter
of resignation was delivered to Secretary of
State Kissinger. Gerald R. Ford thus became
the thirty-eighth President, and was sworn
into office by Chief Justice Burger at 12:03
P.M.

RETIREMENT

August 20. President Ford named former New
York Governor Rockefeller as his choice for
Vice President.

The House of Representatives passed a resolution 412-3 accepting the report of the Judiciary Committee on its impeachment inquiry.
Included was a signed statement by the eleven
representatives who had originally dissented
from Article I, which charged a criminal conspiracy to cover-up the Watergate break-in,
that the new evidence released by Nixon on
August 5 caused them to reverse their position.

September 7. C.I.A. director Colby testified
before a Congressional committee in April,
reported the New York Times, that the Nixon
Administration had authorized the spending
of $8 million for covert activities in Chile
against President Salvador Allende Gossens.

September 8. President Ford announced that
he was granting an unconditional pardon to
former President Nixon for all federal crimes
that he "committed or may have committed or
taken part in" while serving as president.
Nixon issued a statement from San Clemente,
California, saying he accepted the pardon
and that he had been wrong in not acting more
forthrightly in dealing with Watergate.

September 9. Widespread criticism was directed against President Ford for his pardon of
Nixon. His own recently appointed Press Secretary resigned as a matter of conscience
in protest over the pardon. Reports that he
contemplated a blanket pardon for Watergate
defendants met such bipartisan criticism that
Ford was led to announce he would not until
the judicial process had been completed. He

insisted that there had been "no deal" before
the Nixon resignation.

September 23. Nixon entered Hospital Center
in Long Beach, California, for tests and
treatment of a new attack of phlebitis. The
statement issued by President Ford, along
with the pardon of Nixon, had alluded to the
ex-President's health.

October 1. The trial of five of President
Nixon's closest aides opened before Judge Sirica in Washington.

October 5. Fred Buzhardt resigned as White
House legal counsel.

October 12. Watergate Special Prosecutor Ja-
worski announced his resignation, effective
November 1. He made it clear that his resig-
nation was in no way a result of President
Ford's unconditional pardon of Nixon. On
October 26, his chief deputy, Henry S. Ruth,
Jr., was sworn in as the third Watergate pro-
secutor.

October 21. District Judge Charles R. Richey
issued a restraining order barring former
President Nixon access to his White House
tapes and papers, as permitted in an earlier
agreement with President Ford.

October 29. After surgery on a potentially
lethal blood clot on his leg, the former
President went into a coma and was on the
critical list for several hours. Nixon had
reentered the hospital on October 23.

November 1. President Ford visited Nixon at
the hospital.

November 4. Henry E. Petersen resigned as
Assistant Attorney General.

November 13. Judge Sirica appointed a panel
of physicians to determine if former President Nixon was physically able to testify in
the Watergate cover-up trial.

November 15. Patrick J. Buchanan resigned
as counselor to the President on political
affairs.

November 20. The Reverend John McLaughlin,
a former counselor to President Nixon, claimed history would rank Nixon as a "great or
near great" president. Participating in a
colloquium on Watergate at Briarcliff College
in Briarcliff Manor, New York, he claimed
Nixon had done no wrong, but had been perse-
cuted by "McCarthyesque" techniques by the
Senate Watergate Committee. The principal
speaker, Sam Dash, counsel to the committee,
the rest of the panel, and the majority of
the audience were in complete disagreement.

November 25. The court-appointed panel of
physicians visited Mr. Nixon in the Long
Beach hospital. Their report to Judge Sirica said that Mr. Nixon could not presently
travel to Washington, but might by February.

December 2. Dean Burch resigned after serving on the White House staff since February.

December 10. Nelson Rockefeller was confirmed for Vice President by a 90-7 vote of the
Senate. A House vote was pending.

December 19. The House voted 287-128 to
confirm Rockefeller as Vice President. He
was then sworn in, before nationwide television, the first event ever televised in
the Senate chamber.

President Ford signed law denying Nixon custody of his presidential documents, which
were to be put in the custody of the General
Services Administration.

Edward L. Morgan sentenced to four months in
prison for conspiring to violate federal tax
laws by backdating the transfer of Nixon's
papers.

DOCUMENTS

DOCUMENTS
My Side of the Story

TRUTH THE BEST ANSWER TO A SMEAR
By RICHARD M. NIXON, *Republican Candidate for Vice President*
Delivered as a nationwide broadcast, Los Angeles, California, September 23, 1952

MY Fellow Americans: I come before you tonight as a candidate for the Vice Presidency and as a man whose honesty and integrity have been questioned.

The usual political thing to do when charges are made against you is to either ignore them or to deny them without giving details.

I believe we've had enough of that in the United States, particularly with the present Administration in Washington, D. C. To me the office of the Vice Presidency of the United States is a great office, and I feel that the people have got to have confidence in the integrity of the men who run for that office and who might obtain it.

I have a theory, too, that the best and only answer to a smear or to an honest misunderstanding of the facts is to tell the truth. And that's why I'm here tonight. I want to tell you my side of the case.

I am sure that you have read the charge and you've heard that I, Senator Nixon, took $18,000 from a group of my supporters.

WAS IT WRONG?

Now, was that wrong? And let me say that it was wrong —I'm saying, incidentally, that it was wrong and not just illegal. Because it isn't a question of whether it was legal or illegal, that isn't enough. The question is, was it morally wrong?

I say that it was morally wrong if any of that $18,000 went to Senator Nixon for my personal use. I say that it was morally wrong if it was secretly given and secretly handled. And I say that it was morally wrong if any of the contributors got special favors for the contributions that they made.

And now to answer those questions let me say this:

Not one cent of the $18,000 or any other money of that type ever went to me for my personal use. Every penny of it was used to pay for political expenses that I did not think should be charged to the taxpayers of the United States.

It was not a secret fund. As a matter of fact, when I was on "Meet the Press," some of you may have seen it last Sunday—Peter Edson came up to me after the program and he

Source: Vital Speeches of the Day, October 15, 1952; City News Publishing Company, Southold, New York. By permission of the publisher.

said, "Dick, what about this fund we hear about?" And I
said, Well, there's no secret about it. Go out and see Dana
Smith, who was the administrator of the fund. And I gave
him his address, and I said that you will find that the purpose of the fund simply was to defray political expenses that
I did not feel should be charged to the Government.

And third, let me point out, and I want to make this particularly clear, that no contributor to this fund, no contributor to any of my campaign, has ever received any consideration that he would not have received as an ordinary constituent.

I just don't believe in that and I can say that never, while
I have been in the Senate of the United States, as far as the
people that contributed to this fund are concerned, have I
made a telephone call for them to an agency, or have I gone
down to an agency in their behalf. And the record will show
that, the records which are in the hands of the Administration.

WHAT FOR AND WHY?

But then some of you will say and rightly, "Well, what
did you use the fund for, Senator? Why did you have to
have it?"

Let me tell you in just a word how a Senate office oper-
ates. First of all, a Senator gets $15,000 a year in salary.
He gets enough money to pay for one trip a year, a round
trip that is, for himself and his family between his home and
Washington, D. C.

And then he gets an allowance to handle the people that
work in his office, to handle his mail. And the allowance
for my State of California is enough to hire thirteen people.

And let me say, incidentally, that that allowance is not
paid to the Senator—it's paid directly to the individuals that
the Senator puts on his payroll, that all of these people and
all of these allowances are for strictly official business. Business, for example, when a constituent writes in and wants
you to go down to the Veterans Administration and get some
information about his GI policy. Items of that type for example.

But there are other expenses which are not covered by the
Government. And I think I can best discuss those expenses
by asking you some questions. Do you think that when I or
any other Senator makes a political speech, has it printed,
should charge the printing of that speech and the mailing of
that speech to the taxpayers?

Do you think, for example, when I or any other Senator
makes a trip to his home state to make a purely political
speech that the cost of that trip should be charged to the taxpayers?

Do you think when a Senator makes political broadcasts
or political television broadcasts, radio or television, that the
expense of those broadcasts should be charged to the taxpayers?

Well, I know what your answer is. The same answer that
audiences give me whenever I discuss this particular prob-

lem. The answer is, "no." The taxpayers shouldn't be required to finance items which are not official business but which are primarily political business.

But then the question arises, you say, "Well, how do you pay for these and how can you do it legally?"

And there are several ways that it can be done, incidentally, and that it is done legally in the United States Senate and in the Congress.

The first way is to be a rich man. I don't happen to be a rich man so I couldn't use that.

Another way that is used is to put your wife on the payroll. Let me say, incidentally, my opponent, my opposite number for the Vice Presidency on the Democratic ticket, does have his wife on the payroll. And has had her on his payroll for the ten years—the past ten years.

Now just let me say this. That's his business and I'm not critical of him for doing that. You will have to pass judgment on that particular point. But I have never done that for this reason. I have found that there are so many deserving stenographers and secretaries in Washington that needed the work that I just didn't feel it was right to put my wife on the payroll.

My wife's sitting over here. She's a wonderful stenographer. She used to teach stenography and she used to teach shorthand in high school. That was when I met her. And I can tell you folks that she's worked many hours at night and many hours on Saturdays and Sundays in my office and she's done a fine job. And I'm proud to say tonight that in the six years I've been in the House and the Senate of the United States, Pat Nixon has never been on the Government payroll.

There are other ways that these finances can be taken care of. Some who are lawyers, and I happen to be a lawyer, continue to practice law. But I haven't been able to do that. I'm so far away from California that I've been so busy with my Senatorial work that I have not engaged in any legal practice.

And also as far as law practice is concerned, it seemed to me that the relationship between an attorney and the client was so personal that you couldn't possibly represent a man as an attorney and then have an unbiased view when he presented his case to you in the event that he had one before the Government.

And so I felt that the best way to handle these necessary political expenses of getting my message to the American people and the speeches I made, the speeches that I had printed, for the most part, concerned this one message—of exposing this Administration, the communism in it, the corruption in it—the only way that I could do that was to accept the aid which people in my home state of California who contributed to my campaign and who continued to make these contributions after I was elected were glad to make.

No Special Favors

And let me say I am proud of the fact that not one of them has ever asked me for a special favor. I'm proud of the fact that not one of them has ever asked me to vote on a bill other than as my own conscience would dictate. And I am proud of the fact that the taxpayers by subterfuge or otherwise have never paid one dime for expenses which I thought were political and shouldn't be charged to the taxpayers.

Let me say, incidentally, that some of you may say, "Well, that's all right, Senator; that's your explanation, but have you got any proof?"

And I'd like to tell you this evening that just about an hour ago we received an independent audit of this entire fund.

I suggested to Gov. Sherman Adams, who is the chief of staff of the Dwight Eisenhower campaign, that an independent audit and legal report be obtained. And I have that audit here in my hand.

It's an audit made by the Price, Waterhouse & Co. firm, and the legal opinion by Gibson, Dunn & Crutcher, lawyers in Los Angeles, the biggest law firm and incidentally one of the best ones in Los Angeles.

I'm proud to be able to report to you tonight that this audit and this legal opinion is being forwarded to General Eisenhower. And I'd like to read to you the opinion that was prepared by Gibson, Dunn & Crutcher and based on all the pertinent laws and statutes, together with the audit report prepared by the certified public accountants.

"It is our conclusion that Senator Nixon did not obtain any financial gain from the collection and disbursement of the fund by Dana Smith; that Senator Nixon did not violate any Federal or state law by reason of the operation of the fund, and that neither the portion of the fund paid by Dana Smith directly to third persons nor the portion paid to Senator Nixon to reimburse him for designated office expenses constituted income to the Senator which was either reportable or taxable as income under applicable tax laws. (signed) Gibson, Dunn & Crutcher by Alma H. Conway."

Now that, my friends, is not Nixon speaking, but that's an independent audit which was requested because I want the American people to know all the facts and I'm not afraid of having independent people go in and check the facts, and that is exactly what they did.

But then I realize that there are still some who may say, and rightly so, and let me say that I recognize that some will continue to smear regardless of what the truth may be, but that there has been understandably some honest misunderstanding on this matter, and there's some that will say:

"Well, maybe you were able, Senator, to fake this thing. How can we believe what you say? After all, is there a possibility that maybe you got some sums in cash? Is there a possibility that you may have feathered your own nest?"

FINANCIAL HISTORY

And so now what I am going to do—and incidentally this is unprecedented in the history of American politics—I am going at this time to give to this television and radio audience a complete financial history; everything I've earned; everything I've spent; everything I owe. And I want you to know the facts. I'll have to start early.

I was born in 1913. Our family was one of modest circumstances and most of my early life was spent in a store out in East Whittier. It was a grocery store—one of those family enterprises. The only reason we were able to make it go was because my mother and dad had five boys and we all worked in the store.

I worked my way through college and to a great extent through law school. And then, in 1940, probably the best thing that ever happened to me happened, I married Pat—sitting over here. We had a rather difficult time after we were married, like so many of the young couples who may be listening to us. I practiced law; she continued to teach School. I went into the service.

Let me say that my service record was not a particularly unusual one. I went to the South Pacific. I guess I'm entitled to a couple of battle stars. I got a couple of letters of commendation but I was just there when the bombs were falling and then I returned. I returned to the United States and in 1946 I ran for the Congress.

When we came out of the war, Pat and I—Pat during the war had worked as a stenographer and in a bank and as an economist for a Government agency—and when we came out the total of our savings from both my law practice, her teaching and all the time that I was in the war—the total for that entire period was just a little less than $10,000. Every cent of that, incidentally, was in Government bonds.

Well, that's where we start when I go into politics. Now what have I earned since I went into politics? Well, here it is—I jotted it down, let me read the notes. First of all I've had my salary as a Congressman and as a Senator. Second, I have received a total in this past six years of $1,600 from estates which were in my law firm at the time that I severed my connection with it.

And, incidentally, as I said before, I have not engaged in any legal practice and have not accepted any fees from business that came into the firm after I went into politics. I have made an average of aproximately $1,500 a year from nonpolitical speaking engagements and lectures. And then, fortunately, we've inherited a little money. Pat sold her interest in her father's estate for $3,000 and I inherited $1,500 from my grandfather.

We live rather modestly. For four years we lived in an apartment in Park Fairfax, in Alexandria, Va. The rent was $80 a month. And we saved for the time that we could buy a house.

Now, that was what we took in. What did we do with this money? What do we have today to show for it? This will surprise you, because it is so little, I suppose, as standards generally go, of people in public life. First of all, we've got a house in Washington which cost $41,000 and on which we owe $20,000.

We have a house in Whittier, Calif., which cost $13,000 and on which we owe $10,000. My folks are living there at the present time.

I have just $4,000 in life insurance, plus my G. I. policy which I've never been able to convert and which will run out in two years. I have no life insurance whatever on Pat. I have no life insurance on our two youngsters, Patricia and Julie. I own a 1950 Oldsmobile car. We have our furniture. We have no stocks and bonds of any type. We have no interest of any kind, direct or indirect, in any business.

What Do We Owe?

Now, that's what we have. What do we owe? Well, in addition to the mortgage, the $20,000 mortgage on the house in Washington, the $10,000 one on the house in Whittier, I owe $4,500 to the Riggs Bank in Washington, D. C. with interest 4½ per cent.

I owe $3,500 to my parents and the interest on that loan which I pay regularly, because it's the part of the savings they made through the years they were working so hard, I pay regularly 4 per cent interest. And then I have a $500 loan which I have on my life insurance.

Well, that's about it. That's what we have and that's what we owe. It isn't very much but Pat and I have the satisfaction that every dime that we've got is honestly ours. I should say this—that Pat doesn't have a mink coat. But she does have a respectable Republican cloth coat. And I always tell her that she'd look good in anything.

One other thing I probably should tell you because if I don't they'll probably be saying this about me too, we did get something—a gift—after the election. A man down in Texas heard Pat on the radio mention the fact that our two youngsters would like to have a dog. And, believe it or not, the day before we left on this campaign trip we got a message from Union Station in Baltimore saying they had a package for us. We went down to get it. You know what it was.

It was a little cocker spaniel dog in a crate that he sent all the way from Texas. Black and white spotted. And our little girl—Trisha, the 6-year-old—named it Checkers. And you know, the kids love the dog and I just want say this right now, that regardless of what they say about it, we're gonna keep it.

It isn't easy to come before a nation-wide audience and air your life as I've done. But I want to say some things before I conclude that I think most of you will agree on. Mr. Mitchell, the chairman of the Democratic National Committee, made the statement that if a man couldn't afford to be in the United States Senate he shouldn't run for the Senate.

And I just want to make my position clear. I don't agree with Mr. Mitchell when he says that only a rich man should serve his Government in the United States Senate or in the Congress.

I don't believe that represents the thinking of the Democratic party, and I know that it doesn't represent the thinking of the Republican Party.

I believe that it's fine that a man like Governor Stevenson who inherited a fortune from his father can run for President. But I also feel that it's essential in this country of ours that a man of modest means can also run for President. Because, you know, remember Abraham Lincoln, you remember what he said: 'God must have loved the common people—he made so many of them.'

COURSES OF CONDUCT

And now I'm going to suggest some courses of conduct.

First of all, you have read in the papers about other funds now. Mr. Stevenson, apparently, had a couple. One of them in which a group of business people paid and helped to supplement the salaries of state employees. Here is where the money went directly into their pockets.

And I think that what Mr. Stevenson should do should be to come before the American people as I have, give the names of the people that have contributed to that fund; give the names of the people who put this money into their pockets at the same time that they were receiving money from their state government, and see what favors, if any, they gave out for that.

I don't condemn Mr. Stevenson for what he did. But until the facts are in there there is a doubt that will be raised.

And as far as Mr. Sparkman is concerned, I would suggest the same thing. He's had his wife on the payroll. I don't condemn him for that. But I think that he should come before the American people and indicate what outside sources of income he has had.

I would suggest that under the circumstances both Mr. Sparkman and Mr. Stevenson should come before the American people as I have and make a complete financial statement as to their financial history. And if they don't it will be an admission that they have something to hide. And I think that you will agree with me.

Because, folks, remember, a man that's to be President of the United States, a man that's to be Vice President of the United States must have the confidence of all the people. And that's why I'm doing what I'm doing, and that's why I suggest that Mr. Stevenson and Mr. Sparkman since they are under attack should do what I am doing.

Now, let me say this: I know that this is not the last of the smears. In spite of my explanation tonight other smears will be made; others have been made in the past. And the purpose of the smears, I know, is this—to silence me, to make me let up.

Well, they just don't know who they're dealing with.

I'm going to tell you this: I remember in the dark days of
the Hiss case some of the same columnists, some of the same
radio commentators who are attacking me now and misre-
presenting my position were violently opposing me at the
time I was after Alger Hiss.

To Continue Fight

But I continued the fight because I knew I was right.
And I can say to this great television and radio audience
that I have no apologies to the American people for my part
in putting Alger Hiss where he is today.

And as far as this is concerned, I intend to continue the
fight.

Why do I feel so deeply? Why do I feel that in spite of
the smears, the misunderstandings, the necessities for a man
to come up here and bare his soul as I have? Why is it necessary for me to continue this fight?

And I want to tell you why. Because, you see, I love my
country. And I think my country is in danger. And I think
that the only man that can save America at this time is the
man that's running for President on my ticket—Dwight
Eisenhower.

You say, "Why do I think it's in danger?" and I say
look at the record. Seven years of the Truman-Acheson Administration and what's happened? Six hundred million people lost to the Communists, and a war in Korea in which
we have lost 117,000 American casualties.

And I say to all of you that a policy that results in a loss
of 600,000,000 to the Communists and a war which costs
us 117,000 American casualties isn't good enough for America.

And I say that those in the State Department that made
the mistakes which caused that war and which resulted in
those losses should be kicked out of the State Department
just as fast as we can get 'em out of there.

And let me say that I know Mr. Stevenson won't do that.
Because he defends the Truman policy and I know that
Dwight Eisenhower will do that, and that he will give
America the leadership that it needs.

Take the problem of corruption. You've read about the
mess in Washington. Mr. Stevenson can't clean it up because he was picked by the man, Truman, under whose Administration the mess was made. You wouldn't trust a man
who made the mess to clean it up—that's Truman. And by
the same token you can't trust the man who was picked by
the man that made the mess to clean it up—and that's
Stevenson.

And so I say, Eisenhower, who owes nothing to Truman,
nothing to the big city bosses, he is the man that can clean
up the mess in Washington.

Take Communism. I say that as far as that subject is
concerned, the danger is great to America. In the Hiss case
they got the secrets which enabled them to break the American secret State Department code. They got secrets in the

atomic bomb case which enabled 'em to get the secret of the
atomic bomb, five years before they would have gotten it by
their own devices.

And I say that any man who called the Alger Hiss case a
"red herring" isn't fit to be President of the United States.
I say that a man who like Mr. Stevenson has pooh-poohed
and ridiculed the Communist threat in the United States—
he said that they are phantoms among ourselves; he's accused
us that have attempted to expose the Communists of looking
for Communists in the Bureau of Fisheries and Wildlife—
I say that a man who says that isn't qualified to be President
of the United States.

And I say that the only man who can lead us in this fight
to rid the Government of both those who are Communists
and those who have corrupted this Government is Eisenhower, because Eisenhower, you can be sure, recognizes the
problem and he knows how to deal with it.

Now let me say that, finally, this evening I want to read
to you just briefly excerpts from a letter which I received,
a letter which, after all this is over, no one can take away
from me. It reads as follows:

"Dear Senator Nixon,

"Since I'm only 19 years of age I can't vote in this Presidential election but believe me if I could you and General
Eisenhower would certainly get my vote. My husband is
in the Fleet Marines in Korea. He's a corpsman on the front
lines and we have a two-month-old son he's never seen. And
I feel confident that with great Americans like you and General Eisenhower in the White House, lonely Americans like
myself will be united with their loved ones now in Korea.

"I only pray to God that you won't be too late. Enclosed
is a small check to help you in your campaign. Living on
$85 a month it is all I can afford at present. But let me know
what else I can do."

Folks, it's a check for $10, and it's one that I will never
cash.

And just let me say this. We hear a lot about prosperity
these days but I say, why can't we have prosperity built on
peace rather than prosperity built on war? Why can't we
have prosperity and an honest government in Washington,
D. C., at the same time. Believe me, we can. And Eisenhower is the man that can lead this crusade to bring us that
kind of prosperity.

And, now, finally, I know that you wonder whether or
not I am going to stay on the Republican ticket or resign.

Let me say this: I don't believe that I ought to quit because I'm not a quitter. And, incidentally, Pat's not a quitter. After all, her name was Patricia Ryan and she was born
on St. Patrick's Day, and you know the Irish never quit.

But the decision, my friends, is not mine. I would do
nothing that would harm the possibilities of Dwight Eisenhower to become President of the United States. And for
that reason I am submitting to the Republican National
Committee tonight through this television broadcast the decision which it is theirs to make.

Let them decide whether my position on the ticket will help or hurt. And I am going to ask you to help them decide. Wire and write the Republican National Committee whether you think I should stay on or whether I should get off. And whatever their decision is, I will abide by it.

But just let me say this last word. Regardless of what happens I'm going to continue this fight. I'm going to campaign up and down America until we drive the crooks and the Communists and those that defend them out of Washington. And remember, folks, Eisenhower is a great man. Believe me. He's a great man. And a vote for Eisenhower is a vote for what's good for America.

PRINCIPLES OF U.S. GOVERNMENT

In 1963 Richard M. Nixon was admitted on
motion to the Bar of the State of New York.
When applying to the Appellate Division he
made the following statement, which so im-
pressed Senator William Proxmire, Democrat of Wisconsin, that he had it reprinted
in the Congressional Record:

Source: Congressional Record, Vol. 109, Pt.
18, December 9, 1963.

The principles underlying the Government of the United States are decentralization of power, separation of power and maintaining a balance between freedom and order.

Above all else, the framers of the Constitution were fearful of the con-
centration of power in either individuals or government. The genius of their
solution in this respect is that they were able to maintain a very definite
but delicate balance between the Federal Government and the State government, on the one hand, and between the executive, legislative, and judicial
branches of the Federal Government, on the other hand.

By contrast, in the British system, the Parliament is supreme. In the
present French system the primary power resides in the executive, and in
some older civilizations the judges were predominant. Throughout American
history there have been times when one or the other branches of Government
would seem to have gained a dominant position, but the pendulum has always
swung back and the balance over the long haul maintained.

The concept of decentralization of power is maintained by what we call
the Federal system. But the principle is much broader in practice. Putting
it most simply, the American ideal is that private or industrial enterprise
should be allowed and encouraged to undertake all functions which it is capable to perform. Only when private enterprise cannot or will not do what
needs to be done should government step in. When Government action is
required, it should be undertaken if possible by that unit of government closest to the people. For example, the progression should be from local, to
State, to Federal Government in that order. In other words, the Federal
Government should step in only when the function to be performed is too
big for the State or local government to undertake.

Inaugural Address

SEARCH FOR PEACE

By RICHARD M. NIXON, *President of the United States*

Delivered as Inaugural Address, Washington, D. C., January 20, 1969

SENATOR DIRKSEN, Mr. Chief Justice, Mr. Vice President, President Johnson, Vice President Humphrey, my fellow Americans and my fellow citizens of the world community: I ask you to share with me today the majesty of this moment. In the orderly transfer of power, we celebrate the unity that keeps us free.

Each moment in history is a fleeting time, precious and unique. But some stand out as moments of beginning, in which courses are set that shape decades or centuries.

This can be such a moment. Forces now are converging that make possible for the first time the hope that many of man's deepest aspirations can at last be realized.

The spiraling pace of change allows us to contemplate, within our own lifetime, advances that once would have taken centuries.

In throwing wide the horizons of space, we have discovered new horizons on earth.

For the first time, because the people of the world want peace and the leaders of the world are afraid of war, the times are on the side of peace.

Eight years from now America will celebrate its 200th anniversary as a nation. And within the lifetime of most people now living, mankind will celebrate that great new year which comes only once in a thousand years—the beginning of the third millennium.

What kind of a nation we will be, what kind of a world we will live in, whether we shape the future in the image of our hopes, is ours to determine by our actions and our choices.

The greatest honor history can bestow is the title of peacemaker. This honor now beckons America—the chance to help lead the world at last out of the valley of turmoil and on to that high ground of peace that man has dreamed of since the dawn of civilization.

If we succeed, generations to come will say of us now living that we mastered our moment, that we helped make the world safe for mankind.

This is our summons to greatness.

And I believe the American people are ready to answer this call.

Source: Vital Speeches of the Day, February 1, 1969; City News Publishing Company, Southold, New York. By permission of the publisher.

The second third of this century has been a time of proud achievement. We have made enormous strides in science and industry and agriculture. We have shared out wealth more broadly than ever, we learned at last to manage a modern economy to assure its continued growth.

We have given freedom new reach, we have begun to make its promise real for black as well as for white.

We see the hope of tomorrow in the youth of today. I know America's youth. I believe in them. We can be proud that they are better educated, more committed, more passionately driven by conscience than any generation in our history.

No people has ever been so close to the achievement of a just and abundant society, or so possessed of the will to achieve it.

And because our strengths are so great, we can afford to appraise our weaknesses with candor and to approach them with hope.

Standing in this same place a third of a century ago, Franklin Delano Roosevelt addressed the nation ravaged by depression gripped in fear. He could say in surveying the nation's troubles: "They concern, thank God, only material things."

Our crisis today is in reverse.

We find ourselves rich in goods, but ragged in spirit; reaching with magnificent precision for the moon, but falling into raucous discord on earth.

We are caught in war, wanting peace. We're torn by division, wanting unity. We see around us empty lives, wanting fulfillment. We see tasks that need doing, waiting for hands to do them.

To a crisis of the spirit, we need an answer of the spirit.

And to find that answer, we need only look within ourselves.

When we listen to "the better angels of our nature," we find that they celebrate the simple things, the basic things, the basic things—such as goodness, decency, love, kindness.

Greatness comes in simple trappings.

The simple things are the ones most needed today if we are to surmount what divides us and cement what unites us. To lower our voices would be a simple thing.

In these difficult years, America has suffered from a fever of words; from inflated rhetoric that promises more than it can deliver; from angry rhetoric that fans discontents into hatreds; from bombastic rhetoric that postures instead of persuading.

We cannot learn from one another until we stop shouting at one another—until we speak quietly enough so that our words can be heard as well as our voices.

For its part, government will listen. We will strive to listen in new ways—to the voices of quiet anguish, the voices that speak without words, the voices of the heart—to the injured voices, the anxious voices, the voices that have despaired of being heard.

Those who have been left out we will try to bring in. Those left behind, we will help to catch up.

For all our people, we will set as our goal the decent order that makes progress possible and our lives secure.

As we reach toward our hopes, our task is to build on what has gone before—not turning away from the old, but turning toward the new.

In this past third of a century, government has passed more laws, spent more money, initiated more programs, than in all our previous history.

In pursuing our goals of full employment, better housing, excellence in education; in rebuilding our cities and improving our rural areas; in protecting our environment, enhancing the quality of life—in all these and more, we will and must press urgently forward.

We shall plan now for the day when our wealth can be transferred from the destruction of war abroad to the urgent needs of our people at home.

The American dream does not come to those who fall asleep.

But we are approaching the limits of what government alone can do.

Our greatest need now is to reach beyond government, to enlist the legions of the concerned and the committed. What has to be done has to be done by government and people together or it will not be done at all. The lesson of past agony is that without the people we can do nothing; with the people we can do everything.

To match the magnitude of our talks, we need the energies of our people—enlisted not only in grand enterprises, but more importantly in those small splendid efforts that make headlines in the neighborhood newspaper instead of the national journal.

With these, we can build a great cathedral of the spirit— each of us raising it one stone at a time, as he reaches out to his neighbor, helping, caring, doing.

I do not offer a life of uninspiring ease. I do not call for a life of grim sacrifice. I ask you to join in a high adventure— one as rich as humanity itself, and exciting as the times we live in.

The essence of freedom is that each of us shares in the shaping of his own destiny. Until he has been part of a cause larger than himself, no man is truly whole.

The way to fulfillment is in the use of our talents; we achieve nobility in the spirit that inspires that use.

As we measure what can be done, we shall promise only what we know we can produce; but as we chart our goals we shall be lifted by our dreams.

No man can be fully free while his neighbor is not. To go forward at all is to go forward together.

This means black and white together, as one nation, not two. The laws have caught up with our conscience. What remains is to give life to what is in the law: to insure at last that as all are born equal in dignity before God, all are born equal in dignity before man.

As we learn to go forward together at home, let us also seek to go forward together with all mankind.

Let us take as our goal: where peace is unknown, make it welcome; where peace is fragile, make it strong; where peace is temporary, make it permanent.

After a period of confrontation, we are entering an era of negotiation. Let all nations know that during this Administration our lines of communication will be open.

We seek an open world—open to ideas, open to the exchange of goods and people, a world in which no people, great or small, will live in angry isolation.

We cannot expect to make everyone our friend, but we can try to make no one our enemy.

Those who would be our adversaries, we invite to a peaceful competition—not in conquering territory or extending dominion, but in enriching the life of man.

As we explore the reaches of space, let us go to the new worlds together—not as new worlds to be conquered, but as a new adventure to be shared.

And with those who are willing to join, let us cooperate to reduce the burden of arms, to strengthen the structure of peace, to lift up the poor and the hungry.

But to all those who would be tempted by weakness, let us leave no doubt that we will be as strong as we need to be for as long as we need to be.

Over the past 20 years, since I first came to this Capitol as a freshman Congressman, I have visited most of the nations of the world.

I have come to know the leaders of the world, the great forces, the hatreds, the fears that divide the world.

I know that peace does not come through wishing for it— that there is no substitute for days and even years of patient and prolonged diplomacy.

I also know the people of the world.

I have seen the hunger of a homeless child, the pain of a man wounded in battle, the grief of a mother who has lost her son. I know these have no ideology, no race.

I know America. I know the heart of America is good.

I speak from my own heart, and the heart of my country, the deep concern we have for those who suffer and those who sorrow.

I have taken an oath today in the presence of God and my countrymen. To uphold and defend the Constitution of the United States. And to that oath, I now add this sacred commitment: I shall consecrate my office, my energies and all the wisdom I can summon, to the cause of peace among nations.

Let this message be heard by strong and weak alike.

The peace we seek—the peace we seek to win—is not victory over any other people, but the peace that comes with healing in its wings; with compassion for those who have suffered; with understanding for those who have opposed us; with the opportunity for all the peoples of this earth to choose their own destiny.

Only a few short weeks ago, we shared the glory of man's first sight of the world as God sees it, as a single sphere reflecting light in the darkness.

As Apollo astronauts flew over the moon's gray surface on Christmas Eve, they spoke to us of the beauty of earth and in that voice so clear across the lunar distance we heard them invoke God's blessing on its goodness.

In that moment, their view from the moon moved poet Archibald MacLeish to write: "To see the earth as it truly is, small and blue and beautiful in that eternal silence where it floats, is to see ourselves as riders on the earth together, brothers in that bright loveliness in the eternal cold—brothers who know now they are truly brothers."

In that moment of surpassing technological triumph, men turned their thoughts toward home and humanity—seeing in that far perspective that man's destiny on earth is not divisible; telling us that however far we reach into the cosmos our destiny lies not in the stars but on earth itself, in our own hands, in our own hearts.

We have endured a long night of the American spirit. But as our eyes catch the dimness of the first rays of dawn, let us not curse the remaining dark. Let us gather the light.

Our destiny offers not the cup of despair, but the chalice of opportunity. So let us seize it, not in fear, but in gladness—and "riders on the earth together," let us go forward, firm in our faith, steadfast in our purpose, cautious of the dangers; but sustained by our confidence in the will of God and the promise of man.

Campus Revolutionaries

THE RIGHTS OF STUDENTS

By RICHARD M. NIXON, *President of the United States*

Delivered at General Beadle State College, Madison, South Dakota, June 3, 1969

FREEDOM. A condition and a process. As we dedicate this beautiful new library, I think this is the time and place to speak of some basic things in American life. It is the time, because we find our fundamental values under bitter and even violent attack; it is the place, because so much that is basic is represented here.

Opportunity for all is represented here.

This is a small college: not rich and famous, like Harvard or Yale; not a vast state university like Berkeley or Michigan. But for almost 90 years it has served the people of South Dakota, opening doors of opportunity for thousands of deserving young men and women.

Like hundreds of other fine small colleges across the nation, General Beadle State College—has offered a chance to people who might not otherwise have had a chance.

The pioneer spirit is represented here, and the progress that has shaped our heritage.

In South Dakota we still can sense the daring that converted a raw frontier into part of the vast heartland of America.

The vitality of thought is represented here.

A college library is a place of living ideas—a place where timeless truths are collected, to become the raw materials of discovery. In addition, the Karl E. Mundt Library will house the papers of a wise and dedicated man who for 30 years has been at the center of public events. Thus, more than most, this is a library of both thought and action, combing the wisdom of past ages with a uniquely personal record of the present time.

As we dedicate this place of ideas, therefore, let us reflect on some of the values we have inherited, which are now under challenge.

We live in a deeply troubled and profoundly unsettled time. Drugs, crime, campus revolts, racial discord, draft resistance— on every hand we find old standards violated, old values discarded, old precepts ignored. A vocal minority of the young are opting out of the process by which a civilization maintains its continuity: the passing on of values from one generation to the next. Old and young across a chasm of misunderstanding —and the more loudly they shout, the wider the chasm grows.

As a result, our institutions are undergoing what may be their severest challenge yet. I speak not of the physical

Source: Vital Speeches of the Day,   July 1, 1969;
          City News Publishing Company, Southold, New
          York. By permission of the publisher.

challenge: the forces and threats of force that have wracked our cities, and now our colleges. Force can be contained.

We have the power to strike back if need be, and to prevail. The nation has survived other attempts at this. It has not been a lack of civil power, but the reluctance of a free people to employ it, that so often has stayed the hand of authorities faced with confrontation.

The challenge I speak of is deeper: the challenge to our values, and to the moral base of the authority that sustains those values.

At the outset, let me draw one clear distinction.

A great deal of today's debate about "values," or about "morality," centers on what essentially are private values and personal codes: patterns of dress and appearance, sexual mores; religious practices; the uses to which a person intends to put his own life.

These are immensely important, but they are not the values I mean to discuss here.

My concern today is not with the length of a person's hair, but with his conduct in relation to his community; not with what he wears, but with his impact on the process by which a free society governs itself.

I speak not of private morality but of public morality—and of "morality" in its broadest sense, as a set of standards by which the community chooses to judge itself.

Some critics call ours an "immoral" society because they disagree with its policies, or they refuse to obey its laws because they claim that those laws have no moral basis. Yet the structure of our laws has rested from the beginning on a foundation of moral purpose.

That moral purpose embodies what is, above all, a deeply humane set of values—rooted in a profound respect for the individual, for the integrity of his person and the dignity of his humanity.

At first glance, there is something homely and unexciting about basic values we have long believed in. We feel apologetic about espousing them; even the profoundest truths become cliches with repetition. But they can be live sleeping giants: slow to rouse, but magnificent in their strength.

Let us look at some of those values—so familiar now, and yet once so revoluntionary:

Liberty: recognizing that liberties can only exist in balance, with the liberty of each stopping at that point at which it would infringe the liberty of another.

Freedom of conscience: meaning that each person has the freedom of his own conscience, and therefore none has the right to dictate the conscience of his neighbor.

Justice: recognizing that true justice is impartial, and that no man can be judge in his own cause.

Human dignity: a dignity that inspires pride, is rooted in self-reliance and provides the satisfaction of being a useful and respected member of the community.

Concern for the disadvantaged and dispossessed: but a concern that neither panders nor patronizes.

The right to participate in public decisions: which carries

with it the duty to abide by those decisions when reached, recognizing that no one can have his own way all the time.

Human fulfillment: in the sense not of unlimited license, but of maximum opportunity.

The right to grow, to reach upward, to be all that we can become, in a system that rewards enterprise, encourages innovation and honors excellence.

In essence, these all are aspects of freedom. They inhere in the concept of freedom; they aim at extending freedom; they celebrate the uses of freedom. They are not new. But they are as timeless and as timely as the human spirit because they are rooted in the human spirit.

Our baic values concern not only what we seek but how we seek it.

Freedom is a condition; it also is a process. And the process is essential to the freedom itself.

We have a Constitution that sets certain limits on what government can do but that allows wide discretion within those limits. We have a system of divided powers, of checks and balances, of periodic elections, all of which are designed to insure that the majority has a chance to work its will—but not to override the rights of the minority or to infringe the rights of the individual.

What this adds up to is a democratic process, carefully constructed and stringently guarded. It is not perfect. No system could be. But it has served the nation well—and nearly two centuries of growth and change testify to its strength and adaptability.

They testify, also, to the fact that avenues of peaceful change do exist. Those who can make a persuasive case for changes they want can achieve them through this orderly process.

To challenge a particular policy is one thing; to challenge the government's right to set it is another—for this denies the process of freedom.

Lately, however, a great many people have become impatient with the democratic process. Some of the more extreme even argue, with curious logic, that there is no majority, because the majority has no right to hold opinions that they disagree with.

Scorning persuasion, they prefer coercion. Awarding themselves what they call a higher morality, they try to bully authorities into yielding to their "demands."

On college campuses, they draw support from faculty members who should know better; in the larger community, they find the usual apologists ready to excuse any tactic in the name of "progress."

It should be self-evident that this sort of self-righteous moral arrogance has no place in a free community. It denies the most fundamental of all the values we hold: respect for the rights of others. This principle of mutual respect is the keystone of the entire structure of ordered liberty that makes freedom possible.

The student who invades an administration building, roughs

up the dean, rifles the files and issues "non-negotiable demands" may have some of his demands met by a permissive university administration. But the greater his "victory" the more he will have undermined the security of his own rights.

In a free society, the rights of none are secure unless the rights of all are respected. It is precisely the structure of law and custom that he has chosen to violate—the process of freedom—by which the rights of all are protected.

We have long considered our colleges and universities citadels of freedom, where the rule of reason prevails. Now both the process of freedom and the rule of reason are under attack. At the same time, our colleges are under pressure to collapse their educational standards in the misguided belief that this would promote "opportunity."

Instead of seeking to raise lagging students up to meet the college standards, the cry now is to lower the standards to meet the students. This is the old, familiar, self-indulgent cry for the easy way. It debases the integrity of the educational process.

There is no easy way to excellence, no short-cut to the truth, no magic wand that can produce a trained and disciplined mind without the hard discipline of learning. To yield to these demands would weaken the institution; more importantly, it would cheat the student of what he comes to a college for: his education.

No group, as a group, should be more zealous defenders of the integrity of academic standards and the rule of reason in academic life than the faculties of our great institutions. If they simply follow the loudest voices, parrot the latest slogan, yield to unreasonable demands, they will have won not the respect but the contempt of their students.

Students have a right to guidance, to leadership, to direction; they have a right to expect their teachers to listen, and to be reasonable, but also to stand for something—and most especially, to stand for the rule of reason against the rule of force.

Our colleges have their weaknesses. Some have become too impersonal, or too ingrown, and curricula have lagged. But with all its faults, the fact remains that the American system of higher education is the best in this whole imperfect world—and it provides, in the United States today, a better education for more students of all economic levels than ever before, anywhere, in the history of the world.

This is no small achievement.

Often, the worst mischief is done by the name of the best cause. In our zeal for instant reform, we should be careful not to destroy our educational standards, and our educational system along with them; and not to undermine the process of freedom, on which all else rests.

The process of freedom will be less threatened in America, however, if we pay more heed to one of the great cries of the young today. I speak now of their demand for honesty: intellectual honesty, personal honesty, public honesty.

Much of what seems to be revolt is really little more than this: an attempt to strip away sham and pretense, to puncture illusion, to get down to the basic nub of truth.

We should welcome this. We have seen too many patterns of deception:

In political life, impossible promises.

In advertising, extravagant claims.

In business, shady deals.

In personal life, we all have witnessed deceits that ranged from the "little white lie" to moral hypocrisy; from cheating on income taxes to bilking insurance companies.

In public life, we have seen reputations destroyed by smear, and gimmicks paraded as panaceas. We have heard shrill voices of hate, shouting lies, and sly voices of malice, twisting facts.

Even in intellectual life, we too often have seen logical gymnastics performed to justify a pet theory, and refusal to accept facts that fail to support it.

Absolute honesty would be ungenerous. Courtesy compels us to welcome the unwanted visitor; kindness leads us to compliment the homely girl on how pretty she looks. But in our public discussions, we sorely need a kind of honesty that has too often been lacking; the honesty of straight talk; a doing away with hyperbole; a careful concern with the gradations of truth, and a frank recognition of the limits of our knowledge about the problems we have to deal with.

We have long demanded financial integrity in public life; we now need the most rigorous kind of intellectual integrity in public debate.

Unless we can find a way to speak plainly, truly, unself-consciously, about the facts of public life, we may find that our grip on the forces of history is too loose to control our own destiny.

The honesty of straight talk leads us to the conclusion that some of our recent social experiments have worked, and some have failed, and that most have achieved something—but less than their advance billing promised.

This same honesty is concerned not with assigning blame, but with discovering what lessons can be drawn from that experience in order to design better programs next time. Perhaps the goals were unattainable; perhaps the means were inadequate; perhaps the program was based on an unrealistic assessment of human nature.

We can learn these lessons only to the extent that we can be candid with one another. We face enormously complex choices. In approaching these, confrontation is no substitute for consultation; passionate concern gets us nowhere without dispassionate analysis. More fundamentally, our structure of faith depends on faith, and faith depends on truth.

The values we cherish are sustained by a fabric of mutual self-restraint, woven of ordinary civil decency, respect for the rights of others, respect for the laws of the community, and respect for the democratic process of orderly change.

The purpose of these restraints is not to protect an

"establishment," but to establish the protection of liberty; not to prevent change, but to insure that change reflects the public will and respects the rights of all.

This process is our most precious resource as a nation. But it depends on public acceptance, public understanding and public faith.

Whether our values are maintained depends ultimately not on the Government, but on the people.

A nation can be only as great as its people want it to be.

A nation can be only as free as its people insist that it be.

A nation's laws are only as strong as its people's will to see them enforced.

A nation's freedoms are only as secure as its people's determination to see them maintained.

A nation's values are only as lasting as the ability of each generation to pass them on to the next.

We often have a tendency to turn away from the familiar because it is familiar, and to seek the new because it is new.

To those intoxicated with the romance of violent revolution, the continuing revolution of democracy may seem unexciting. But no system has ever liberated the spirits of so many so fully. Nothing has ever "turned on" man's energies, his imagination, his unfettered creativity, the way the ideal of freedom has.

Some see America's vast wealth and protest that this has made us "materialistic." But we should not be apologetic about our abundance. We should not fall into the easy trap of confusing the production of things with the worship of things. We produce abundantly; but our values turn not on what we have, but on what we believe.

We believe in liberty, and decency, and the process of freedom. On these beliefs we rest our pride as a nation; in these beliefs, we rest our hopes for the future; and by our fidelity to the process of freedom, we can assure to ourselves and our posterity the blessings of freedom.

America's Role In The World
THE NEED FOR STRENGTH

By RICHARD M. NIXON, *President of the United States*

Delivered at the Commencement Exercises at the Air Force Academy, June 4, 1969

FOR EACH OF you, and for your parents and your countrymen, this is a moment of quiet pride. After years of study and training, you have earned the right to be saluted.

But the members of the graduating class of the Air Force Academy are beginning their careers at a difficult moment in military life.

On a fighting front, you are asked to be ready to make unlimited sacrifice in a limited war.

On the home front, you are under attack from those who question the need for a strong national defense, and indeed see a danger in the power of the defenders.

You are entering the military service of your country when the nation's potential adversaries abroad were never stronger and your critics at home were never more numerous.

It is open season on the armed forces. Military programs are ridiculed as needless if not deliberate waste. The military profession is derided in some of the best circles. Patriotism is considered by some to be a backward, unfashionable fetish of the uneducated and unsophisticated. Nationalism is hailed and applauded as a panacea for the ills of every nation—except the United States.

This paradox of military power is a symptom of something far deeper that is stirring in our body politic. It goes beyond the dissent about the war in Vietnam. It goes behind the fear of the "military industrial complex."

The underlying questions are really these:

What is America's role in the world? What are the responsibilities of a great nation toward protecting freedom beyond its shores? Can we ever be *left* in peace if we do not actively assume the burden of *keeping* the peace?

When great questions are posed, fundamental differences of opinion come into focus. It serves no purpose to gloss over these differences, or to try to pretend they are mere matters of degree.

One school of thought holds that the road to understanding with the Soviet Union and Communist China lies through a downgrading of our own alliances and what amounts to a unilateral reduction of our arms—as a demonstration of our "good faith."

Source: Vital Speeches of the Day, July 1, 1969;
City News Publishing Company, Southhold, New
York. By permission of the publisher.

They believe that we can be conciliatory and accommodating only if we do not have the strength to be otherwise. They believe America will be able to deal with the possibility of peace only when we are unable to cope with the threat of war.

Those who think that way have grown weary of the weight of free world leadership that fell upon us in the wake of World War II, and they argue that we are as much responsible for the tensions in the world as any adversary we face.

They assert that the United States is blocking the road to peace by maintaining its military strength at home and its defense forces abroad. If we would only reduce our forces, they contend, tensions would disappear and the chances for peace brighten.

America's presence on the world scene, they believe makes peace abroad improbable and peace in our society impossible.

We should never underestimate the appeal of the isolationist school of thought. Their slogans are simplistic and powerful: "Charity begins at home." "Let's first solve our own problems and then we can deal with the problems of the world."

This simple formula touches a responsive chord with many an overburdened taxpayer. It would be easy to buy some popularity by going along with the new isolationists. But it would be disastrous for our nation and the world.

I hold a totally different view of the world, and I come to a different conclusion about the direction America must take.

Imagine what would happen to this world if the American presence were swept from the scene. As every world leader knows, and as even the most outspoken of America's critics will admit, the rest of the world would be living in terror.

If America were to turn its back on the world, a deadening form of peace would settle over this planet—the kind of peace that suffocated freedom in Czechoslovakia.

The danger to us has changed, but it has not vanished. We must revitalize our alliances, not abandon them.

We must rule out unilateral disarmament. In the real world that simply will not work. If we pursue arms control as an end in itself, we will not achieve our end. The adversaries in the world today are not in conflict because they are armed. They are armed because they are in conflict, and have not yet learned peaceful ways to resolve their conflicting national interests.

The aggressors of this world are not going to give the United States a period of grace in which to put our domestic house in order—just as the crises within our society cannot be put on a back burner until we resolve the problem of Vietnam.

Programs solving our domestic problems will be meaningless if we are not around to enjoy them. Nor can we conduct a successful policy of peace abroad if our society is at war with itself at home.

There is no advancement for Americans at home in a retreat from the problems of the world. America has a vital national interest in world stability, and no other nation can uphold that interest for us.

We stand at a crossroad in our history. We shall reaffirm our aspiration to greatness or we shall choose instead to withdraw into ourselves. The choice will affect far more than our foreign policy; it will determine the quality of our lives.

A nation needs many qualities, but it needs faith and confidence above all. Skeptics do not build societies; the idealists are the builders. Only societies that believe in themselves can rise to their challenges. Let us not, then, pose a false choice between meeting our responsibilities abroad and meeting the needs of our people at home. We shall meet both or we shall meet neither.

This is why my disagreement with the skeptics and the isolationists is fundamental. They have lost the vision indispensable to great leadership. They observe the problems that confront us; they measure our resources; and they despair. When the first vessels set out from Europe for the New World, these men would have weighed the risks, and stayed behind. When the colonists on the Eastern seaboard started across the Appalachians to the unknown reaches of the Ohio Valley, these men would have calculated the odds, and stayed behind.

Our current exploration of space makes the point vividly: Here is testimony to man's vision and man's courage. The journey of the astronauts is more than a technical achievement; it is a reaching-out of the human spirit. It lifts our sights; it demonstrates that magnificent conceptions can be made real.

They inspire us and at the same time teach us true humility. What could bring home to us more the limitations of the human scale than the hauntingly beautiful picture of our earth seen from the moon?

Every man achieves his own greatness by reaching out beyond himself. So it is with nations. When a nation believes in itself—as Athenians did in their golden age, as Italians did in the Renaissance—that nation can perform miracles. Only when a nation means something to itself can it mean something to others.

That is why I believe a resurgence of American idealism can bring about a modern miracle—a world order of peace and justice.

I know that every member of this graduating class is, in that sense, an idealist.

In the years to come, you may hear your commitment to America's responsibility in the world derided as a form of militarism. It is important that you recognize the strawman issue for what it is: The outward sign of a desire by some to turn America inward—to have America turn away from greatness.

I am not speaking about those responsible critics who reveal waste and inefficiency in our defense establishment, who demand clear answers on procurement policies, who want to make sure a new weapons system will truly add to our defense.

On the contrary, you should be in the vanguard of that movement. Nor do I speak of those with sharp eyes and sharp pencils who are examining our post-Vietnam planning with other pressing national priorities in mind. I count myself as one of those.

As your Commander-in-Chief, I want to relay to you as future officers of our armed forces some of my thoughts on these issues of national moment.

I worked closely with President Eisenhower. I know what he meant when he said ". . . we must guard against the acquisition of unwarranted influence, whether sought or unsought, by the military industrial complex."

Many people conveniently forget that he followed that warning with another: "We must also be alert to the equal and opposite danger that public policy could itself become the captive of a scientific-technological elite."

And in that same Farewell Address, President Eisenhower made quite clear the need for national security. As he put it: "A vital element in keeping the peace is our military establishment. Our arms must be mighty, ready for instant action, so that no potential aggressor may be tempted to risk his own destruction."

The American defense establishment should never be a sacred cow, nor should the American military be anybody's scapegoat.

America's wealth is enormous but it is not limitless. Every dollar available to the Federal Government has been taken from the American people in taxes. A responsible government has a duty to be prudent when it spends the people's money. There is no more justification for wasting money on unnecessary military hardware than there is for wasting it on unwarranted social programs.

There can be no question that we should not spend "unnecessarily" for defense. But we must also not confuse our priorities.

The question in defense spending is "how much is necessary?" The President of the United States is the man charged with making that judgment. After a complete review of our foreign and defense policies I have submitted requests to the Congress for military appropriations—some of them admittedly controversial. These requests represent the minimum I believe essential for the United States to meet its current and long-range obligations to itself and to the free world. I have asked only for those programs and those expenditures that I believe are necessary to guarantee the security of this country and to honor our obligations. I will bear the responsibility for these judgments. I do not consider my recommendations infallible. But if I have made a mistake I pray that it is on the side of too much and not too little. If we do too much, it will cost us our money; if we do too little, it may cost us our lives.

Mistakes in military policy can be irretrievable. Time lost in this age of science can never be regained. I have no choice in my decisions but to come down on the side of security. History has dealt harshly with those nations who have taken the other course.

In that spirit, let me offer this credo for the defenders of our nation:

I believe that we must balance our need for survival as a nation with our need for survival as a people. Americans, soldiers and civilians, must remember that defense is not an end in itself—it is a way of holding fast to the deepest values known to civilized man.

I believe that our defense establishment will remain the servant of our national policy of bringing about peace in this world, and that those in any way connected with the military must scrupulously avoid even the appearance of becoming the master of that policy.

I believe that every man in uniform is a citizen first and a serviceman second, and that we must resist any attempt to isolate or separate the defenders from the defended. In this regard, those who agitate for the removal of the ROTC from college campuses only contribute to an unwanted militarism.

I believe that the basis for decisions on defense spending must be "what do we need for our security" and not "what will this mean for business and employment." The Defense Department must never be considered a modern-day WPA: There are far better ways for government to help ensure a sound prosperity and high employment.

I believe that moderation has a moral significance only in those who have another choice. The weak can only plead maganimity and restraint gain moral meaning coming from the strong.

I believe that defense decisions must be made on the hard realities of the offensive capabilities of our adversaries, and not on our fervent hopes about their intentions. With Thomas Jefferson, we can prefer "the flatteries of hope" to the gloom of despair, but we cannot survive in the real world if we plan our defense in a dream world.

I believe we must take risks for peace—but calculated risks, not foolish risks. We shall not trade our defenses for a disarming smile or honeyed words. We are prepared for new initiatives in the control of arms in the context of other specific moves to reduce tensions around the world.

I believe that America is not about to become a Garrison State, or a Welfare State, or a Police State— because we will defend our values from those forces, external or internal, that would challenge or erode them.

And I believe this above all: That this nation shall continue to be a source of world leadership and a source of freedom's strength in creating a just world order that will bring an end to war.

Let me conclude with a personal word.

A President shares a special bond with the men and women of the nation's armed services. He feels that bond strongly at moments like these, facing all of you who have pledged your lives, your fortunes and your sacred honor to the service of your country. He feels that bond most strongly when he presents a Medal of Honor to an 8-year-old boy who will not see his father again. Because of that bond, let me say this to you now:

In the past generation, since 1941, this nation has paid for fourteen years of peace with fourteen years of war. The American war dead of this generation has been far greater than all of the preceding generations of Americans combined. In terms of human suffering, this has been the costliest generation in the two centuries of our history.

Perhaps this is why my generation is so fiercely determined to pass on a different legacy. We want to redeem that sacrifice. We want to be remembered, not as the generation that suffered, but as the generation that was tempered in its fire for a great purpose: to make the kind of peace that the next generation will be able to keep.

This is a challenge worthy of the idealism which I know motivates every man who will receive his diploma today.

I am proud to have served in America's armed forces in a war which ended before members of this class were born.

It is my deepest hope and my belief that each of you will be able to look back on your career with pride, not because of the wars in which you served but because of the peace and freedom which your service made possible for America and the world.

President's
State Of The Union Message

By RICHARD M. NIXON, *President of the United States*

Delivered before the Congress of the United States, Washington, D. C., January 22, 1970 [*]

MR. SPEAKER, Mr. President, my colleagues in the Congress, our distinguished guests and my fellow Americans. To address a joint session of the Congress in this great chamber in which I was once privileged to serve is an honor for which I am deeply grateful.

The State of the Union Address is traditionally an occasion for a lengthy and detailed account by the President of what he has accomplished in the past, what he wants the Congress to do in the future, and, in an election year, to lay the basis for the political issues which might be decisive in the fall.

Occasionally there comes a time when profound and far-reaching events command a break with tradition. This is such a time.

I say this not only because 1970 marks the beginning of a new decade in which America will celebrate its 200th birthday; I say it because new knowledge and hard e xperience argue persuasively that both our programs and our institutions in America need to be reformed.

The moment has arrived to harness the vast energies and abundance of this land to the creation of a new American experience, an experience richer and deeper and more truly a reflection of the goodness and grace of the human spirit.

The seventies will be a time of new beginnings, a time of exploring both on the earth and in the heavens, a time of discovery.

But the time has also come for emphasis on developing better ways of managing what we have and of completing what man's genius has begun but left unfinished.

Our land, this land that is ours together, is a great and a good land. It is also an unfinished land and the challenge of perfecting it is the summons of the Seventies.

It is in that spirit that I address myself to those great issues facing our nation which are above partisanship.

When we speak of America's priorities, the first priority must always be peace for America and the world.

The major immediate goal of our foreign policy is to bring an end to the war in Vietnam in a way that our generation will be remembered not so much as the generation that suffered in war but more for the fact that we had the courage and character to win the kind of a just peace that the next generation was able to keep.

We are making progress toward that goal. The prospects for peace are far greater today than they were a year ago. A major part of the credit for this development goes to the members of this Congress who, despite their differences on the conduct of the war, have overwhelmingly indicated their support of a just peace.

By this action you have completely demolished the enemy's hopes that they can gain in Washington the victory our fighting men have denied them in Vietnam.

No goal could be greater than to make the next generation the first in this century in which America was at peace with every nation in the world.

I shall discuss in detail the new concepts and programs designed to achieve this goal in a separate report on foreign policy which I shall submit to the Congress at a later date.

Today let me describe the directions of our new policies.

We have based our policies on an evaluation of the world as it is, not as it was 25 years ago at the conclusion of World War II.

Many of the policies which were necessary and right then are obsolete today. Then, because of America's overwhelming military and economic strength, because of the weakness of other major free world powers and the inability of scores of newly independent nations to defend or even govern themselves, America had to assume the major burden for the defense of freedom in the world.

In two wars, first in Korea and now in Vietnam, we furnished most of the money, most of the arms, most of the men to help other nations defend their freedom.

Today the great industrial nations of Europe as well as Japan have regained their economic strength and the nations of Latin America and many of the nations who acquired their freedom from colonialism after World War II in Asia and Africa have a new sense of pride and dignity and a determination to assume the responsibility for their own defense.

That is the basis of the doctrine I announced at Guam. Neither the defense nor the development of other nations can be exclusively or primarily an American undertaking.

The nations of each part of the world should assume the primary responsibility for their own well being and they themselves should determine the terms of that well being.

We shall be faithful to our treaty commitments but we shall reduce our involvement and our presence in other nations' affairs.

To insist that other nations play a role is not a retreat from responsibility; it is a sharing of responsibility.

The result of this new policy has been not to weaken our alliances but to give them new life, new strength, a new sense of common purpose.

Relations with our European allies are once again strong and healthy, based on mutual consultation and mutual responsibility.

We have initiated a new approach to Latin America in which we deal with those nations as partners rather than patrons.

The new partnership concept has been welcomed in Asia. We have developed an historic new basis for Japanese-American friendship and cooperation, which is the linchpin for peace in the Pacific.

And if we are to have peace in the last third of the century, a major factor will be the development of a new relationship between the United States and the Soviet Union.

I would not underestimate our differences, but we are moving with precision and purpose from an era of confrontation to an era of negotiation.

Our negotiations on strategic arms limitations and in other areas will have far greater chance for success if both sides enter them motivated by mutual self-interest rather than naive sentimentality.

It is with this -- this is the same spirit with which we have resumed discussions with Communist China in our talks at Warsaw.

Our concern and our relations with both these nations is to avoid a catastrophic collision and to build a solid basis for peaceful settlement of our differences.

I would be the last to suggest that the road to peace is not difficult and dangerous, but I believe our new policies have contributed to the prospect that America may have the best chance since World War II to enjoy a generation of uninterrupted peace, and that chance will be enormously increased if we continue to have a relationship between Congress and the executive in which, despite differences in detail where the security of America and the peace of mankind are concerned, we act not as Republicans, not as Democrats, but as Americans.

As we move into the decade of the seventies we have the greatest opportunity for progress at home of any people in world history.

Our gross national product will increase by $500-billion in the next 10 years. This increase alone is greater than the entire growth of the American economy from 1790 to 1950.

The critical question is not whether we will grow but how we will use that growth. The decade of the sixties was also a period of great growth economically. But in that same 10-year period we witnessed the greatest growth of crime, the greatest increase in inflation, the greatest social unrest in America in 100 years. Never has a nation seemed to have had more and enjoyed it less.

At heart the issue is effectivenss of government. Ours has become, as it continues to be and should remain, a society of large expectations. Government helped to generate those expectations. It undertook to meet them.

Yet increasingly it proved unable to do so. As a people we had too many visions and too little vision.

Now as we enter the seventies we should enter also a great age of reform of the institutions of American government.

Our purpose in this period should not be simply better management of the programs of the past. The time has come for a new quest -- a quest not for a greater quantity of what we have but for a new quality of life in America.

A major part of the substance for an unprecedented advance in this nation's approach to its problems and opportunities is contained in more than two-score legislative proposals which I sent to the Congress last year and which still awa t enactment.

I will offer at least a dozen more major programs in the course of this session.

At this point I do not intend to go through a detailed listing of what I have proposed or will propose. But I would like to mention three areas in which urgent priorities demand that we move and move now.

First, we cannot delay longer in accomplishing a total reform of our welfare system. When a system penalizes work, breaks up homes, robs recipients of dignity there is no alternative to abolishing that system and adopting in its place the program of income support, job training and work incentive which I recommended to the Congress last year.

Second, the time has come to assess and reform all of our institutions of government at the Federal, state and local level. It is time for a new federalism in which after 190 years of power flowing from the people and local and state governments to Washington, D.C., it will begin to flow from Washington back to the states and to the people of the United States.

Third, we must adopt reforms which will expand the range of opportunities for all Americans. We can fulfill the American dream only when each person has a fair chance to fulfill his own dreams. This means equal voting rights, equal employment opportunity and new opportunities for expanded ownership. Because in order to be secure in their human rights people need access to property rights.

I could give similar examples of the need for reform in our programs for health, education, housing, transportation as well as other critical areas which directly affect the well being of millions of Americans.

The people of the United States should wait no longer for these reforms that would so deeply enhance the quality of their lives.

When I speak of actions which would be beneficial to the American people I can think of none more important than for the Congress to join this Administration in the battle to stop the rise in the cost of living.

Now I realize it is tempting to blame someone else for inflation. Some blame business for raising prices and some blame unions for asking for more wages. But a review of the stark fiscal facts of the 1960's clearly demonstrates where the primary blame for rising prices must be placed.

In the decade of the sixties the Federal Government spent $57-billion more than it took in in taxes. In that same decade the American people paid the bill for that deficit in price increases which raised the cost of living for the average family of four by $200 per month in America.

Now millions of Americans are forced to go into debt today because the Federal Government decided to go into debt yesterday. We must balance our Federal budget so that American families will have a better chance to balance their family budgets.

Only with the cooperation of the Congress can we meet this highest priority objective of responsible government. We're on the right track. We had a balanced budget in 1969. This Administration cut more than $7-billion out of spending plans in order to produce a surplus in 1970, and in spite of the fact that Congress reduced revenues by $3-billion, I shall recommend a balanced budget for 1971.

But I can assure you that not only to present but to stay within a balanced budget requires some very hard decisions.

It means rejecting pending programs which would benefit some of the people when their net effect would result in price increases for all the people.

It is time to quit putting good money into bad programs; otherwise, we will end up with bad money and bad programs.

I recognize the political popularity of spending programs, particularly in an election year. But unless we stop the rise in prices, the cost of living for millions of American families will become unbearable and government's ability to plan programs for progress for the future will become impossible.

In referring to budget cuts, here is one area where I have ordered an increase rather than a cut. And that is the requests of those agencies with the responsibilities for law enforcement.

We've heard a great deal of over-blown rhetoric during the sixties in which the word war has perhaps too often been used. The war on poverty, the war on misery, the war on disease, the war on hunger. But if there is one area where the word war is appropriate it is in the fight against crime. We must declare and win the war against the criminal elements which increasingly threaten our cities, our homes and our lives.

We have a tragic example of this problem in the nation's capital for whose safety the Congress and the executive have the primary responsibility. I doubt if many members of this Congress who live more than a few blocks from here would dare leave their cars in the Capitol garage and walk home alone tonight.

This year this Administration sent to the Congress 13 separate pieces of legislation dealing with organized crime, pornography, street crime, narcotics crime in the District of Columbia. None of these bills have reached my desk for signature.

I am confident that the Congress will act now to adopt the legislation I placed before you last year.

We in the executive have done everything we can under existing law but new and stronger weapons are needed in that fight.

While it is true that state and local law enforcement agencies are the cutting edge in the effort to eliminate street crime, burglaries, murders, my proposals to you have embodied my belief that the Federal Government should play a greater role in working in partnership with these agencies.

That is why 1971 Federal spending for local law enforcement will double that budgeted for 1970.

The primary responsibility for crimes that affect individuals is with local and state rather than with Federal Government. But in the field of organized crime, narcotics and pornography the Federal Government has a special responsibility it should fulfill and we should make Washington, D.C., where we have the primary responsibility, an example to the nation and the world of respect for law rather than lawlessness.

I now turn to a subject which next to our desire for peace may well become the major concern of the American people in the decade of the seventies.

In the next 10 years we shall increase our wealth by 50 per cent. The profound question is: does this mean we will be 50 per cent richer in a real sense, 50 per cent better off, 50 per cent happier, or does it mean that in the year 1980 the President standing in this place will look back on a decade in which 70 per cent of our people lived in metropolitan areas choked by traffic, suffocated by smog, poisoned by water, deafened by noise and terrorized by crime?

These are not the great questions that concern world leaders at summit conferences. But people do not live at the summit. They live in the foothills of everyday experience and it is time for all of us to concern ourselves with the way real people live in real life.

The great question of the seventies is: Shall we surrender to our surroundings or shall we make our peace with nature and begin to make reparations for the damage we have done to our air, to our land and to our water?

Restoring nature to its natural state is a cause beyond party and beyond factions. It has become a common cause of all the people of this country. It is the cause of particular concern to young Americans because they more than we will reap the grim consequences of our failure to act on the programs which are needed now if we are to prevent disaster later -- clean air, clean water, open spaces. These should once again be the birthright of every American. If we act now they can be.

We still think of air as free. But clean air is not free. And neither is clean water. The price tag on pollution control is high. Through our years of past carelessness we incurred a debt to nature and now that debt is being called.

The program I shall propose to Congress will be the most comprehensive and costly program in this field in America's history. It is not a program for just one year. A year's plan in this field is no plan at all. This is the time to look ahead not a year but five years or 10 years, whatever time is required to do the job.

I shall propose to this Congress a $10-billion nationwide clean waters program to put modern municipal waste treatment plants in every place in America where they are needed to make our waters clean again and do it now.

We have the industrial capacity if we begin now to build within five years.

As our cities and suburbs relentlessly expand, those priceless open spaces needed for recreation areas accessible to their people are swallowed up, often forever. Unless we preserve these spaces while they are still available we will have none to preserve.

Therefore I shall propose new financing methods for purchasing open space and parklands now before they are last to us.

The automobile is our worst polluter of the air. Adequate control requires further advances in engine design and fuel composition. We shall intensify our research, set increasingly strict standards and strengthen enforcement procedures, and we shall do it now.

We can no longer afford to consider air and water common property, free to be abused by anyone without regard to the consequences. Instead we should begin now to treat them as scarce resources which we are no more free to contaminate than we are free to throw garbage into our neighbor's yard.

This requires comprehensive new regulations. It also requires that to the extent possible the price of goods should be made to include the costs of producing and disposing of them without damage to the environment.

Now I realize that the argument is often made that there is a fundamental contradiction between economic growth and the quality of life, so that to have one we must forsake the other.

The answer is not to abandon growth but to redirect it. For example, we should turn toward ending congestion and eliminating smog the same reservoir of inventive genius that created them in the first place.

Continued vigorous economic growth provides us with the means to enrich life itself and to enhance our planet as a place hospitable to man.

Each individual must enlist in this fight if it is to be won.

It has been said that no matter how many national parks and historical monuments we buy and develop, the truly significant environment for each of us is that in which we spend 80 per cent of our time, in our homes, in our places of work, the streets over which we travel.

Street litter, rundown parking strips and yards, dilapidated fences, broken windows, smoking automobiles, dingy working places, all should be the object of our fresh view.

We have been too tolerant of our surroundings and too willing to leave it to others to clean up our environment. It is time for those who make massive demands on society to make some minimal demands on themselves.

Each of us must resolve that each day he will leave his home, his property, the public places of the city or town a little cleaner, a little better, a little more pleasant for himself and those around him.

With the help of people we can do anything, and without their help, we can do nothing.

In this spirit together we can reclaim our land for ours and generations to come.

Between now and the year 2000, over 100 million children will be born in the United States. Where they grow up and how will more than any one thing measure the quality of American life in these years ahead.

This should be a warning to us.

For the past 30 years, our population has also been growing and shifting. The result is exemplified in the vast areas of rural America, emptying out of people and of promise. A third of our counties lost population in the sixties. The violent and decayed central cities of our great metropolitan complexes are the most conspicuous area of failure in American life today.

I propose that before these problems become insoluble the nation develop a national growth policy.

In the future, government decisions as to where to build highways, locate airports, acquire land or sell land should be made with the clear objective of aiding a balanced growth for America.

An in particular the Federal Government must be in a position to assist in the building of new cities and the rebuilding of old ones.

At the same time we will carry our concern with the quality of life in America to the farm as well as the suburb, to the village as well as to the city. What rural America needs most is a new kind of assistance. It needs to be dealt with not as a separate nation but as part of an overall growth policy for America.

We must create a new rural environment which will not only stem the migration to urban centers but reverse it. If we seize our growth as a challenge we can make the 1970's an historic period when by conscious choice we transformed our land into what we want it to become.

America, which has pioneered in the new abundance and in the new technology, is called upon today to pioneer in meeting the concerns which have followed in their wake in turning the wonders of science to the service of man.

In the majesty of this great chamber we hear the echoes of America's history, of debates that rocked the union and those that repaired it, of the summons to war and the search for peace, of the uniting of the people, the building of a nation. Those echoes of history remind us of our roots and our strengths.

They remind us also of that special genius of American democracy which at one critical turning point after another has led us to the spot the new road to the future and given us the wisdom and the courage to take it.

As I look down that new road which I tried to map out today I see a new America as we celebrate our 200th anniversary six years from now. I see an America in which we have abolished hunger, provided the means for every family in the nation to obtain a minimum income, made enormous progress in providing better housing, faster transportation, improved health and superior education.

I see an America in which we've checked inflation and waged a winning war against crime. I see an America in which we made great strides in stopping the pollution of our air, cleaning up our water, opening up our parks, continuing to explore in space.

And most important, I see an America at peace with all the nations of the world. This is not an impossible dream. These goals are all within our reach.

In times past our forefathers had the vision but not the means to achieve such goals. Let it not be recorded that we were the first American generation that had the means but not the vision to make this dream come true.

But let us above all recognize the fundamental truth: we can be the best clothed, best fed, best housed people in the world enjoying clean air, clean water, beautiful parks. But we could still be the unhappiest people in the world without an indefinable spirit, the lift of a driving dream which has made America from its beginning the hope of the world.

Two hundred years ago this was a new nation of three million people, weak militarily, poor economically. But America meant something to the world then which could not be measured in dollars -- something far more important than military might.

Listen to President Thomas Jeffereson in 1802: "We act not for ourselves alone but for the whole human race." We had a spiritual quality then which caught the imagination of millions of people in the world.

Today when we are the richest and strongest nation in the world let it not be recorded that we lacked the moral and spiritual idealism which made us the hope of the world at the time of our birth.

The demands of us in 1976 are even greater than 1776. It's no longer enough to live and let live. Now we must live and help live.

We need a fresh climate in America. One in which a person can breathe freely and breathe in freely.

Our recognition of the truth that wealth and happiness are not the same thing requires us to measure success or failure by new criteria.

Even more than the programs I have described today, what this nation needs is an example from its elected leaders in providing the spiritual and moral leadership which no programs for material progress can satisfy.

Above all, let us inspire young Americans with a sense of excitement, a sense of destiny, a sense of involvement in meeting the challenges we face in this great period of our history. Only then are they going to have any sense of satisfaction in their lives.

The greatest privilege an individual can have is to serve in a cause bigger than himself.

We have such a cause.

How we seize the opportunities I have described today will determine not only our future but the future of peace and freedom in this world in the last third of the century.

May God give us the wisdom, the strenght, and, above all, the idealism to be worthy of that challenge so that America can fulfill its destiny of being the world's best hope for liberty, for opportunity, for progress and peace, for all peoples.

---

* Source: Vital Speeches of the Day,   February 1, 1970;
            City News Publishing Company, Southold, New
            York.   By permission of the publisher.

Cambodia

A DIFFICULT DECISION

By RICHARD M. NIXON, *President of the United States*

Delivered over national TV, April 31, 1970

GOOD EVENING my fellow Americans. Ten days ago in my report to the nation on Vietnam I announced a decision to withdraw an additional 150,000 Americans from Vietnam over the next year. I said then that I was making that decision despite our concern over increased enemy activity in Laos, in Cambodia and in South Vietnam.

And at that time I warned that if I concluded that increased enemy activity in any of these areas endangered the lives of Americans remaining in Vietnam, I would not hesitate to take strong and effective measures to deal with that situation.

Despite that warning, North Vietnam has increased its military aggression in all these areas, and particularly in Cambodia.

After full consultation with the National Security Council, Ambassador Bunker, General Abrams and my other advisors, I have concluded that the actions of the enemy in the last 10 days clearly endanger the lives of Americans who are in Vietnam now and would constitute an unacceptable risk to those who will be there after withdrawal of another 150,000.

To protect our men who are in Vietnam, and to guarantee the continued success of our withdrawal and Vietnamization program, I have concluded that the time has come for action.

Tonight, I shall describe the actions of the enemy, the actions I have ordered to deal with that situation, and the reasons for my decision.

Cambodia—a small country of seven million people—has been a neutral nation since the Geneva Agreement of 1954, an agreement, incidentally, which was signed by the government of North Vietnam.

American policy since then has been to scrupulously respect the neutrality of the Cambodian people. We have maintained a skeleton diplomatic mission of fewer than 15 in Cambodia's capital, and that only since last August.

For the previous four years, from 1965 to 1969 we did not have any diplomatic mission whatever in Cambodia, and for the past five years we have provided no military assistance whatever and no economic assistance to Cambodia.

Source: Vital Speeches of the Day, May 15, 1970;
         City News Publishing Company, Southold, New
         York. By permission of the publisher.

North Vietnam, however, has not respected that neutrality. For the past five years, as indicated on this map, as you see here, North Vietnam has occupied military sanctuaries all along the Cambodian frontier with South Vietnam. Some of these extend up to 20 miles into Cambodia.

The sanctuaries are in red, and as you note they are on both sides of the border.

They are used for hit-and-run attacks on American and South Vietnamese forces in South Vietnam. These Communist-occupied territories contain major base camps, training sites, logistics facilities, weapons and ammunition factories, airstrips and prisoner of war compounds.

And for five years neither the United States nor South Vietnam has moved against these enemy sanctuaries because we did not wish to violate the territory of a neutral nation.

Even after the Vietnamese Communists began to expand these sanctuaries four weeks ago, we counseled patience to our South Vietnamese allies and imposed restraints on our own commanders.

In contrast to our policy the enemy in the past two weeks has stepped up his guerrilla actions and he is concentrating his main force in these sanctuaries that you see in this map, where they are building up the large massive attacks on our forces and those of South Vietnam.

North Vietnam in the last two weeks has stripped away all pretense of respecting the sovereignty or the neutrality of Cambodia. Thousands of their soldiers are invading the country from the sanctuaries. They are encircling the capital of Pnompenh. Coming from these sanctuaries as you see here, they had moved into Cambodia and are encircling the capital.

Cambodia, as a result of this, has sent out a call to the United States, to a number of other nations, for assistance. Because if this enemy effort succeeds, Cambodia would become a vast enemy staging area and a springboard for attacks on South Vietnam along 600 miles of frontier: a refuge where enemy troops could return from combat without fear of retaliation.

North Vietnamese men and supplies could then be poured into that country, jeopardizing not only the lives of our men but the people of South Vietnam as well.

Now confronted with this situation we had three options:

First, we can do nothing. Now, the ultimate result of that course of action is clear. Unless we indulge in wishful thinking, the lives of Americans remaining in Vietnam after our next withdrawal of 150,000 would be gravely threatened.

Let us go to the map again.

Here is South Vietnam. Here is North Vietnam. North Vietnam already occupies this part of Laos. If North Vietnam also occupied this whole band in Cambodia or the entire country, it would mean that South Vietnam was completely outflanked and the forces of Americans in this area as well as the South Vietnamese would be in an untenable military position.

Our second choice is to provide massive military assistance to Cambodia itself and, unfortunately, while we deeply sympathize with the plight of seven million Cambodians whose country has been invaded, massive amounts of military assistance could not be rapidly and effectively utilized by this small Cambodian Army against the immediate trap.

With other nations we shall do our best to provide the small arms and other equipment which the Cambodian Army of 40,000 needs and can use for its defense.

But the aid we will provide will be limited for the purpose of enabling Cambodia to defend its neutrality and not for the purpose of making it an active belligerent on one side or the other.

Our third choice is to go to the heart of the trouble.

And that means cleaning out major North Vietnamese- and Vietcong-occupied territories, these sanctuaries which serve as bases for attacks on both Cambodia and American and South Vietnamese forces in South Vietnam.

Some of these, incidentally are as close to Saigon as Baltimore is to Washington. This one, for example, is called the Parrots' Beak—it's only 33 miles from Saigon.

Now faced with these three options, this is the decision I have made. In co-operation with the armed forces of South Vietnam, attacks are being launched this week to clean out major enemy sanctuaries on the Cambodian-Vietnam border. A major responsibility for the ground operation is being assumed by South Vietnamese forces.

For example, the attacks in several areas, including the parrot's beak, that I referred to a moment ago, are exclusively South Vietnamese ground operations, under South Vietnamese command, with the United States providing air and logistical support.

There is one area however, immediately above the parrot's beak where I have concluded that a combined American and South Vietnamese operation is necessary.

And now, let me give you the reasons for my decision.

A majority of the American people, a majority of you listening to me are for the withdrawal of our forces from Vietnam. The action I have taken tonight is indispensable for the continuing success of that withdrawal program.

A majority of the American people want to end this war rather than to have it drag on interminably.

The action I have taken tonight will serve that purpose.

A majority of the American people want to keep the casualties of our brave men in Vietnam at an absolute minimum.

Tonight, American and South Vietnamese units will attack the headquarters for the entire Communist military operation in South Vietnam. This key control center has been occupied by the North Vietnamese and Vietcong for five years in blatant violation of Cambodia's neutrality.

This is not an invasion of Cambodia. The areas in which these attacks will be launched are completely occupied and controlled by North Vietnamese forces.

Our purpose is not to occupy the areas. Once enemy forces

are driven out of these sanctuaries and once their military supplies are destroyed, we will withdraw.

These actions are in no way directed to security interests of any nation. Any government that chooses to use these actions as a pretext for harming relations with the United States will be doing so on its own responsibility and on its own initiative and we will draw the appropriate conclusions.

The action I take tonight is essential if we are to accomplish that goal.

We take this action not for the purpose of expanding the war into Cambodia but for the purpose of ending the war in Vietnam, and winning the just peace we all desire.

We have made and will continue to make every possible effort to end this war through negotiation at the conference table rather than through more fighting in the battlefield.

Let's look again at the record.

We stopped the bombing of North Vietnam. We have cut air operations by over 20 per cent. We've announced the withdrawal of over 250,000 of our men. We've offered to withdraw all of our men if they will withdraw theirs. We've offered to negotiate all issues with only one condition: and that is that the future of South Vietnam be determined, not by North Vietnam, and not by the United States, but by the people of South Vietnam themselves.

The answer of the enemy has been intransigeance at the conference table, belligerence at Hanoi, massive military aggression in Laos and Cambodia and stepped-up attacks in South Vietnam designed to increase American casualties.

This attitude has become intolerable.

We will not react to this threat to American lives merely by plaintive diplomatic protests.

If we did, credibility of the United States would be destroyed in every area of the world where only the power of the United States deters aggression.

Tonight, I again warn the North Vietnamese that if they continue to escalate the fighting when the United States is withdrawing its forces, I shall meet my responsibility as commander and chief of our armed forces to take the action I consider necessary to defend the security of our American men.

The action I have announced tonight puts the leaders of North Vietnam on notice that we will be patient in working for peace. We will be conciliatory at the conference table, but we will not be humiliated. We will not be defeated.

We will not allow American men by the thousands to be killed by an enemy from privileged sanctuary.

The time came long ago to end this war through peaceful negotiations. We stand ready for those negotiations. We've made major efforts many of which must remain secret.

I say tonight all the offers and approaches made previously remain on the conference table whenever Hanoi is ready to negotiate seriously.

But if the enemy response to our most conciliatory offers for peaceful negotiation continues to be to increase its attacks and humiliate and defeat us, we shall react accordingly.

My fellow Americans, we live in an age of anarchy, both abroad and at home. We see mindless attacks on all the great institutions which have been created by free civilizations in the last 500 years. Even here in the United States, great universities are being systematically destroyed.

Small nations all over the world find themselves under attack from within and from without. If when the chips are down the world's most powerful nation—the United States of America—acts like a pitiful, helpless giant, the forces of totalitarianism and anarchy will threaten free nations and free institutions throughout the world.

It is not our power but our will and character that is being tested tonight.

The question all Americans must ask and answer tonight is this:

Does the richest and strongest nation in the history of the world have the character to meet a direct challenge by a group which rejects every effort to win a just peace, ignores our warning, tramples on solemn agreements, violates the neutrality of an unarmed people and uses our prisoners as hostages?

If we fail to meet this challenge all other nations will be on notice that despite its overwhelming power the United States when a real crisis comes will be found wanting.

During my campaign for the Presidency, I pledged to bring Americans home from Vietnam. They are coming home. I promised to end this war. I shall keep that promise. I promised to win a just peace. I shall keep that promise.

We shall avoid a wider war, but we are also determined to put an end to this war.

In this room, Woodrow Wilson made the great decision which led to victory in World War I.

Franklin Roosevelt made the decisions which led to our victory in World War II.

Dwight D. Eisenhower made decisions which ended the war in Korea and avoided war in the Middle East.

John F. Kennedy in his finest hour made the great decision which removed Soviet nuclear missiles from Cuba and the western hemisphere.

I have noted that there's been a great deal of discussion with regard to this decision I have made. And I should point out that I do not contend that it is in the same magnitude as these decisions that I have just mentioned.

But between those decisions and this decision, there is a difference that is very fundamental. In those decisions the American people were not assailed by counsels of doubt and defeat from some of the most widely known opinion leaders of the nation.

I have noted, for example, that a Republican Senator has said that this action I have taken means that my party has lost all chance of winning the November elections, and others are saying today that this move against enemy sanctuaries will make me a one-term President.

No one is more aware than I am of the political consequences of the action I've taken. It is tempting to take the easy political path, to blame this war on previous Administrations, and to bring all of our men home immediately—regardless of the consequences, even though that would mean defeat for the United States; to desert 18 million South Vietnamese people who have put their trust in us; to expose them to the same slaughter and savagery which the leaders of North Vietnam inflicted on hundreds of thousands of North Vietnamese who chose freedom when the Communists took over North Vietnam in 1954.

To get peace at any price now, even though I know that a peace of humiliation for the United States would lead to a bigger war or surrender later.

I have rejected all political considerations in making this decision. Whether my party gains in November is nothing compared to the lives of 400,000 brave Americans fighting for our country and for the cause of peace and freedom in Vietnam.

Whether I may be a one-term President is insignificant compared to whether by our failure to act in this crisis the United States proves itself to be unworthy to lead the forces of freedom in this critical period in world history.

I would rather be a one-term President and do what I believe was right than to be a two-term President at the cost of seeing America become a second-rate power and to see this nation accept the first defeat in its proud 190-year history.

I realize in this war there are honest, deep differences in this country about whether we should have become involved, that there are differences to how the war should have been conducted.

But the decision I announce tonight transcends those differences, for the lives of American men are involved. The opportunity for a 150,000 Americans to come home in the next 12 months is involved. The future of 18-million people in South Vietnam and 7-million people in Cambodia is involved, the possibility of winning a just peace in Vietnam and in the Pacific is at stake.

It is customary to conclude a speech from the White House by asking support for the President of the United States.

Tonight, I depart from that precedent. What I ask is far more important. I ask for your support for our brave men fighting tonight halfway around the world, not for territory, not for glory but so that their younger brothers and their sons and your sons can have a chance to grow up in a world of peace and freedom, and justice.

Thank you, and good night.

State of the Union Message

1971

RICHARD M. NIXON, *President of the United States*

Delivered to a joint session of Congress, Washington, D. C., January 22, 1971

MR. SPEAKER, MR. PRESIDENT, my colleagues in the Congress, our distinguished guests, my fellow Americans—as this 92d Congress begins its session, America has lost a great Senator, and all of us who had the privilege to know him have lost a loyal friend.

I had the privilege of visiting Senator Russell in the hospital just a few days before he died. He never spoke about himself. He only spoke eloquently about the need for a strong national defense.

In tribute to one of the most magnificent Americans of all time, I respectfully ask that all those here will rise in silent prayer for Senator Russell.

Thank you. Thank you.

Mr. Speaker, before I begin my formal address, I want to use this opportunity to congratulate all of those who were winners in the rather spirited contests for leadership positions in the House and the Senate, and also to express my condolences to the losers. I know how both of you feel.

And I particularly want to join with all of the members of the House and the Senate as well in congratulating the new Speaker of the United States Congress.

And to those new members of this house who may have some doubts about the possibilities for advancement in the years ahead, I would remind you that the Speaker and I met just 24 years ago in this chamber as freshmen members of the 80th Congress. As you see, we both have come up in the world since then.

Mr. Speaker, this 92d Congress has a chance to be recorded as the greatest Congress in America's history.

In these troubled years just past, America has been going through a long nightmare of war and division, of crime and inflation. Even more deeply, we have gone through a long, dark night of the American spirit. But now that night is ending. Now we must let our spirits soar again. Now we are ready for the lift of a driving dream.

The people of this nation are eager to get on with the quest for new greatness. They see challenges and are prepared to

Source: Vital Speeches of the Day, February 1, 1971; City News Publishing Company, Southold, New York. By permission of the publisher.

meet those challenges. It is for us here to open the doors that will set free again the real greatness of this nation—the genius of the American people.

How shall we meet this challenge? How can we truly open the doors, and set free the full genius of our people?

The way in which the 92d Congress answers these questions will determine its place in history. But, more important, it can determine this nation's place in history as we enter the third century of our independence.

Tonight, I shall present to the Congress six great goals. I shall ask not simply for more new programs in the old framework. I shall ask to change the framework of government itself—to reform the entire structure of American government so we can make it again fully responsive to the needs and the wishes of the American people.

If we act boldly—if we seize this moment and achieve these goals—we can close the gap between promise and performance in American government. We can bring together the resources of this nation and the spirit of the American people.

In discussing these great goals, I shall deal tonight only with matters on the domestic side of the nation's agenda. I shall make a separate report to the Congress and the nation next month on developments in our foreign policy.

The first of these great goals is already before the Congress.

I urge that the unfinished business of the 91st Congress be made the first priority business of the 92d.

Over the next two weeks, I will call upon Congress to take action on more than 35 pieces of proposed legislation on which action was not completed last year.

The most important is welfare reform.

The present welfare system has become a monstrous, consuming outrage—an outrage against the community, against the taxpayer, and particularly against the children it is supposed to help.

Now, we honestly disagree, as we do, on what to do about it. But we can all agree that we must meet the challenge not by pouring more money into a bad program but by abolishing the present welfare system and adopting a new one.

And, so, let us place a floor under the income of every family with children in America—and without those demeaning, soul-stifling affronts to human dignity that so blight the lives of welfare children today. But let us also establish an effective work incentive, an effective work requirement.

Let us provide the means by which more can help themselves. This shall be our goal. Let us generously help those who are not able to help themselves. But let us stop helping those who are able to help themselves but refuse to do so.

The second great goal is to achieve what Americans have not enjoyed since 1957—full prosperity in peacetime.

The tide of inflation has turned. The rise in the cost of living, which had been gathering dangerous momentum in the late sixties, was reduced last year. Inflation will be further reduced this year.

But as we have moved from runaway inflation toward reasonable price stability, and at the same time, as we have been moving from a wartime economy to a peacetime economy, we have paid a price in increased unemployment.

We should take no comfort from the fact that the level of unemployment in this transition from a wartime to a peacetime economy is lower than in any peacetime year of the sixties.

This is not good enough for the man who is unemployed in the seventies. We must do better for workers in peacetime and we will do better.

And to achieve this, I will submit an expansionary budget this year—one that will help stimulate the economy and thereby open up new job opportunities for millions of Americans.

It will be a full-employment budget, a budget designed to be in balance if the economy were operating at its peak potential. By spending as if we were at full employment, we will help to bring about full employment.

I ask the Congress to accept these expansionary policies—to accept the concept of the full-employment budget.

And at the same time, I ask the Congress to cooperate in resisting expenditures that go beyond the limits of the full-employment budget. For as we wage a campaign to bring about a widely shared prosperity, we must not re-ignite the fires of inflation and so undermine that prosperity.

With the stimulus and the discipline of the full-employment budget; with the commitment of the independent Federal Reserve System to provide fully for the monetary needs of a growing economy; and with a much greater effort on the part of labor and management to make their wage and price decisions in the light of the national interest and their own self-interest—then for the worker, the farmer, the consumer, for Americans everywhere we shall gain the goal of a new prosperity; more jobs, more income, more profits, without inflation and without war.

This is a great goal, and one that we can achieve together.

The third great goal is to continue the effort so dramatically begun last year: to restore and enhance our natural environment.

Building on the foundation laid in the 37-point program that I submitted to Congress last year, I will propose a strong new set of initiatives to clean up our air and water, to combat noise, and to preserve and restore our surroundings.

I will propose programs to make better use of our land, to encourage a balanced national growth—growth that will revitalize our rural heartland and enhance the quality of life in America.

And not only to meet today's needs but to anticipate those of tomorrow, I will put forward the most extensive program ever proposed by a President of the United States to expand the nation's parks, recreation areas, open spaces in a way that truly brings parks to the people where the people are. For only if we have a legacy of parks will the next generation have parks to enjoy.

As a fourth great goal, I will offer a far-reaching set of proposals for improving America's health care and making it available more fairly to more people.

I will propose:

A program to insure that no American family will be prevented from obtaining basic medical care by inability to pay.

I will propose a major increase in and redirection of aid to medical schools, to greatly increase the number of doctors and other health personnel.

Incentives to improve the delivery of health services, to get more medical care resources into those areas that have not been adequately served, to make greater use of medical assistants and to slow the alarming rise in the costs of medical care.

New Programs to encourage better preventive medicine, by attacking the causes of disease and injury, and by providing incentives to doctors to keep people well rather than just to treat them when they are sick.

I will also ask for an appropriation of an extra $100-million to launch an intensive campaign to find a cure for cancer, and I will ask later for whatever additional funds can effectively be used. The time has come in America when the same kind of concentrated effort that split the atom and took man to the moon should be turned toward conquering this dread disease. Let us make a total national commitment to achieve this goal.

America has long been the wealthiest nation in the world. Now it is time we became the healthiest nation in the world.

The fifth great goal is to strengthen and to renew our state and local governments.

As we approach our 200th anniversary in 1976, we remember that this nation launched itself as a loose confederation of separate states, without a workable central government. At the time, the mark of its leaders' vision was that they quickly saw the need to balance the separate powers of the states with a government of central powers.

And so they gave us a Constitution of balanced powers, of unity with diversity—and so clear was their vision that it survives today as the oldest written Constitution still in force in the world.

For almost two centuries since—and dramatically in the nineteen-thirties—at those great turning points when the question has been between the states and the Federal Government, that question had been resolved in favor of a stronger central Federal Government.

During this time the nation grew and the nation prospered. But one thing history tells us is that no great movement goes in the same direction forever. Nations change, they adapt, or they slowly die.

The time has now come in America to reverse the flow of power and resources from the states and communities to Washington and start power and resources flowing back from Washington to the states and communities and, more important, to the people, all across America.

The time has come for a new partnership between the Federal Government and the states and localities—a partnership in which we entrust the states and localities with a larger share of the nation's repsonsibilities, and in which we share our Federal revenues with them so that they can meet those responsibilities.

To achieve this goal, I propose to the Congress tonight that we enact a plan of revenue sharing historic in scope and bold in concept.

All across America today, states and cities are confronted with a financial crisis. Some have already been cutting back on essential services—for example, just recently San Diego and Cleveland cut back on trash collections. Most are caught between the prospects of bankruptcy, on the one hand, and adding to an already crushing tax burden, on the other.

One indication of the rising costs of local government, I discovered the other day that my home town of Whittier, Calif.—which has a population of 67,000—has a larger budget for 1971 than the entire Federal budget was in 1791.

Now the time has come to take a new direction, and once again to introduce a new and more creative balance to our approach to government.

And, so, let us put the money where the needs are. And let us put the power to spend it where the people are.

I propose that the Congress make a $16-billion investment in renewing state and local government—$5-billion of this will be in new and unrestricted funds, to be used as the states and localities see fit. The other $11-billion will be provided by allocating $1-billion of new funds and converting one-third of the money going to the present narrow-purpose aid programs into Federal revenue-sharing funds for six broad purposes—for urban development, rural development education, transportation, job training, and law enforcement—but with states and localities making their own decisions on how it should be spent within each category.

For the next fiscal year, this would increase total Federal aid to the states and localities more than 25 per cent over the present level.

The revenue-sharing proposals I send to the Congress will include the safeguards against discrimination that accompany all other Federal funds allocated to the states. Neither the President nor the Congress nor the conscience of this nation can permit money which comes from all the people to be used in a way which discriminates against some of them.

The Federal Government will still have a large and vital role to play in achieving our national purposes. Established functions that are clearly and essentially Federal in nature will still be performed by the Federal Government. New functions that need to be sponsored or performed by the Federal

Government—such as those I have urged tonight in welfare and health—will be added to the Federal agenda. Whenever it makes the best sense for us to act as a whole nation, the Federal Government should and will lead the way. But where state or local governments can better do what needs to be done, let us see that they have the resources to do it there.

Under this plan, the Federal Government will provide the states and localities with more money and less interference—and by cutting down the interference the same amount of money will go a lot further:

Let us share them to rescue the states and localities from the brink of financial crisis.

Let us share them to give homeowners and wage earners a chance to escape from ever higher property taxes and sales taxes.

Let us share our resources for two other reasons as well.

The first of these reasons has to do with government itself, and the second has to do with each of us—with the individual.

Let's face it. Most Americans today are simply fed up with government at all· levels. They will not—and they should not—continue to tolerate the gap between promise and performance in government.

The fact is that we made the Federal Government so strong it grows musclebound and the states and localities so weak they approach impotence.

If we put more power in more places, we can make government more creative in more places. That way we multiply the number of people with the ability to make things happen. We can open the way to a new burst of creative energy throughout America.

The final reason I urge this historic shift is much more personal, for each and every one of us.

As everything seems to have grown bigger and more complex in America, as the forces that shape our lives seem to have grown more distant and more impersonal, a great feeling of frustration has crept across this land.

Whether it is the workingman who feels neglected, the black man who feels oppressed or the mother concerned about her children, there has been a growing feeling that "things are in the saddle, and ride mankind."

Millions of frustrated young Americans today are crying out—asking not what will government do for me, but what can I do, what can I contribute, how can I matter?

And so, let us answer them. Let us say to them and let us say to all Americans: "We hear you. We will give you a chance. We are going to give you a new chance to have more to say about the decisions that affect your future—a chance to participate in government—because we are going to provide more centers of power where what you do can make a difference that you can see and feel in your own lives and the life of your whole community."

The further away government is from people, the stronger government becomes and the weaker people become. And a nation with a strong government and a weak people is an empty shell.

I reject the patronizing idea that government in Washington, D. C., is inevitably more wise, more honest and more efficient than government at the local or state level. The honesty and efficiency of government depends on people. Government at all levels has good people and bad people. And the way to get more good people into government is to give them more opportunity to do good things.

The idea that a bureaucratic élite in Washington knows best what is best for people everywhere and that you cannot trust local government is really a contention that you cannot trust people to govern themselves. This notion is completely foreign to the American experience. Local government is the government closest to the people; it's most responsive to the individual person; it is people's government in a far more intimate way than the Government in Washington can ever be.

People came to America because they wanted to determine their own future rather than to live in a country where others determined their future for them.

What this change means is that once again in America we are placing our trust in people.

I have faith in people. I trust the judgment of people. Let us give the people of America a chance, a bigger voice in deciding for themselves those questions that so greatly affect their lives.

The sixth great goal is the complete reform of the Federal Government itself.

Based on a long and intensive study with the aid of the best advice obtainable, I have concluded that a sweeping reorganization of the executive branch is needed if the Government is to keep up with the times and with the needs of the people.

I propose therefore that we reduce the present 12 Cabinet departments to eight. I propose that the Department of State, Treasury, Defense and Justice remain, but that all the other departments be consolidated into four: human resources, community development, natural resources, and economic development.

Let us look at what these would be:

First, a department dealing with the concerns of people—as individuals, as members of a family—a department focused on human needs.

Second, a department concerned with the community—rural communities and urban communities—and with all that it takes to make a community function as a community.

And, third, a department concerned with our physical environment, with the preservation and balanced use of those great natural resources on which our nation depends.

And, fourth, a department concerned with our prosperity—with our jobs, our businesses, and those many activities that keep our economy running smoothy and well.

Under this plan, rather than dividing up our departments by narrow subjects, we would organize them around the great purposes of government. Rather than scattering responsibility by adding new levels of bureaucracy, we would focus and concentrate the responsibility for getting problems solved.

With these four departments, when we have a problem we will know where to go—and the department will have the authority and the resources to do something about it.

Over the years we have added departments and created agencies at the Federal level, each to serve a new constituency or to handle a particular task—and these have grown and multiplied in what has become a hopeless confusion of form and function.

The time has come to match our structure to our purposes—to look with a fresh eye, to organize the Government by conscious, comprehensive design to meet the new needs of a new era.

One hundred years ago, Abraham Lincoln stood on a battlefield and spoke of a government of the people, by the people and for the people. Too often since then, we have become a nation of the Government, by the Government, and for the Government.

By enacting these reforms, we can renew that principle that Lincoln stated so simply and so well.

By giving everyone's voice a chance to be heard, we have Government that truly is of the people.

By creating more centers of meaningful power, more places where decisions that really count can be made, by giving more people a chance to do something, we can have government that truly is by the people.

And by setting up a completely modern, functional system of Government at the national level, we in Washington will at last be able to provide Government that truly is for the people.

I realize that what I am asking is that not only the executive branch in Washington but that even this Congress will have to change by giving up some of its power.

Change is hard. But without change there can be no progress. And for each of us the question then becomes, not "Will change cause me inconvenience?" but "Will change bring progress for America?"

Giving up power is hard. But I would urge all of you, as leaders of this country, to remember that the truly revered leaders in world history are those who gave power to people, not those who took it away.

As we consider these reforms we will be acting, not for the next two years or for the next 10 years, but for the next hundred years.

So let us approach these six great goals with a sense, not only of the moment in history, but also of history itself.

Let us act with the willingness to work together and the vision and the boldness and the courage of those great Americans who met in Philadelphia almost 190 years ago to write a Constitution.

Let us leave a heritage as they did—not just for our children but for millions yet unborn—of a nation where every American will have a chance not only to live in peace and to enjoy prosperity and opportunity, but to participate in a system of government where he knows not only his votes but his ideas count—a system of government which will provide the means for America to reach heights of achievement undreamed of before.

Those men who met in Philadelphia left a great heritage because they had a vision—not only of what the nation was, but of what it could become.

When I think of that vision, I recall that America was founded as the land of the open door—a haven for the oppressed, a land of opportunity, a place of refuge and hope.

When the first settlers opened the door of America three and a half centuries ago, they came to escape persecution and to find opportunity—and they left wide the door of welcome for others to follow.

When the 13 colonies declared their independence almost two centuries ago, they opened the door to a new vision of liberty and of human fulfillment—not just for an élite, but for all.

To the generations that followed, America's was the open door that beckoned millions from the old world to the new in search of a better life, a freer life, a fuller life, and in which by their own decisions they could shape their own destinies.

For the black American, the Indian, the Mexican-American, and for those others in our land who have not had an equal chance, the nation at last has begun to confront the need tó press open the door of full and equal opportunity, and of human dignity.

For all Americans, with these changes I have proposed tonight, we can open the door to a new era of opportunity. We can open the door to full and effective participation in the decisions that affect their lives. We can open the door to a new partnership among governments of all levels—between those governments and the people themselves. And by so doing, we can open wide the doors of human fulfillment for millions of people here in America now and in the years to come.

In the next few weeks I will spell out in greater detail the way I propose that we achieve these six great goals. I ask this Congress to be responsive. If it is, then the 92nd Congress—your Congress, our Congress—at the end of its term, will be able to look back on a record more splendid than any in our history.

This can be the Congress that helped us end the longest war in the nation's history, and end it in a way that will give us at last a genuine chance to enjoy what we have not had in this century—a full generation of peace.

This can be the Congress that helped achieve an expanding economy, with full employment and without inflation—and without the deadly stimulus of war.

This can be the Congress that reformed a welfare system that has robbed recipients of their dignity and robbed states and cities of their resources.

This can be the Congress that pressed forward the rescue of our environment, and established for the next generation an enduring legacy of parks for the people.

This can be the Congress that launched a new era in American medicine, in which the quality of medical care was enhanced while the costs were made less burdensome.

But above all, what this Congress can be remembered for is opening the way to a New American Revolution—a peaceful revolution in which power was turned back to the people—in which government at all levels was refreshed and renewed, and made truly responsive. This can be a revolution as profound, as far-reaching, as exciting, as that first revolution almost 200 years ago—and it can mean that just five years from now America will enter its third century as a young nation new in spirit, with all the vigor and the freshness with which it began its first century.

My colleagues in the Congress—these are great goals. They can make the sessions of this Congress a great moment for America. And so, let us pledge together to go forward together—by achieving these goals to give America the foundation today for a new greatness tomorrow and in all the years to come—and in so doing to make this the greatest Congress in the history of this great and good country.

United States— Peoples Republic Of China

A JOURNEY FOR PEACE

By RICHARD M. NIXON, *President of the United States*

Delivered on National TV, July 15, 1971

G OOD EVENING: I have requested this television time tonight to announce a major development in our efforts to build a lasting peace in the world.

As I have pointed out on a number of occasions over the past three years, there can be no stable peace and enduring peace without the participation of the People's Republic of China and its 750 million people. That is why I have undertaken initiatives in several areas to open the door for more normal relations between our two countries.

In pursuance of that goal, I sent Dr. Kissinger, my Assistant for National Security Affairs, to Peking during his recent world tour for the purpose of having talks with Premier Chou En-lai.

The announcement I shall now read is being issued simultaneously in Peking and in the United States:

"Premier Chou En-lai and Dr. Henry Kissinger, President Nixon's Assistant for National Security Affairs, held talks in Peking from July 9 to 11, 1971. Knowing of President Nixon's expressed desire to visit the People's Republic of China, Premier Chou En-Lai on behalf of the Government of the People's Republic of China has extended an invitation to President Nixon to visit China at an appropriate date before May, 1972.

"President Nixon has accepted the invitation with pleasure.

"The meeting between the leaders of China and the United States is to seek the normalization of relations between the two countries and also to exchange views on questions of concern to the two sides."

In anticipation of the inevitable speculation which will follow this announcement, I want to put our policy in the clearest possible context. Our action in seeking a new relationship with the People's Republic of China will not be at the expense of our old friends.

Source: Vital Speeches of the Day,   July 15, 1971;
          City News Publishing Company, Southold, New
          York.   By permission of the publisher.

It is not directed against any other nation. We seek friendly relations with all nations. Any nation can be our friend without being any other nation's enemy.

I have taken this action because of my profound conviction that all nations will gain from a reduction of tensions and a better relationship between the United States and the People's Republic of China.

It is in this spirit that I will undertake what I deeply hope will become a journey for peace, peace not just for our generation but for future generations on this earth we share together.

Thank you and good night.

A New Economic Policy

TEMPORARY WAGE & PRICE CONTROLS

By RICHARD M. NIXON, *President of the United States*

Broadcast on Television, Washington, D. C., August 15, 1971

G OOD EVENING. I've addressed the nation a number of times over the past two years on the problems of ending the war. Because of the progress we have made toward achieving that goal, this Sunday evening is an appropriate time for us to turn our attention to the challenges of peace.

America today has the best opportunity in this century to achieve two of its greatest ideals: to bring about a full generation of peace and to create a new prosperity without war.

This not only requires bold leadership ready to take bold action; it calls for the greatness in a great people.

Prosperity without war requires action on three fronts. We must create more and better jobs; we must stop the rise in the cost of living; we must protect the dollar from the attacks of international money speculators.

We are going to take that action—not timidly, not halfheartedly and not in piecemeal fashion. We are going to move forward to the new prosperity without war as befits a great people, all together and along a broad front.

The time has come for a new economic policy for the United States. Its targets are unemployment, inflation and international speculation, and this is how we are going to attack those targets:

First, on the subject of jobs. We all know why we have an unemployment problem. Two million workers have been released from the armed forces and defense plants because of our success in winding down the war in Vietnam. Putting those people back to work is one of the challenges of peace, and we have begun to make progress. Our unemployment rate today is below the average of the four peace-time years of the nineteen-sixties, but we can and we must do better than that.

The time has come for American industry, which has produced more jobs at higher real wages than any other industrial system in history, to embark on a bold program of new investment of production for peace. To give that system a powerful new stimulus I shall ask the Congress when it reconvenes after its summer recess to consider as its first priority the enactment of the Job Development Act of 1971.

Source: Vital Speeches of the Day, September 1, 1971;
         City News Publishing Company, Southold, New
         York. By permission of the publisher.

I will propose to provide the strongest short-term incentive in our history to invest in new machinery and equipment that will create new jobs for Americans: a 10 per cent job development credit for one year effective as of today with a 5 per cent credit after Aug. 15, 1972.

This tax credit for investment in new equipment will not only generate new jobs. It will raise productivity; it will make our goods more competitive in the years ahead.

Second, I will propose to repeal the 7 per cent excise tax on automobiles effective today. This will mean a reduction in price of about $200 per car.

I shall insist that the American auto industry pass this tax reduction on to the nearly 8 million customers who are buying automobiles this year. Lower prices will mean that more people will be able to afford new cars, and every additional 100,000 cars sold means 25,000 new jobs.

Third, I propose to speed up the personal-income-tax exemptions scheduled for Jan. 1, 1973, to Jan. 1, 1972, so that taxpayers can deduct an extra $50 for each exemption one year earlier than planned.

This increase in consumer spending power will provide a strong boost to the economy in general and to employment in particular.

The tax reductions I am recommending, together with this broad upturn of the economy, which has taken place in the first half of this year, will move us strongly forward toward a goal this nation has not reached since 1956, fifteen years ago: prosperity with full employment in peacetime.

Looking to the future, I have directed the Secretary of the Treasury to recommend to the Congress in January new tax proposals for stimulating research and development of new industries and new techniques to help provide the 20 million new jobs that America needs for the young people who will be coming into the job market in the next decade.

To offset the loss of revenue from these tax cuts, which directly stimulate new jobs, I have ordered today a $4.7-billion cut in Federal spending.

Tax cuts to stimulate employment must be matched by spending cuts to restrain inflation. To check the rise in the cost of government I have ordered a postponement of pay raises and a 5 per cent cut in Government personnel.

I have ordered a 10 per cent cut in foreign economic aid. In addition, since the Congress has already delayed action on two of the great initiatives of this Administration, I will ask Congress to amend my proposals to postpone the implementation of revenue sharing for three months and welfare reform for one year.

In this way, I am reordering our budget piorities so as to concentrate more on achieving our goal of full employment.

The second indispensable element of the new prosperity is to stop the rise in the cost of living. One of the cruelest legacies of the artificial prosperity produced by war is inflation. Inflation robs every American, every one of you. The 20 million who are retired and living on fixed incomes—they are particularly hard hit. Homemakers find it harder than ever to balance the family budget. And 80 million American wage earners have been on a treadmill.

For example, in the four war years between 1965 and 1969, your wage increases were completely eaten up by price increases. Your paychecks were higher, but you were no better off. We have made progress against the rise in the cost of living. From the high point of 6 per cent a year in 1969, the rise in consumer prices has been cut to 4 per cent in the first half of 1971. But just as is the case in our fight against unemployment, we can and we must do better than that. The time has come for decisive action—action that will break the vicious circle of spiraling prices and costs.

I am today ordering a freeze on all prices and wages throughout the United States for a period of 90 days.

In addition I call upon corporations to extend the wage-price freeze to all dividends. I have today appointed a Cost-of-Living Council within the Government. I have directed this council to work with leaders of labor and business to set up the proper mechanism for achieving continued price and wage stability after the 90-day freeze is over.

Let me emphasize two characteristics of this action. First, it is temporary. To put the strong vigorous American economy into a permanent staitjacket would lock in unfairness; it would stifle the expansion of our free-enterprise system, and second, while the wage-price freeze will be backed by Government sanctions, if necessary, it will not be accompanied by the establishment of a huge price-control bureaucracy.

I am relying on the voluntary cooperation of all Americans—each one of you: workers, employers, consumers—to make this freeze work. Working together, we will break the back of inflation, and we will do it without the mandatory wage and price controls that crush economic and personal freedom.

The third indispensable element in building the new prosperity is closely related to creating new jobs and halting inflation. We must protect the position of the American dollar as a pillar of monetary stability around the world.

In the past seven years, there's been an average of one international monetary crisis every year. Now who gains from these crises? Not the working man, not the investor, not the real producers of wealth. The gainers are the international money speculators: because they thrive on crises, they help to create them.

In recent weeks, the speculators have been waging an all-out war on the American dollar. The strength of a nation's currency is based on the strength of that nation's ecnomy, and the American economy is by far the strongest in the world.

Accordingly, I have directed the Secretary of the Treasury to take the action necessary to defend the dollar against the speculators.

I directed Secretary Connally to suspend temporarily the convertibility of the dollar into gold or other reserve assets except in amounts and conditions determined to be in the interest of monetary stability and in the best interests of the United States.

Now what is this action—which is very technical—what does it mean to you? Let me lay to rest the bugaboo of what is called "devaluation." If you want to buy a foreign car or take a trip abroad, market conditions may cause your dollar to buy slightly less.

But, if you are among the overwhelming majority of Americans who buy American-made products, in America, your dollar will be worth just as much tomorrow as it is today.

The effect of this action, in other words, will be to stabilize the dollar. Now this action will not win us any friends among the international money traders. But our primary concern is with the American workers, and with their competition around the world.

To our friends abroad, including the many responsible members of the international banking community who are dedicated to stability in the flow of trade, I give this assurance: The United States has always been and will continue to be a forward-looking and trustworthy trading partner.

In full cooperation with the International Monetary Fund and those who trade with us, we will press for the necessary reforms to set up an urgently needed new international monetary system. Stability and equal treatment is in everybody's best interest. I am determined that the American dollar must never again be a hostage in the hands of international speculators.

I am taking one further step to protect the dollar, to improve our balance of payments and to increase jobs for Americans. As a temporary measure I am today imposing an additional tax of 10 per cent on goods imported into the United States.

This is a better solution for international trade than direct controls on the amount of imports. This import tax is a temporary action. It isn't directed against any other country. It's an action to make certain that American products will not be at a disadvantage because of unfair exchange rates.

When the unfair treatment is ended, the import tax will end as well. As a result of these actions the product of American labor will be more competitive and the unfair edge that some of our foreign competition has will be removed.

This is a mjaor reason why our trade balance has eroded over the past 15 years.

At the end of World War II, the economies of the major industrial nations of Europe and Asia were shattered. To help them get on their feet and to protect their freedom, the United States has provided over the past 25 years $143-billion in foreign aid.

That was the right thing for us to do. Today, largely with our help, they have regained their vitality. They have become our strong competitors, and we welcome their success.

But now that other nations are economically strong, the time has come for them to bear their fair share of the burden of defending freedom around the world. The time has come for exchange rates to be set straight, and for the major nations to compete as equals.

There is no longer any need for the United States to compete with one hand tied behind her back.

The range of actions I have taken and proposed tonight on the job front, on the inflation front, on the monetary front, is the most comprehensive new economic policy to be undertaken in this nation in four decades.

We are fortunate to live in a nation with an economic system capable of producing for its people the highest standard of living in the world, a system flexible enough to change its ways dramatically when circumstances call for change, and most important, a system resourceful enough to produce prosperity with freedom and opportunity unmatched in the history of nations.

The purposes of the Government actions I have announced tonight are to lay the basis for renewed confidence, to make it possible for us to compete fairly with the rest of the world, to open the door to new prosperity.

But Government with all of its powers does not hold the key to the success of a people. That key, my fellow Americans, is in your hands. A nation, like a person, has to have a certain inner drive in order to succeed. In economic affairs that inner drive is called the competitive spirit.

Every action I have taken tonight is designed to nurture and stimulate that competitive spirit, to help us snap out of the self-doubt, the self-disparagement that saps our energy and erodes our confidence in ourselves.

Whether this nation stays number one in the world's economy or resigns itself to second, third or fourth place, whether we as a people have faith in ourselves or lose that faith, whether we hold fast to the strength that makes peace and freedom possible in this world or lose our grip—all that depends on you.

All that depends on you, on your competitive spirit, your sense of personal destiny, your pride in your country and in yourself.

We can be certain of this: As the threat of war recedes, the challenge of peaceful competition in the world will greatly increase. And we welcome competition because America is at her greatest when she is called on to compete.

As there has always been in our history, there will be voices urging us to shrink from that challange of competition, to build a protective wall around ourselves, to crawl into a shell as the rest of the world moves ahead.

Two hundred years ago a man wrote in his diary these words: "Many thinking people believe America has seen its best days." That was written in 1775, just before the American Revolution, the dawn of the most exciting era in the history of man.

And today we hear the echoes of those voices preaching a gospel of gloom and defeat, saying the same thing: We have seen our best days. I say, "Let Americans reply, 'Our best days lie ahead'." As we move into a generation of peace, as we blaze the trail toward the new prosperity, I say to every American:

Let us raise our spirits, let us raise our sights, let all of us contribute all we can to this great and good country that has contributed so much to the progress of mankind. Let us invest in our nation's future. And let us revitalize that faith in ourselves that built a great nation in the past and that will shape the world of the future.

Thank you, and good evening.

The Economic Plan

PHASE II

By RICHARD M. NIXON, *President of the United States*
Delivered over National Radio and Television, to the American People,
October 7, 1971

GOOD EVENING. Seven weeks ago, I announced a new economic policy to stop the rise in prices, to create new jobs and to protect the American dollar. Tonight, I want to report to you about how that new policy has been working and to describe how that policy will be continued.

On the international front, I am glad to report substantial progress in our campaign to create a new monetary stability and to bring a new fairness to world trade. This nation welcomes foreign competition. But we have a right to expect that our trading partners abroad will welcome American competition.

It is a healthy development that the world has come to understand that America believes in free trade as long as it is fair trade. This will mean more sales of American goods abroad and more jobs for American workers at home.

Further on the job front, the House of Representatives just yesterday passed a tax program based on my recommendations that will create an additional half-million jobs in the coming year.

I call upon the United States Senate, which has begun hearings on this bill today, to act as promptly as the House; so that we can move forward to our goal of full employment in peace time.

Secretary Connally and I will be meeting tomorrow morning at breakfast with Chairman Long of Louisiana, of the Senate Finance Committee, to work toward this goal.

On the inflation front, I can report to you tonight that the wage-price freeze has been remarkably successful.

As you heard on your evening news, the figures bear out that statement. Wholesale prices in September posted the biggest decline in five years. And the price of industrial commodities has gone down for the first time in seven years.

The primary credit for the success of this first step in the fight against rising prices belongs to you—it belongs to the American people. It is you who have shown a willingness to cooperate in the campaign against inflation. It is you who have answered the call to put the public interest ahead of the special interest.

Source: Vital Speeches of the Day, October 15, 1971;
         City News Publishing Company, Southold, New
         York. By permission of the publisher.

Thousands of letters have come to this desk since I made the announcement of the wage-price freeze seven weeks ago. Listen to what people all across America from all walks of life have written to me, the President, about this program.

Here's a letter from a schoolteacher in New Jersey. "I am a widow raising two sons on my teacher salary. I will lose about $300 because of that freeze. Yet I sincerely feel that we must all support your efforts to bring the economy into balance."

And here's a letter from a wage earner in Wantagh, N. Y. "As one who is expecting an increase in income this December, let me say that I will gladly go without it if that will curtail inflation."

The wife of a Government employe in Texas writes, "We are willing as a family to forgo our pay raises in order to see stability in prices."

Let us all hope that Americans will once again realize that we must be willing to sacrifice for a long-term goal and once again have pride in our country.

And then from a man in Klamath Falls, Ore. "Your Administration's recent freeze on wages and prices means that I will not receive the 4 per cent raise that was written into my contract this year. Nevertheless, I support your efforts to halt inflation, including the wage freeze. The fight against inflation is everybody's fight."

I want to express my appreciation to the thousands of others of you who have written me letters like this. And I want you to know how much it has meant to me to hear that most Americans will put their country's interest above their personal interest in fighting this battle.

Now, let's look at the future.

Because of our strong beginning, because of the determination Americans have shown to pull together during the freeze, I am confident that our further action in stopping inflation will succeed as well.

Over the past seven weeks I have consulted with scores of representatives of labor and business, of farmers and consumers, of the Congress and state and local government. They have been virtually unanimous in their belief that the battle against inflation must be fought here and now. They are together in their determination to win that battle.

And consequently, I am announcing tonight that when the 90-day freeze is over on Nov. 13 we shall continue our program of wage and price restraint.

We began this battle against inflation for the purpose of winning and we're going to stay in it 'till we do win it.

I am appointing a Price Commission to hold down prices. It will be made up of persons outside of Government, all public members, not beholden to any special interest group.

The Price Commission will develop yardsticks and will be empowered to restrain prices and rent increases to the necessary minimum and to prevent windfall profits.

Its goal will be to continue to drive down the rate of inflation.

This goal, however, can only be achieved with the active

cooperation of working men and business men, farmers and
consumers, members of the Congress, of our state and local
government. That means all of us.

I'm also appointing a Pay Board to stop inflationary wage
and salary increases—the kind of increases that don't really
benefit the working man.

For example, in the past six years, workers have received big
wage increases. But every wife of a worker who has to do the
family shopping will tell you that those increases have
practically all been eaten up by rises in the cost of living.

The Pay Board will be made up of representatives of labor,
management and the public. Both the Price Commission and
the Pay Board will seek voluntary cooperation from business
and labor. But they will be backed by the authority of law to
make their decisions stick.

Their staffs will be small. Stabilization must be made to
work not by an army of bureaucrats but by an all-volunteer
army of patriotic citizens in every walk of life.

The Cost of Living Council, which is headed by the
Secretary of the Treasury, will have the power to back up the
Pay Board and the Price Commission with Government
sanctions where necessary.

I have today named Counselor Rumsfeld as a member of
that council and he will spend full time as the director of
operations for the council.

Secretary Connally, the chairman of the council, will be on
television tomorrow at noon to answer technical questions
with regard to the continuing program.

All experience over the past seven weeks proves conclusive-
ly that the vast majority of Americans will cooperate
wholeheartedly with a system of voluntary restraint. But, if
there are some who try to take advantage of the patriotic
cooperation of their fellow Americans, I can assure you that
the Government must be and will be prepared to act against
them.

For that reason, in a meeting with the bipartisan legislative
leaders today in the Cabinet Room, I have asked the Congress
to extend for one year the Economic Stabilization Act, which
gives the President the power he needs to stop inflation.

Holding the line against inflation means holding all of that
line. Consequently, I am appointing a Government Committee
on Interest and Dividends to apply a yardstick to both of those
areas.

That committee will be headed by Dr. Arthur Burns,
chairman of the board of governors of the Federal Reserve
System.

The nation needs interest rates as low as they can be to meet
the credit requirements of American families on equitable
terms as they stimulate non-inflationary economic expansion.

I am confident that this can be accomplished on a voluntary
basis.

As a safeguard, however, as I informed the bipartisan
leaders today, I will ask the Congress for standby controls over
interest rates and dividends.

Let me turn now to the subject of profits. Many of my good

friends in the field of politics have advised me that the only politically popular position to take is to be against profits.

But let us recognize an unassailable fact of economic life. All Americans will benefit from more profits. More profits fuel the expansion that generates more jobs.

More profits means more investment, which will make our goods more competitive in America and in the world.

And more profits means there will be more tax revenue to pay for the programs that help people in need. That's why higher profits in the American economy would be good for every person in America.

Windfall profits, however, as I will describe them, are quite another thing. When wages and other costs are held down by the Government, even though prices are also held down, circumstances could arise in some cases that might generate exorbitant profit.

In other words, someone will profit from the wage-price stabilization program.

In the few cases where this happens, rather than tax such excess profits, the Price Commission's policy will be that business should pass along a fair share of its cost savings to the consumer by cutting prices.

We've lived too long in this country with an inflation psychology. Everybody just assumes that the only direction of prices is to go up. The time has come for some price reduction psychology.

Let's see some prices go down. This is not only in the public interest, it makes good competitive business sense.

Summing up these actions to stop the rise in the cost of living, here is what we will do and what we will not do:

We will permit some adjustments of prices and wages. Adjustments that fairness and equity demand. But we will not permit inflation to flare up again.

We will concentrate on those major portions of the economy that are the primary causes of inflation. But we will not hesitate to take action against any part of the economy that fails to comply.

We will continue wage and price restraints until inflationary pressures are brought under control. But we are not going to make controls a permanent feature of American life.

When controls are no longer needed, we will get rid of them. We will rely primarily on the good faith and voluntary cooperation of the American people to make this program work. But we will not let any selfish interest escape the fair enforcement of the law.

I call upon all you tonight to look at this program, not as Democrats or Republicans, workers or businessmen, farmers or consumers, but as Americans.

Let us recognize this profound truth: What is best for all of us is best for each of us. We cannot afford a business-as-usual attitude anywheres because fighting inflation is everybody's business.

Let us look for a moment into the future.

Some of you have heard me say that 1972 will be a very good year for the American economy.

Let me broaden that estimate tonight. The coming year can be more than a very good year for the American economy.

It can be a great year for America and the world.

It can be a year for the first time in 15 years in which we can achieve our goal of prosperity in a time of peace.

It can be a year in which great progress can be made toward our goal of full employment without the inflation that robs working people of the full value of the dollars they earn.

It can be a year in which the American competitive spirit is reborn, as we open up new markets for our goods abroad and new careers and job opportunities for our working men at home.

It can be a year in which we and our international trading partners build upon the most significant initiative in monetary affairs in 25 years, a year in which we replace the crisis-prone system of the past with a new system tuned to the future.

It can be a year in which historic events will take place on the international scene, events that could affect the peace of the world in the next generation, even in the next century.

We often hear people say these are troubled times. I say these are great and exciting times. We are at the threshold of a great new era, an age of movement in challenge and change. We have an unparalleled opportunity to create a better world for ourselves, for our children.

Let us dedicate ourselves tonight to make the most of that opportunity. To join in a great common effort to stop inflation and to create a new prosperity in a world of peace.

State Of The Union Message
1972

RICHARD M. NIXON, *President of the United States*

Delivered to a joint session of Congress, Washington, D. C., January 20, 1972

MR. SPEAKER, Mr. President, my colleagues in the Congress, our distinguished guests, my fellow Americans: Twenty-five years ago I sat here as a freshman Congressman along with Speaker Albert and listened for the first time to the President address the State of the Union.

I shall never forget that moment. The Senate, the diplomatic corps, the Supreme Court, the Cabinet entered the chamber and then the President of the United States.

As all of you are aware, I had some differences with President Truman. He had some with me.

But I remember that on that day, the day he addressed that joint session of the newly elected Republican 80th Congress he spoke not as a partisan but as President of all the people, calling upon the Congress to put aside partisan considerations in the national interest.

The Greek-Turkish aid program, the Marshall Plan, the great foreign policy initiatives which have been responsible for avoiding a world war for over 25 years were approved by the 80th Congress by a bipartisan majority of which I was proud to be a part.

Nineteen seventy-two is now before us. It holds precious time in which to accomplish good for the nation. We must not waste it.

I know the political pressures in this session of the Congress will be great. There are more candidates for the Presidency in this chamber today than there probably have been at any one time in the whole history of the republic.

And there is an honest difference of opinion, not only between the parties, but within each party, on some foreign policy issues and on some domestic policy issues.

However, there are great national problems that are so vital that they transcend partisanship. And so let us have our debates, let us have our honest differences but let us join in keeping the national interest first.

Let us join in making sure that legislation the nation needs does not become hostage to the political interests of any party or any person.

Source: Vital Speeches of the Day, February 1, 1972;
City News Publishing Company, Southold, New
York. By permission of the publisher.

There is ample precedent in this election year for me to present you with a huge list of new proposals, knowing full well that there wouldn't be any possibility of your passing them if you worked night and day.

I shall not do that. I presented to the leaders of the Congress today a message of 15,000 words discussing in some detail where the nation stands and setting forth specific legislative items on which I have asked the Congress to act.

Much of this is legislation which I proposed in 1969 and 1970 and also in the first session of this 92d Congress, and on which I feel it is essential that action be completed this year.

I am not presenting proposals which have attractive labels but no hope of passage. I am presenting only vital programs which are within the capacity of this Congress to enact, within the capacity of the budget to finance, and which I believe should be above partisanship—programs which deal with urgent priorities for the nation, which should and must be the subject of bipartisan action by this Congress in the interests of the country in 1972.

When I took the oath of office on the steps of this building just three years ago today, the nation was ending one of the most tortured decades in its history.

The 1960's were a time of great progress in many areas. But as we all know, they were also times of great agony—the agonies of war, of inflation, of rapidly rising crime, of deteriorating cities, of hopes raised and disappointed and of anger and frustration that led finally to violence and to the worst civil disorder in a century.

I recall these troubles not to point any fingers of blame. The nation was so torn in those final years of the '60's that many in both parties questioned whether America could be governed at all.

The nation has made significant progress in these first years of the '70's.

Our cities are no longer engulfed by civil disorders.

Our colleges and universities have again become places of learning instead of battle grounds.

A beginning has been made on preserving and protecting our environment.

The rate of increase in crime has been slowed and here in the District of Columbia, the one city where the Federal Government has direct jurisdiction, serious crime in 1971 was actually reduced by 13 per cent from the year before.

Most important, because of the beginnings that have been made, we can say today that this year 1972 can be the year in which America may make the greatest progress in 25 years toward achieving our goal of being at peace with all the nations of the world.

As our involvement in the war in Vietnam comes to an end, we must now go on to build a generation of peace.

To achieve that goal, we must first face realistically the need to maintain our defense.

In the past three years, we have reduced the burden of arms. For the first time in 20 years, spending on defense has been brought below spending on human resources.

As we look to the future, we find encouraging progress in our negotiations with the Soviet Union on limitation of strategic arms. And looking further into the future, we hope there can eventually be agreement on the mutual reduction of arms. But until there is such a mutual agreement, we must maintain the strength necessary to deter war.

And that is why—because of rising research-and-development costs, because of increases in military and civilian pay, because of the need to proceed with new weapons systems—my budget for the coming fiscal year will provide for an increase in defense spending.

Strong military defenses are not the enemy of peace. They are the guardians of peace. And there could be no more misguided set of priorities than one which would tempt others by weakening America, and thereby endanger the peace of the world.

In our foreign policy we have entered a new era. The world has changed greatly in the 11 years since President John Kennedy said, in his inaugural address, "We shall pay any price, bear any burden, meet any hardship, support any friend, oppose any foe, to assure the survival and the success of liberty."

Our policy has been carefully and deliberately adjusted to meet the new realities of the new world we live in. We make today only those commitments we are able and prepared to meet.

Our commitment to freedom remains strong and unshakable. But others must bear their share of the burden of defending freedom around the world.

And so this, then, is our policy:

¶We will maintain a nuclear deterrent adequate to meet any threat to the security of the United States or of our allies.

¶We will help other nations develop the capability of defending themselves.

¶We will faithfully honor all of our treaty commitments.

¶We will act to defend our interests whenever and wherever they are threatened any place in the world.

¶But where our interests or our treaty commitments are not involved our role will be limited.

¶We will not intervene militarily.

¶But we will use our influence to prevent war.

¶If war comes we will use our influence to stop it.

¶And once it is over we will do our share in helping to bind up the wounds of those who have participated in it.

As you know, I will soon be visiting the Peoples Republic of China and the Soviet Union.

I go there with no illusions. We have great differences with both powers. We shall continue to have great differences. But peace depends on the ability of great powers to live together on the same planet despite their differences.

We would not be true to our obligation to generations yet unborn if we failed to seize this moment to do everything in our power to insure that we will be able to talk about those differences rather than to fight about them in the future.

And as we look back over this century, let us in the highest spirit of bipartisanship recognize that we can be proud of our nation's record in foreign affairs. America has given more generously of itself toward maintaining freedom, preserving peace, alleviating human suffering around the globe than any nation has ever done in the history of man.

We have fought four wars in this century but our power has never been used to break the peace, only to keep it; never been used to destroy freedom, only to defend it.

We now have within our reach the goal of insuring that the next generation can be the first generation in this century to be spared the scourges of war.

Turning to our problems at home, we are making progress toward our goal of a new prosperity without war. Industrial production, consumer spending, retail sales, personal income— all have been rising. Total employment, real income are the highest in history.

New home-building starts this past year reached the highest level ever. Business and consumer confidence have both been rising. Interest rates are down. The rate of inflation is down. We can look with confidence to 1972 as the year when the back of inflation will be broken.

Now this is a good record, but it is not good enough. Not when we still have an unemployment rate of 6 per cent. It's not enough to point out that this was the rate of the early peacetime years of the sixties or that if the more than two million men released from the armed forces and defense-related industries were still in their wartime jobs then unemployment would be far lower.

Our goal in this country is full employment in peacetime. We intend to meet that goal and we can.

The Congress has helped to meet that goal by passing our job-creating tax program last month.

The historic monetary agreements—agreements that we have reached with the major European nations, Canada and Japan—will help meet it by providing new markets for American products, new jobs for American workers.

Our budget will help meet it by being expansionary without being inflationary, a job-producing budget that will help take up the gap as the economy expands to full employment.

Our program to raise farm income will help to meet it by helping to revitalize rural America, by giving up to America's farmers their fair share of America's increasing productivity.

And we also will help meet our goal of full employment in peacetime with a set of major initiatives to stimulate more imaginative use of America's great capacity for technological advance and direct it toward improving the quality of life for every American.

In reaching the moon we demonstrated what miracles American technology is capable of achieving. And now the time has come to move more deliberately toward making full use of that technology here on earth, of harnessing the wonders of science to the service of men.

I shall soon send to the Congress a special message proposing a new program of Federal partnership in technological research and development with Federal incentives to increase private research, federally supported research and projects designed to improve our everyday lives in ways that will range from improving mass transit to developing new systems of emergency health care that could save thousands of lives annually.

Historically, our superior technology and high productivity have made it possible for American workers to be the highest paid in the world, by far, and yet for our goods still to compete in world markets.

Now we face a new situation. As other nations move rapidly forward in technology, the answer to the new competition is not to build a wall around America but rather to remain competitive by improving our own technology still further and by increasing productivity in American industry.

Our new monetary and trade agreements will make it possible for American goods to compete thoroughly in the world's markets but they still must compete. The new technology program will put to use the skills of many highly trained Americans, skills that might otherwise be wasted.

It will also meet the growing technological challenge from abroad and it will thus help to create new industries as well as creating more jobs for America's workers in producing for the world's markets.

This second session of the 92d Congress already has before it more than 90 major Administration proposals which still await action.

I have discussed these in the extensive written message that I have presented to the Congress today.

They include among others our programs to improve life for the aging, to combat crime and drug abuse, to improve health services, to insure that no one will be denied needed health care because of inability to pay, to protect workers' pensions rights, to promote equal opportunity for members of minorities and others who have been left behind, to expand consumer protection, to improve the environment, to revitalize rural America, to help the cities, to launch new initiatives in education, to improve transportation and to put an end to costly labor tie-ups in transportation.

The West Coast dock strike is a case in point. This nation cannot and will not tolerate that kind of irresponsible labor tie-up in the future.

The messages also include basic reforms which are essential if our structure of government is to be adequate in the decades ahead.

They include reform of our wasteful and outmoded welfare system, substitution of a new system that provides work requirements and work incentives for those who can help themselves, income support for those who cannot help themselves and fairness to the working poor.

They include a $17-billion program of Federal revenue sharing with the states and localities as an investment in their renewal and an investment also of faith in the American people.

They also include a sweeping reorganization of the

executive branch of the Federal Government so that it will be more efficient, more responsive and able to meet the challenges of the decades ahead.

One year ago standing in this place, I laid before the opening session of this Congress six great goals.

One of these was welfare reform. That proposal has been before the Congress for nearly 2½ years.

My proposals on revenue sharing, government reorganization, health care and the environment have now been before the Congress for nearly a year. Many of the other major proposals that I have referred to have been here that long or longer.

Now 1971, we can say, was a year of consideration of these measures. Now let us join in making 1972 a year of action on them, action by the Congress for the nation and for the people of America.

Now in addition, there is one pressing need which I have not previously covered but which must be placed on the national agenda.

We long have looked in this nation to the local property tax at the main source of financing for public primary and secondary education.

As a result, soaring school costs, soaring property tax rates now threaten both our communities and our schools. They threaten communities because property taxes—which more than doubled in the years from 1960 to 1970—have become one of the most oppressive and discriminatory of all taxes, hitting most cruelly at the elderly and the retired; and they threaten schools, as hard-pressed voters understandably reject new bond issues at the polls.

The problem has been given even greater urgency by four recent court decisions, which have held that the conventional method of financing schools through local property taxes is discriminatory and unconstitutional.

Nearly two years ago, I named a special Presidential commission to study the problems of school finance, and I also directed the Federal departments to look into the same problems. We are developing comprehensive proposals to meet these problems.

This issue involves two complex and interrelated sets of problems: support of the schools, and the basic relationships of Federal, state and local governments in any tax reforms.

Under the leadership of the Secretary of the Treasury, we are carefully reviewing all of the tax aspects; and I have this week enlisted the Advisory Committee on Intergovernmental Relations in addressing the intergovernmental relations aspects.

I have asked this bipartisan commission to review our proposal for Federal action to cope with the gathering crisis of school finance and property taxes.

Later in the year, when both commissions have completed their studies, I shall make my final recommendations for relieving the burden of property taxes and providing both fair and adequate financing for our children's education.

These recommendations will be revolutionary, but all these

recommendations, however, will be rooted in one fundamental principle with which there can be no compromise: local school boards must have control over local schools.

As we look ahead over the coming decades, vast new growth and change are not only certainties, they will be the dominant reality of this world and particularly of our life in America.

Surveying the certainty of rapid change, we can be like a fallen rider caught in the stirrups or we can sit high in the saddle, the masters of change, directing it on a course we choose.

The secret of mastering change in today's world is to reach back to old and proven principles and to adapt them with imagination and intelligence to the new realities of a new age, and that's what we have done in the proposals that I've laid before the Congress.

They are rooted in basic principles that are as enduring as human nature, as robust as the American experience. And they are responsive to new conditions. Thus, they represent a spirit of change that is truly renewal.

As we look back at those old principles we find them as timely as they are timeless.

We believe in independence and self reliance and the creative value of the competitive spirit.

We believe in full and equal opportunity for all Americans and in the protection of individual rights and liberties.

We believe in the family as the keystone of the community and the community as the keystone of the nation.

We believe in compassion for those in need. We believe in a system of law, justice and order as the basis of a genuinely free society.

We believe that a person should get what he works for and that those who can should work for what they get.

We believe in the capacity of people to make their own decisions in their own lives in their own communities and we believe in their right to make those decisions.

In applying these principles we have done so with the full understanding that what we seek in the '70's, what our quest is, is not merely for more but for better—for a better quality of life for all Americans.

Thus, for example, we are giving a new measure of attention to cleaning up our air and water, making our surroundings more attractive.

We're providing broader support for the arts, helping to stimulate a deeper appreciation of what they can contribute to the nation's activities and to our individual lives.

But nothing really matters more to the quality of our lives than the way we treat one another—than our capacity to live respectfully together as a unified society with a full generous regard for the rights of others and also for the feelings of others.

As we recover from the turmoil and violence of recent years, as we learn once again to speak with one another instead of shouting at one another, we are regaining that capacity.

As is customary here on this occasion, I've been talking

about programs. Programs are important. But even more important than programs is what we are as a nation, what we mean as a nation to ourselves and to the world.

In New York Harbor stands one of the most famous statues in the world—the Statue of Liberty, the gift in 1886 of the people of France to the people of the United States.

This statue is more than a landmark; it is a symbol—a symbol of what America has meant to the world.

It reminds us that what America has meant is not its wealth and not its power but its spirit and purpose—a land that enshrines liberty and opportunity and that has held out a hand of welcome to millions in search of a better and fuller and, above all, a freer life.

The world's hopes poured into America along with its people and those hopes, those dreams that have been brought here from every corner of the world, have become a part of the hope that we now hold out to the world.

Four years from now, America will celebrate the 200th anniversary of its founding as a nation.

And there are those who say that the old spirit of '76 is dead, that we no longer have the strength of character, the idealism, the faith in our founding purposes, that that spirit represents.

Those who say this do not know America.

We have been undergoing self doubts, self criticism. But these are only the other side of our growing sensitivity to the persistence of want in the midst of plenty of our impatience with the slowness with which age-old ills are being overcome.

If we were indifferent to the shortcomings of our society or complacent about our institutions or blind to the lingering inequities, then we would have lost our way.

But the fact that we have those concerns is evidence that our ideals, deep down, are still strong. Indeed, they remind us that what is really best about America is its compassion. They remind us that in the final analysis America is great. Not because it is strong, not because it is rich, but because this is a good country.

Let us reject the narrow visions of those who would tell us that we are evil because we are not yet perfect; that we are corrupt because we are not yet pure; that all the sweat and toil and sacrifice that have gone into the building of America were for naught because the building is not yet done.

Let us see that the path we are traveling is wide, with room in it for all of us and that its direction is toward a better nation in a more peaceful world.

And never has it mattered more than we go forward together.

Look at this chamber.

The leadership of America is here today. The Supreme Court, the Cabinet, the Senate, the House of Representatives. Together we hold the future of the nation and the conscience of the nation in our hands.

Because this year is an election year it will be a time of

great pressure. If we yield to that pressure and fail to deal seriously with the historic challenges that we face, we will have failed the trust of millions of Americans and shaken the confidence they have a right to place in us, in their Government.

Never has a Congress had a greater opportunity to leave a legacy of a profound and constructive reform for the nation than this Congress. If we succeed in these tasks, there will be credit enough for all, not only for doing what is right but doing it in the right way—by rising above partisan interest to serve the national interest.

And if we fail, more than any one of us, America will be the loser.

And that is why my call upon the Congress today is for a high statesmanship so that in the years to come Americans will look back and say because it withstood the intense pressures of a political year and achieved such great good for the American people and for the future of this nation, this was truly a great Congress.

A Trip For World Peace

TO RE-ESTABLISH COMMUNICATIONS

By RICHARD M. NIXON, *President of the United States*

Delivered at Andrews Air Force Base, Maryland, February 28, 1972

MR. VICE PRESIDENT, members of the Congress, members of the Cabinet, members of the diplomatic corps, and ladies and gentlemen: I want to express my very deep appreciation and the appreciation of all of us for this wonderfully warm welcome that you've given us and for the support that we have had on the trip that we just completed from Americans of both political parties in all walks of life across this land.

And because of the superb efforts of the hard-working members of the press who accompanied us—they got even less sleep than I did—millions of Americans in this past week have seen more of China than I did.

Consequently tonight, I would like to talk to you not about what we saw but about what we did, to sum up the results of the trip and to put it in perspective.

When I announced this trip last July, I described it as a journey for peace. In the last 30 years Americans have in three different wars gone off in the hundreds of thousands to fight and some to die in Asia and in the Pacific.

One of the central motives behind my journey to China was to prevent that from happening a fourth time to another generation of Americans.

As I've often said, peace means more than the mere absence of war. In a technical sense we were at peace with the People's Republic of China before this trip. But a gulf of almost 12,000 miles and 22 years of noncommunication and hostility separated the United States of America from the 750 million people who live in the People's Republic of China—and that's one-fourth of all the people in the world.

As a result of this trip we have started the long process of building a bridge across that gulf, and even now we have something better than the mere absence of war.

Not only have we completed a week of intensive talks at the highest levels, we have set up a procedure whereby we can continue to have discussions in the future.

We have demonstrated that nations with very deep and fundamental differences can learn to discuss those differences calmly, rationally and frankly without compromising their principles.

Source: Vital Speeches of the Day, March 15, 1972;
          City News Publishing Company, Southold, New
          York. By permission of the publisher.

This is the basis of a structure for peace; where we can talk about differences rather than fight about them.

The primary goal of this trip was to re-establish communication with the People's Republic of China after a generation of hostility. We achieved that goal.

Let me turn now to our joint communique. We did not bring back any written or unwritten agreements that will guarantee peace in our time. We did not bring home any magic formula which will make unnecessary the efforts of the American people to continue to maintain the strength so that we can continue to be free.

We made some necessary and important beginnings however, in several areas.

We entered into agreements to expand cultural, educational and journalistic contacts between the Chinese and the American people.

We agreed to work to begin and broaden trade between our two countries.

We have agreed that the communications that have now been established between our Governments will be strengthened and expanded.

Most important, we have agreed on some rules of international conduct which will reduce the risk of confrontation and war in Asia and in the Pacific.

We agreed that we are opposed to domination of the Pacific area by any one power.

We agreed that international disputes be settled without the use of the threat of force, and we agreed that we are prepared to apply this principle to our mutual relations.

With respect to Taiwan, we stated our established policy that our forces overseas will be reduced gradually as tensions ease, and that our ultimate objective is to withdraw our forces as a peaceful settlement is achieved.

We've agreed that we will not negotiate the fate of other nations behind their back and we did not do so in Peking. There were no secret deals of any kind.

We have done all this without giving up any United States commitment to any other country.

In our talks—the talks that I had with the leaders of the People's Republic and that the Secretary of State had with the office of the Government of the People's Republic in the foreign affairs area—we both realized that a bridge of understanding that spans almost 12,000 miles and 22 years of hostility can't be built in one week of discussions, but we have agreed to begin to build that bridge, recognizing that our work will require years of patient effort.

We made no attempt to pretend that major differences did not exist between our two governments, because they do exist.

This communique was unique in honestly setting forth differences rather than trying to cover them up with diplomatic double-talk.

One of the gifts that we left behind in Hangchow was the planted sapling of the American redwood tree. As all

Californians know, and as most Americans know, redwoods grow from saplings into giants of the forest. But the process is not one of days, or even years—it is a process of centuries.

Just as we hope that those saplings—those tiny saplings that we left in China—will grow one day into mighty redwoods, so we hope, too, that the seeds planted on this journey for peace will grow and prosper into a more enduring structure for peace and security in the Western Pacific.

But peace, peace is too urgent to wait for centuries. We must seize the moment to move toward that goal now, and this is what we have done on this journey.

As I am sure you realize, it was a great experience for us to see the timeless wonders of ancient China, the changes that are being made in modern China.

And one fact stands out among many others from my talks with the Chinese leaders. It is their total belief, their total dedication to their system of government. That is their right, just as it is the right of any country to choose the kind of government it wants.

But as I return from this trip, just as has been the case on my return from other trips abroad which have taken me to over 80 countries, I come back to America with an even stronger faith in our system of government.

As I flew across America today, all the way from Alaska, over the Rockies, the Plains, and then on to Washington, I thought of the greatness of our country.

And most of all, I thought of the freedom, the opportunity, the progress that 200 million Americans are privileged to enjoy.

I realized again, this is a beautiful country.

And tonight my prayer, and my hope, is that as a result of this trip our children will have a better chance to grow up in a peaceful world.

Thank you.

Address To The People Of The Soviet Union

A WORLD FREE OF FEAR

By RICHARD M. NIXON, *President of the United States*
Delivered as Radio and Television Address from the Green Room of the
Grand Kremlin Palace, Moscow, USSR, May 28, 1972

D OBRYY VECHER. I deeply appreciate this opportunity your Government has given me to speak directly with the people of the Soviet Union, to bring you a message of friendship from all the people of the United States and to share with you some of my thoughts about the relations between our two countries and about the way to peace and progress in the world.

This is my fourth visit to the Soviet Union. On these visits I have gained a great respect for the peoples of the Soviet Union, for your strength, your generosity, your determination, for the diversity and richness of your cultural heritage, for your many achievements.

In the 3 years I have been in office, one of my principal aims has been to establish a better relationship between the United States and the Soviet Union. Our two countries have much in common. Most important of all, we have never fought one another in war. On the contrary, the memory of your soldiers and ours embracing at the Elbe, as allies, in 1945, remains strong in millions of hearts in both of our countries. It is my hope that that memory can serve as an inspiration for the renewal of Soviet-American cooperation in the 1970's.

As great powers, we shall sometimes be competitors, but we need never be enemies.

Thirteen years ago, when I visited your country as Vice President, I addressed the people of the Soviet Union on radio and television, as I am addressing you tonight. I said then, "Let us have peaceful competition, not only in producing the best factories, but in producing better lives for our people. Let us cooperate in our exploration of outer space . . . Let our aim be not victory over other peoples, but the victory of all mankind over hunger, want, misery, and disease, wherever it exists in the world."

In our meetings this week, we have begun to bring some of those hopes to fruition. Shortly after we arrived here on Monday afternoon, a brief rain fell on Moscow, of a kind that I am told is called a mushroom rain, a warm rain, with sunshine breaking through, that makes the mushrooms grow and is therefore considered a good omen. The month of May is early for mushrooms, but as our talks progressed this week,

Source: Vital Speeches of the Day, August 15, 1972; City News Publishing Company, Southold, New York. By permission of the publisher.

what did grow was even better. A far-reaching set of agreements that can lead to a better life for both of our peoples, to a better chance for peace in the world.

We have agreed on joint ventures in space. We have agreed on ways of working together to protect the environment, to advance health, to cooperate in science and technology. We have agreed on means of preventing incidents at sea. We have established a commission to expand trade between our two nations.

Most important, we have taken an historic first step in the limitation of nuclear strategic arms. This arms control agreement is not for the purpose of giving either side an advantage over the other. Both of our nations are strong, each respects the strength of the other, each will maintain the strength necessary to defend its independence.

But in an unchecked arms race between two great nations, there would be no winners, only losers. By setting this limitation together, the people of both of our nations, and of all nations, can be winners. If we continue in the spirit of serious purpose that has marked our discussions this week, these agreements can start us on a new road of cooperation for the benefit of our people, for the benefit of all peoples.

There is an old proverb that says, "Make peace with man and quarrel with your sins." The hardships and evils that beset all men and all nations, these and these alone are what we should make war upon.

As we look at the prospects for peace, we see that we have made significant progress at reducing the possible sources of direct conflict between us. But history tells us that great nations have often been dragged into war without intending it, by conflicts between smaller nations. As great powers, we can and should use our influence to prevent this from happening. Our goal should be to discourage aggression in other parts of the world and particularly among those smaller nations that look to us for leadership and example.

With great power goes great responsibility. When a man walks with a giant tread, he must be careful where he sets his feet. There can be true peace only when the weak are as safe as the strong. The wealthier and more powerful our own nations become, the more we have to lose from war and the threat of war, anywhere in the world.

Speaking for the United States, I can say this: We covet no one else's territory, we seek no dominion over any other people, we seek the right to live in peace, not only for ourselves, but for all the peoples of this earth. Our power will only be used to keep the peace, never to break it, only to defend freedom, never to destroy it. No nation that does not threaten its neighbors has anything to fear from the United States.

Soviet citizens have often asked me, "Does America truly want peace?"

I believe that our actions answer that question far better than any words could do. If we did not want peace, we would not have reduced the size of our armed forces by a million men, by almost one-third, during the past 3 years. If we did not want peace, we would not have worked so hard at reaching an agreement on the limitation of nuclear arms, at achieving a settlement of Berlin, at maintaining peace in the Middle East, at establishing better relations with the Soviet Union, with the People's Republic of China, with other nations of the world.

Mrs. Nixon and I feel very fortunate to have had the opportunity to visit the Soviet Union, to get to know the people of the Soviet Union, friendly and hospitable, courageous and strong. Most Americans will never have a chance to visit the Soviet Union and most Soviet citizens will never have a chance to visit America. Most of you know our country only through what you read in your newspapers and what you hear and see on radio and television and motion pictures. This is only a part of the real America.

I would like to take this opportunity to try to convey to you something of what America is really like, not in terms of its scenic beauties, its great cities, its factories, its farms, or its highways, but in terms of its people.

In many ways, the people of our two countries are very much alike. Like the Soviet Union, ours is a large and diverse nation. Our people, like yours, are hard-working. Like you, we Americans have a strong spirit of competition, but we also have a great love of music and poetry, of sports, and of humor. Above all, we, like you, are an open, natural, and friendly people. We love our country. We love our children. And we want for you and for your children the same peace and abundance that we want for ourselves and for our children.

We Americans are idealists. We believe deeply in our system of government. We cherish our personal liberty. We would fight to defend it, if necessary, as we have done before. But we also believe deeply in the right of each nation to choose its own system. Therefore, however much we like our own system for ourselves, we have no desire to impose it on anyone else.

As we conclude this week of talks, there are certain fundamental premises of the American point of view which I believe deserve emphasis. In conducting these talks, it has not been our aim to divide up the world into spheres of influence, to establish a condominium, or in any way to conspire together against the interests of any other nation. Rather we have sought to construct a better framework of understanding between our two nations, to make progress in our bilateral relationships, to find ways of ensuring that future frictions between us would never embroil our two nations, and therefore, the world, in war.

While ours are both great and powerful nations, the world is no longer dominated by two superpowers. The world is a better and safer place because its power and resources are more widely distributed.

Beyond this, since World War II, more than 70 new nations have come into being. We cannot have true peace unless they, and all nations, can feel that they share it.

America seeks better relations, not only with the Soviet Union, but with all nations. The only sound basis for a peaceful and progressive international order is sovereign equality and mutual respect. We believe in the right of each nation to chart its own course, to choose its own system, to go its own way, without interference from other nations.

As we look to the longer term, peace depends also on continued progress in the developing nations. Together with other advanced industrial countries, the United States and the Soviet Union share a twofold responsibility in this regard.

On the one hand, to practice restraint in those activities, such as the supply of arms, that might endanger the peace of developing nations. And second, to assist them in their orderly economic and social development, without political interference.

Some of you may have heard an old story told in Russia of a traveler who was walking to another village. He knew the way, but not the distance. Finally he came upon a woodsman chopping wood by the side of the road and he asked the woodsman, "How long will it take to reach the village?"

The woodsman replied, "I don't know."

The traveler was angry, because he was sure the woodsman was from the village and therefore knew how far it was. And so he started off down the road again. After he had gone a few steps, the woodsman called out, "Stop. It will take you about 15 minutes."

The traveler turned and demanded, "Why didn't you tell me that in the first place?"

The woodsman replied, "Because then I didn't know the length of your stride."

In our talks this week with the leaders of the Soviet Union, both sides have had a chance to measure the length of our strides toward peace and security. I believe that those strides have been substantial and that now we have well begun the long journey which will lead us to a new age in the relations between our two countries. It is important to both of our peoples that we continue those strides.

As our two countries learn to work together, our people will be able to get to know one another better. Greater cooperation can also mean a great deal in our daily lives. As we learn to cooperate in space, in health and the environment, in science and technology, our cooperation can help sick people get well. It can help industries produce more consumer goods. It can help all of us enjoy cleaner air and water. It can increase our knowledge of the world around us.

As we expand our trade, each of our countries can buy more of the other's goods and market more of our own. As we gain experience with arms control, we can bring closer the day when further agreements can lessen the arms burden of our two nations and lessen the threat of war in the world.

Through all the pages of history, through all the centuries, the world's people have struggled to be free from fear, whether fear of the elements or fear of hunger or fear of their own rulers or fear of their neighbors in other countries. And yet, time and again, people have vanquished the source of one fear only to fall prey to another.

Let our goal now be a world free of fear. A world in which nation will no longer prey upon nation, in which human energies will be turned away from production for war and toward more production for peace, away from conquest and toward invention, development, creation. A world in which together we can establish that peace which is more than the absence of war, which enables man to pursue those higher goals that the spirit yearns for.

Yesterday, I laid a wreath at the cemetery which commemorates the brave people who died during the siege of Leningrad in World War II. At the cemetery, I saw the picture of a 12-year-old girl. She was a beautiful child. Her name was Tanya. The pages of her diary tell the terrible story of war. In the simple words of a child, she wrote of the deaths of the members of her family: Zhenya in December. Grannie in January. Leka then next. Then Uncle Vasya. Then Uncle Lyosha. Then Mama. And then the Savichevs. And then finally, these words, the last words in her diary, "All are dead. Only Tanya is left."

As we work toward a more peaceful world, let us think of Tanya and of the other Tanyas and their brothers and sisters everywhere. Let us do all that we can to insure that no other children will have to endure what Tanya did and that your children and ours, all the children of the world can live their full lives together in friendship and in peace.

Spasibo y do svidaniye.

The Moscow Summit

A GOOD BEGINNING

By RICHARD M. NIXON, *President of the United States*

Delivered before a Joint Session of Congress, Washington, D. C., June 1, 1972

MR. SPEAKER, MR. PRESIDENT, members of the Congress, our distinguished guests, my fellow Americans: Your welcome in this great chamber tonight has a very special meaning to Mrs. Nixon and to me. We feel very fortunate to have traveled abroad so often, representing the United States of America.

But we both agree, after each journey, that the best part of any trip abroad is coming home to America again.

During the past 13 days we have flown more than 16,000 miles and we visited four countries. And everywhere we went—to Austria, the Soviet Union, Iran, Poland—we could feel the quickening pace of change in old international relationship and the people's genuine desire for friendship with the American people.

Everywhere new hopes are rising for a world no longer shadowed by fear and want and war. And as Americans, we can be proud that we now have an historic opportunity to play a great role in helping to achieve man's oldest dream, a world in which all nations can enjoy the blessings of peace.

On this journey we saw many memorable sights, but one picture will always remain indelible in our memory—the flag of the United States of America flying high in the spring breeze above Moscow's ancient Kremlin fortress.

To millions of Americans for the past quarter century the Kremlin has stood for implacable hostility toward all that we cherish, and to millions of Russians the American flag has long been held up as a symbol of evil. No one would have believed even a short time ago that these two apparently irreconcilable symbols would be seen together as we saw them for those few days.

Now this does not mean that we bring back from Moscow the promise of instant peace, but we do bring the beginning of a process that can lead to a lasting peace.

And that's why I've taken the extraordinary action of requesting this special joint session of the Congress; because we have before us an extraordinary opportunity.

I have not come here this evening to make new announcements in a dramatic setting. This summit has already made its news. It has barely begun, however, to make its mark on our world.

Source: Vital Speeches of the Day, June 15, 1972; City News Publishing Company, Southold, New York. By permission of the publisher.

And I ask you to join me tonight, while events are fresh, while the iron is hot, in starting to consider how we can help to make that mark what we want it to be. The foundation has been laid for a new relationship between the two most powerful nations in the world.

And now it is up to us—to all of us here in this chamber, to all of us across America—to join with other nations in building a new house upon that foundation; one that can be a home for the hopes of mankind and a shelter against the storms of conflict.

As a preliminary, therefore, to requesting your concurrence in some of the agreements we reached and your approval of funds to carry out others, and also as a keynote for the unity in which this Government and this nation must go forward from here, I am rendering this immediate report to the Congress on the results of the Moscow summit.

The pattern of U. S.-Soviet summit diplomacy in the cold war era is well known to all those in this chamber. One meeting after another produced a brief euphoric mood—the spirit of Geneva, the spirit of Camp David, the spirit of Vienna, the spirit of Glassboro—but without producing significant progress on the really difficult issues.

And so early in this Administration I stated that the prospect of concrete results, not atmospherics, would be our criterion for meetings at the highest level. And I also announced our intention to pursue negotiations with the Soviet Union across a broad front of related issues, with the purpose of creating a momentum of achievement in which progress in one area could contribute to progress in others.

This is the basis on which we prepared for and conducted last week's talks. This was a working summit. We sought to establish not a superficial spirit of Moscow but a solid record of progress on solving the difficult issues which for so long had divided our two nations and also have divided the world.

Reviewing the number and the scope of agreements that emerged, I think we've accomplished that goal. Recognizing the responsibility of the advanced industrial nations to set an example in combating mankind's enemies, the United States and the Soviet Union have agreed to cooperate in efforts to reduce pollution and enhance environmental quality. We have agreed to work together in the field of medical science and public health—particularly in the conquest of cancer and heart disease. Recognizing that the quest for useful knowledge transcends differences between ideologies and social systems, we have agreed to expand United States and Soviet cooperation in many areas of science and technology. We have joined in plans for an exciting new adventure—a new adventure in the cooperative exploration of space which will begin subject to Congressional approval of funding with a joint orbital mission of an Apollo vehicle and a Soviet spacecraft in 1975.

By forming habits of cooperation and strengthening institutional ties in areas of peaceful enterprise, these four agreements to which I have referred will create on both sides a steadily growing vested interest in the maintenance of good relations between our two countries.

Expanded United States-Soviet trade will also yield advantages to both of our nations. When the two largest economies in the world start trading with each other on a much larger scale, living standards in both nations will rise, and the stake which both have in peace will increase.

Progress in this area is proceeding on schedule. At the summit, we established a joint commercial commission which will complete the negotiations for a comprehensive trade agreement between the United States and the U.S.S.R. And we expect the final terms of this agreement to be settled later this year.

Two further accords which were reached last week have a much more direct bearing on the search for peace and security in the world.

One is the agreement between the American and Soviet navies aimed at significantly reducing the chances of dangerous incidents between our ships and aircraft at sea.

And second and most important, there is the treaty and the related executive agreement which will limit for the first time both offensive and defensive strategic nuclear weapons in the arsenals of the United States and the Soviet Union.

Three-fifths of all the people alive in the world today have spent their whole lifetimes under the shadow of a nuclear war which could be touched off by the arms race among the great powers.

Last Friday in Moscow we witnesesd the beginning of the end of that era, which began in 1945. We took the first step toward a new era of mutually agreed restraint in arms limitation between the two principal nuclear powers.

With this step we have enhanced the security of both nations. We have begun to check the wasteful and dangerous spiral of nuclear arms which has dominated relations between our two countries for a generation.

We have begun to reduce the level of fear by reducing the causes of fear for our two peoples and for all peoples in the world.

The ABM treaty will be submitted promptly for the Senate's advice and consent for ratification, and the interim agreement limiting certain offensive weapons will be submitted to both Houses for a concurrence, because we can undertake agreements as important as these only on a basis of full partnership between the executive and legislative branches of our Government.

I ask from this Congress—and I ask from the nation—the fullest scrutiny of these accords. I am confident such examination will underscore the truth of what I told the Soviet people on television just a few nights ago—that this is an agreement in the interest of both nations. From the standpoint of the United States when we consider what the strategic balance would have looked like later in the seventies if there had been no arms limitation, it is clear that the agreements forestall a major spiraling of the arms race, one which would have worked to our disadvantage since we have no current building programs for the categories of weapons which have been frozen and since no new building program could have produced any new weapons in those categories during the period of the freeze.

My colleagues in the Congress, I have studied the strategic balance in great detail with my senior advisers for more than three years. And I can assure you, the members of the Congress and the American people tonight, that the present and planned strategic forces of the United States are without question sufficient for the maintenance of our security and the protection of our vital interests.

No power on earth is stronger than the United States of America today. And none will be stronger than the United States of America in the future.

This is the only national defense posture which can ever be acceptable to the United States and this is the posture I ask the Senate and the Congress to protect by approving the arms-limitation agreements to which I have referred.

And this is the posture which with the responsible cooperation of the Congress I will take all necessary steps to maintain in our future defense programs.

In addition to the talks which led to the specific agreements I have listed, I also had full, very frank and extensive discussions with General Secretary Brezhnev and his colleagues about several parts of the world where American and Soviet interests have come in conflict.

With regard to the reduction of tensions in Europe, we recorded our intention of proceeding later this year with multilateral consultations looking toward a conference on security and cooperation in all of Europe.

We have also jointly agreed to move forward with negotiations on mutual and balanced force reductions in central Europe.

The problem of ending the Vietnam war, which engages the hopes of all Americans, was one of the most extensively discussed subjects on our agenda.

It would only jeopardize the search for peace if I were to review here all that was said on that subject.

I will simply say this: each side obviously has its own point of view and its own approach to this very difficult issue. But at the same time, both the United States and the Soviet Union share an overriding desire to achieve a more stable peace in the world.

I emphasize to you once again this Administration has no higher goal, a goal that I know all of you share, than bringing the Vietnam war to an early and honorable end. We are ending the war in Vietnam, but we shall end it in a way which will not betray our friends, risk the lives of the courageous Americans still serving in Vietnam, break faith with those held prisoners by the enemy, or stain the honor of the United States of America.

Another area where we had very full, frank and extensive discussions was the Middle East. I reiterated the American people's commitment to the survival of the state of Israel and of a settlement just to all the countries in the area. Both sides stated in the communiqué their intention to support the Jarring peace mission and other appropriate efforts to achieve this objective.

The final achievement of the Moscow conference was the signing of a landmark declaration entitled "Basic Principles of Mutual Relations Between the United States and the U.S.S.R."

As these 12 basic principles are put into practice, they can provide a solid framework for the future development of better American-Soviet relations.

They begin with the recognition that two nuclear nations, each of which has the power to destroy humanity, have no alternative but to coexist peacefully because in a nuclear war there would be no winners—only losers.

The basic principles commit both sides to avoid direct military confrontation and to exercise constructive leadership and restraint with respect to smaller conflicts in other parts of the world which could drag the major powers into war.

We disavow any intention to create spheres of influence or to conspire against the interests of any other nation and to exercise constructive leadership, saying once again tonight that America values its ties with all nations, from our oldest allies in Europe and Asia—as I emphasized by my visit to Iran—to our good friends in the third world and to our new relationship with the People's Republic of China.

The improvement of relations depends not only, of course, on words, but far more on actions. The principles to which we agreed in Moscow are like a road map. Now that the map has been laid out, it is up to each country to follow it. The United States intends to adhere to these principles.

The leaders of the Soviet Union have indicated a similar intention. However, we must remember that Soviet ideology still proclamis hostility to some of America's most basic values.

The Soviet leaders remain committed to that ideology. Like the nation they lead, they are and they will continue to be totally dedicated competitors of the United States of America.

As we shape our policies for the period ahead, therefore, we must maintain our defenses at an adequate level until there is mutual agreement to limit forces. The time-tested policies of vigilance and firmness which have brought us to this summit are the ones that can safely carry us forward to further progress in reaching agreements to reduce the danger of war.

Our successes in the strategic arms talks and in the Berlin negotiations which opened the road to Moscow came about because over the past three years we have consistently refused proposals for unilaterally abandoning the ABM, unilaterally pulling back our forces from Europe and drastically cutting the defense budget.

And the Congress deserves the appreciation of the American people for having the courage to vote such proposals down and to maintain the strength America needs to protect its interests.

As we continue the strategic arms talks seeking a permanent offensive-weapons treaty, we must bear the lessons of the earlier talks well in mind.

By the same token, we must stand steadfastly with our NATO partners if negotiations leading to a new détente and a mutual reduction of forces in Europe are to be productive.

Maintaining the strength, integrity and steadfastness of our free world alliances is the foundation on which all of our other initiatives for peace and security in the world must rest.

As we seek better relations with those who have been our adversaries, we will not let down our friends and allies around the world.

And in this period we must keep our economy vigorous and competitive, if the opening for greater East-West trade is to mean anything at all and if we do not wish to be shouldered aside in world markets by the growing potential of the economies of Japan, Western Europe, the Soviet Union, the People's Republic of China.

For America to continue its role of helping to build a more peaceful world we must keep American No. 1 economically in the world.

And we must maintain our own momentum of domestic innovation and growth and reform if the opportunities for joint action with the Soviets are to fulfill their promises.

As we seek agreements to build peace abroad, we must keep America moving forward at home.

Most importantly, if the new age we seek is ever to become a reality, we must keep America strong in spirit, a nation proud of its greatness as a free society, confident of its mission in the world.

Let us be committed to our way of life, as wholeheartedly as the Communist leaders, with whom we seek a new relationship, are committed to their system.

Let us always be proud to show in our words and actions what we know in our hearts that we believe in America.

These are just some of the challenges of peace. They are in some ways even more difficult than the challenges of war. But we are equal to them. And as we meet them we will be able to go forward and explore the sweeping possibilities for peace which this season of summits has now opened up for the world.

For decades, America has been locked in hostile confrontation with the two great Communist powers—the Soviet Union and the People's Republic of China. We were engaged with the one at many points; and almost totally isolated from the other. But our relationships with both had reached a deadly impasse.

All three countries were victims of the kind of bondage about which George Washington long ago warned in these words: "The nation which indulges toward an habitual hatred is a slave to its own animosity."

But now, in the brief space of four months, these journeys

to Peking and Moscow, have begun to free us from perpetual confrontation. We have moved toward better understanding, mutual respect, point-by-point settlement of differences with both of the major Communist powers.

Now this one series of meetings has not rendered an imperfect world suddenly perfect. There still are deep philosophical differences. There still are parts of the world in which age-old hatreds persist. The threat of war has not been eliminated—it has been reduced.

We are making progress toward a world in which leaders of nations will settle their differences by negotiation, not by force, and in which they learn to live with their differences so that their sons will not have to die for those differences.

It is particularly fitting that this trip aimed at building such a world has concluded in Poland. No country in the world has suffered more from war than Poland, and no country has more to gain from peace. The faces of the people who gave us such a heartwarming welcome in Warsaw yesterday and then again this morning and this afternoon told an eloquent story of suffering from war in the past and of hope for peace in the future.

One could see it in their faces.

It made me more determined than ever that America must do all in its power to help that hope for peace come true for all people in the world.

As we continue that effort, our unity of purpose and action will be all important. For the summits of 1972 have not belonged just to one person or to one party or to one branch of our Government alone.

Rather, they are part of a great national journey for peace. Every American can claim a share in the credit for the success of that journey so far, and every American has a major stake in the success for the future.

An unparalleled opportunity has been placed in America's hands. Never has there been a time when hope was more justified or when complacency was more dangerous.

We have made a good beginning. And because we have begun, history now lays upon us a special obligation to see it through. We can seize this moment or we can lose it. We can make good this opportunity to build a new structure of peace in the world, or we can let it slip away.

Together, therefore, let us seize the moment so that our children and the world's children can live free of the fears and free of the hatreds that have been the lot of mankind through the centuries.

And then the historians of some future age will write of the year 1972, not that this was the year America went up to the summit and then down to the depths of the valley again; but that this was the year when America helped to lead the world up out of the lowlands of constant war and on to the high plateau of lasting peace.

The Republican Candidate For President

ACCEPTANCE SPEECH

By RICHARD M. NIXON, *President of the United States*
Broadcast Live on Radio and Television from Miami Beach, Florida, at the
Republican National Convention, August 23, 1972

MR. CHAIRMAN, DELEGATES to this convention, my fellow Americans: Four years ago, standing in this very place, I proudly accepted your nomination for President of the United States.

With your help and with the votes of millions of Americans, we won a great victory in 1968.

Tonight, I again proudly accept your nomination for President of the United States.

Let us pledge ourselves to win an even greater victory this November in 1972.

I congratulate Chairman Ford. I congratulate Chairman Dole, Anne Armstrong, and the hundreds of others who have laid the foundation for that victory by their work at this great convention.

Our platform is a dynamic program for progress for America and for peace in the world.

Speaking in a very personal sense, I express my deep gratitude to this convention for the tribute you have paid to the best campaigner in the Nixon family—my wife Pat. In honoring her, you have honored millions of women in America who have contributed in the past and will contribute in the future so very much to better government in this country.

Again, as I did last night, when I was not at the convention, I express the appreciation of all of the delegates and of all America for letting us see young America at its best at our convention. As I express my appreciation to you, I want to say that you have inspired us with your enthusiasm, with your intelligence, with your dedication at this convention. You have made us realize that this is a year when we can prove the experts' predictions wrong, because we can set as our goal winning a majority of the new voters for *our* ticket this November.

I pledge to you, all of the new voters in America who are listening on television and listening here in this convention hall, that I will do everything that I can over these next 4 years

Source: Vital Speeches of the Day, September 15, 1972; City News Publishing Company, Southold, New York. By permission of the publisher.

to make your support be one that you can be proud of, because, as I said to you last night, and I feel it very deeply in my heart: Years from now I want you to look back and be able to say that your first vote was one of the best votes you ever cast in your life.

Mr. Chairman, I congratulate the delegates to this convention for renominating as my running-mate the man who has just so eloquently and graciously introduced me, Vice President Ted Agnew.

I thought he was the best man for the job 4 years ago.

I think he is the best man for the job today.

And I am not going to change my mind tomorrow.

Finally, as the Vice President has indicated, you have demonstrated to the Nation that we can have an open convention without dividing Americans into quotas.

Let us commit ourselves to rule out every vestige of discrimination in this country of ours. But my fellow Americans, the way to end discrimination against some is not to begin discrimination against others.

Dividing Americans into quotas is totally alien to the American traditions.

Americans don't want to be part of a quota. They want to be part of America. This Nation proudly calls itself the United States of America. Let us reject any philosophy that would make us the divided people of America.

In that spirit, I address you tonight, my fellow Americans, not as a partisan of party, which would divide us, but as a partisan of principles which can unite us.

Six weeks ago our opponents at their convention rejected many of the great principles of the Democratic Party. To those millions who have been driven out of their home in the Democratic Party, we say come home. We say come home not to another party, but we say come home to the great principles we Americans believe in together.

And I ask you, my fellow Americans, tonight to join us not in a coalition held together only by a desire to gain power. I ask you to join us as members of a new American majority bound together by our common ideals.

I ask everyone listening to me tonight—Democrats, Republicans, Independents, to join our new majority—not on the basis of the party label you wear in your lapel, but on the basis of what you believe in your hearts.

In asking for your support I shall not dwell on the record of our Administration which has been praised perhaps too generously by others at this convention.

We have made great progress in these past 4 years.

It can truly be said that we have changed America and that America has changed the world. As a result of what we have done, America today is a better place and the world is a safer place to live in than was the case 4 years ago.

We can be proud of that record, but we shall never be satisfied. A record is not something to stand on; it is something to build on.

Tonight I do not ask you to join our new majority because of what we have done in the past. I ask your support of the principles I believe should determine America's future.

The choice in this election is not between radical change and no change. The choice in this election is between change that works and change that won't work.

I begin with an article of faith.

It has become fashionable in recent years to point up what is wrong with what is called the American system. The critics contend it is so unfair, so corrupt, so unjust, that we should tear it down and substitute something else in its place.

I totally disagree. I believe in the American system.

I have traveled to 80 countries in the past 25 years, and I have seen Communist systems, I have seen Socialist systems, I have seen systems that are half Socialist and half free.

Every time I come home to America, I realize how fortunate we are to live in this great and good country.

Every time I am reminded that we have more freedom, more opportunity, more prosperity than any people in the world; that we have the highest rate of growth of any industrial nation; that Americans have more jobs at higher wages than in any country in the world; that our rate of inflation is less than that of any industrial nation; that the incomparable productivity of America's farmers has made it possible for us to launch a winning war against hunger in the United States; and that the productivity of our farmers also makes us the best fed people in the world with the lowest percentage of the family budget going to food of any country in the world.

We can be very grateful in this country that the people on welfare in America would be rich in most of the nations of the world today.

Now, my fellow Americans, in pointing up those things, we do not overlook the fact that our system has its problems.

Our Administration, as you know, has provided the biggest tax cut in history, but taxes are still too high.

That is why one of the goals of our next Administration is to reduce the property tax which is such an unfair and heavy burden on the poor, the elderly, the wage earner, the farmer, and those on fixed incomes.

As all of you know, we have cut inflation in half in this Administration, but we have got to cut it further. We must cut it further so that we can continue to expand on the greatest accomplishment of our new economic policy: For the first time in 5 years wage increases in America are not being eaten up by price increases.

As a result of the millions of new jobs created by our new economic policies, unemployment today in America is less than the peacetime average of the sixties, but we must continue the unparalleled increase in new jobs so that we can achieve the great goal of our new prosperity—a job for every American who wants to work, without war and without inflation. The way to reach this goal is to stay on the new road we have charted to move America forward and not to take a sharp detour to the left, which would lead to a dead end for the hopes of the American people.

This points up one of the clearest choices in this campaign. Our opponents believe in a different philosophy.

Theirs is the politics of paternalism, where master planners in Washington make decisions for people.

Ours is the politics of people—where people make decisions for themselves.

The proposal that they have made to pay $1,000 to every person in America insults the intelligence of the American voters.

Because you know that every politician's promise has a price—the taxpayer pays the bill.

The American people are not going to be taken in by any scheme where Government gives money with one hand and then takes it away with the other.

Their platform promises everything to everybody, but at an increased net in the budget of $144 billion, but listen to what it means to you, the taxpayers of the country. That would mean an increase of 50 per cent in what the taxpayers of America pay. I oppose any new spending programs which will increase the tax burden on the already overburdened American taxpayer.

And they have proposed legislation which would add 82 million people to the welfare rolls.

I say that instead of providing incentives for millions of more Americans to go on welfare, we need a program which will provide incentives for people to get off of welfare and to get to work.

We believe that it is wrong for anyone to receive more on welfare than for someone who works. Let us be generous to those who can't work without increasing the tax burden of those who do work.

And while we are talking about welfare, let us quit treating our senior citizens in this country like welfare recipients. They have worked hard all of their lives to build America. And as the builders of America, they have not asked for a handout. What they ask for is what they have earned—and that is retirement in dignity and self-respect. Let's give that to our senior citizens.

Now, when you add up the cost of all of the programs our opponents have proposed, you reach only one conclusion: They would destroy the system which has made America number one in the world economically.

Listen to these facts: Americans today pay one-third of all of their income in taxes. If their programs were adopted, Americans would pay over one-half of what they earn in taxes. This means that if their programs are adopted, American wage earners would be working more for the government than they would for themselves.

Once we cross this line, we cannot turn back because the incentive which makes the American economic system the most productive in the world would be destroyed.

Theirs is not a new approach. It has been tried before in countries abroad, and I can tell you that those who have tried it have lived to regret it.

We cannot and we will not let them do this to America.

Let us always be true to the principle that has made America the world's most prosperous nation—that here in America a person should get what he works for and work for what he gets.

Let me illustrate the difference in our philosophies. Because of our free economic system, what we have done is to build a great building of economic wealth and money in America. It is by far the tallest building in the world and we are still adding to it. Now because some of the windows are broken, they say tear it down and start again. We say, replace the windows and keep building. That is the difference.

Let me turn now to a second area where my beliefs are totally different from those of our opponents.

Four years ago crime was rising all over America at an unprecedented rate. Even our Nation's Capital was called the crime capital of the world. I pledged to stop the rise in crime. In order to keep that pledge, I promised in the election campaign that I would appoint judges to the Federal courts, and particularly to the Supreme Court, who would recognize that the first civil right of every American is to be free from domestic violence.

I have kept that promise. I am proud of the appointments I have made to the courts, and particularly proud of those I have made to the Supreme Court of the United States. And I pledge again tonight, as I did 4 years ago, that whenever I have the opportunity to make more appointments to the courts, I shall continue to appoint judges who share my philosophy that we must strengthen the peace forces as against the criminal forces in the United States.

We have launched an all-out offensive against crime, against narcotics, against permissiveness in our country.

I want the peace officers across America to know that they have the total backing of their President in their fight against crime.

My fellow Americans, as we move toward peace abroad, I ask you to support our programs which will keep the peace at home.

Now, I turn to an issue of overriding importance not only to this election, but for generations to come—the progress we have made in building a new structure of peace in the world.

Peace is too important for partisanship. There have been five Presidents in my political lifetime—Franklin D. Roosevelt, Harry Truman, Dwight Eisenhower, John F. Kennedy, and Lyndon Johnson.

They had differences on some issues, but they were united in their belief that where the security of America or the peace of the world is involved we are not Republicans, we are not Democrats. We are Americans, first, last, and always.

These five Presidents were united in their total opposition to isolation for America and in their belief that the interests of the United States and the interests of world peace require that America be strong enough and intelligent enough to assume the responsibilities of leadership in the world.

They were united in the conviction that the United States should have a defense second to none in the world.

They were all men who hated war and were dedicated to peace.

But not one of these five men and no President in our history believed that America should ask an enemy for peace on terms that would betray our allies and destroy respect for the United States all over the world.

As your President, I pledge that I shall always uphold that proud bipartisan tradition. Standing in this Convention Hall 4 years ago, I pledged to seek an honorable end to the war in Vietnam. We have made great progress toward that end. We have brought over half a million men home and more will be coming home. We have ended America's ground combat role. No draftees are being sent to Vietnam. We have reduced our casualties by 98 per cent. We have gone the extra mile, in fact, we have gone tens of thousands of miles trying to seek a negotiated settlement of the war. We have offered a cease-fire, a total withdrawal of all American forces, an exchange of all prisoners of war, internationally supervised free elections with the Communists participating in the elections and in the supervision.

There are three things, however, that we have not and that we will not offer.

We will never abandon our prisoners of war.

Second, we will not join our enemies in imposing a Communist government on our allies—the 17 million people of South Vietnam.

And we will never stain the honor of the United States of America.

Now I realize that many, particularly in this political year, wonder why we insist on an honorable peace in Vietnam. From a political standpoint they suggest that since I was not in office when over a half million American men were sent there, that I should end the war by agreeing to impose a Communist government on the people of South Vietnam and just blame the whole catastrophe on my predecessors.

This might be good politics, but it would be disastrous to the cause of peace in the world. If, at this time, we betray our allies, it will discourage our friends abroad and it will encourage our enemies to engage in aggression.

In areas like the Mideast, which are danger areas, small nations who rely on the friendship and support of the United States would be in deadly jeopardy.

To our friends and allies in Europe, Asia, the Mideast, and Latin America, I say the United States will continue its great bipartisan tradition—to stand by our friends and never to desert them.

Now in discussing Vietnam, I have noted that in this election year there has been a great deal of talk about providing amnesty for those few hundred Americans who chose to desert their country rather than to serve it in Vietnam. I think it is time that we put the emphasis where it belongs. The real heroes are two and one-half million young Americans who chose to serve their country rather than desert it. I say to you tonight, in these times when there is so much of a tendency to run down those who have served America in the past and who serve it today, let us give those who serve in our Armed Forces and those who have served in Vietnam the honor and the respect that they deserve and that they have earned.

Finally, in this connection, let one thing be clearly understood in this election campaign: The American people will not tolerate any attempt by our enemies to interfere in the cherished right of the American voter to make his own decision with regard to what is best for America without outside intervention.

Now it is understandable that Vietnam has been a major concern in foreign policy. But we have not allowed the war in Vietnam to paralyze our capacity to initiate historic new policies to construct a lasting and just peace in the world.

When the history of this period is written, I believe it will be recorded that our most significant contributions to peace resulted from our trips to Peking and to Moscow.

The dialogue that we have begun with the People's Republic of China has reduced the danger of war and has increased the chance for peaceful cooperation between two great peoples.

Within the space of 4 years in our relations with the Soviet Union we have moved from confrontation to negotiation, and then to cooperation in the interest of peace.

We have taken the first step in limiting the nuclear arms race.

We have laid the foundation for further limitations on nuclear weapons and eventually of reducing the armaments in the nuclear area.

We can thereby not only reduce the enormous cost of arms for both our countries, but we can increase the chances for peace.

More than on any other single issue, I ask you, my fellow Americans, to give us the chance to continue these great initiatives that can contribute so much to the future of peace in the world.

It can truly be said that as a result of our initiatives, the danger of war is less today than it was; the chances for peace are greater.

But a note of warning needs to be sounded. We cannot be complacent. Our opponents have proposed massive cuts in our defense budget which would have the inevitable effect of making the United States the second strongest nation in the world.

For the United States unilaterally to reduce its strength with the naive hope that other nations would do likewise would increase the danger of war in the world.

It would completely remove any incentive of other nations to agree to a mutual limitation or reduction of arms.

The promising initatives we have undertaken to limit arms would be destroyed.

The security of the United States and all the nations in the world who depend upon our friendship and support would be threatened.

Let's look at the record on defense expenditures. We have cut spending in our Administration. It now takes the lowest percentage of our national product in 20 years. We should not spend more on defense than we need. But we must never spend less than we need.

What we must understand is, spending what we need on defense will cost us money. Spending less than we need could cost us our lives or our freedom.

So tonight, my fellow Americans, I say, let us take risks for peace, but let us never risk the security of the United States of America.

It is for that reason that I pledge that we will continue to seek peace and the mutual reduction of arms. The United States, during this period, however, will always have a defense second to none.

There are those who believe that we can entrust the security of America to the good will of our adversaries.

Those who hold this view do not know the real world. We can negotiate limitation of arms and we have done so. We can make agreements to reduce the danger of war, and we have done so.

But one unchangeable rule of international diplomacy that I have learned over many, many years is that, in negotiations between great powers, you can only get something if you have something to give in return.

That is why I say tonight: Let us always be sure that when the President of the United States goes to the conference table, he never has to negotiate from weakness.

There is no such thing as a retreat to peace.

My fellow Americans, we stand today on the threshold of one of the most exciting and challenging eras in the history of relations between nations.

We have the opportunity in our time to be the peacemakers of the world, because the world trusts and respects us, and because the world knows that we shall only use our power to defend freedom, never to destroy it; to keep the peace, never to break it.

A strong America is not the enemy of peace; it is the guardian of peace.

The initiatives that we have begun can result in reducing the danger of arms, as well as the danger of war which hangs over the world today.

Even more important, it means that the enormous creative energies of the Russian people and the Chinese people and the American people and all the great peoples of the world can be turned away from production of war and turned toward production for peace.

In America it means that we can undertake programs for progress at home that will be just as exciting as the great initiatives we have undertaken in building a new structure of peace abroad.

My fellow Americans, the peace dividend that we hear so much about has too often been described solely in monetary terms—how much money we could take out of the arms budget and apply to our domestic needs. By far the biggest dividend, however, is that achieving our goal of a lasting peace in the world would reflect the deepest hopes and ideals of all of the American people.

Speaking on behalf of the American people, I was proud to be able to say in my television address to the Russian people in May: "We covet no one else's territory. We seek no dominion over any other nation. We seek peace not only for ourselves, but for all the people of the world."

This dedication to idealism runs through America's history.

During the tragic War Between the States, Abraham Lincoln was asked whether God was on his side. He replied, "My concern is not whether God is on our side, but whether we are on God's side."

May that always be our prayer for America.

We hold the future of peace in the world and our own future in our hands. Let us reject therefore the policies of those who whine and whimper about our frustrations and call on us to turn inward.

Let us not turn away from greatness.

The chance America now has to lead the way to a lasting peace in the world may never come again.

With faith in God and faith in ourselves and faith in our country, let us have the vision and the courage to seize the moment and meet the challenge before it slips away.

On your television screen last night, you saw the cemetery in Leningrad I visited on my trip to the Soviet Union—where 300,000 people died in the siege of that city during World War II.

At the cemetery I saw the picture of a 12-year-old girl. She was a beautiful child. Her name was Tanya.

I read her diary. It tells the terrible story of war. In the simple words of a child she wrote of the deaths of the members of her family. Zhenya in December. Grannie in January. Then Leka. Then Uncle Vasya. Then Uncle Lyosha. Then Mama in May. And finally—these were the last words in her diary: "All are dead. Only Tanya is left."

Let us think of Tanya and of the other Tanyas and their brothers and sisters everywhere in Russia, in China, in America, as we proudly meet our responsibilities for leadership in the world in a way worthy of a great people.

I ask you, my fellow Americans, to join our new majority not just in the cause of winning an election, but in achieving a hope that mankind has had since the beginning of civilization. Let us build a peace that our children and all the children of the world can enjoy for generations to come.

Second Inaugural Address

A LASTING PEACE

By RICHARD M. NIXON, *President of the United States*

Delivered in Washington, D. C., January 20, 1973

MR. VICE PRESIDENT, Mr. Speaker, Mr. Chief Justice, Senator Cook, Mrs. Eisenhower, and my fellow citizens of this great and good country we share together:

When we met here 4 years ago, America was bleak in spirit, depressed by the prospect of seemingly endless war abroad and of destructive conflict at home.

As we meet here today, we stand on the threshold of a new era of peace in the world.

The central question before us is: How shall we use that peace?

Let us resolve that this era we are about to enter will not be what other postwar periods have so often been: a time of retreat and isolation that leads to stagnation at home and invites new danger abroad.

Let us resolve that this will be what it can become: a time of great responsibilities greatly borne, in which we renew the spirit and the promise of America as we enter our third century as a Nation.

This past year saw far-reaching results from our new policies for peace. By continuing to revitalize our traditional friendships, and by our missions to Peking and to Moscow, we were able to establish the base for a new and more durable pattern of relationships among the nations of the world. Because of America's bold initiatives, 1972 will be long remembered as the year of the greatest progress since the end of World War II toward a lasting peace in the world.

The peace we seek in the world is not the flimsy peace which is merely an interlude between wars, but a peace which can endure for generations to come.

It is important that we understand both the necessity and the limitations of America's role in maintaining that peace.

Unless we in America work to preserve the peace, there will be no peace.

Unless we in America work to preserve freedom, there will be no freedom.

But let us clearly understand the new nature of America's role, as a result of the new policies we have adopted over these past 4 years.

We shall respect our treaty commitments.

We shall support vigorously the principle that no country has the right to impose its will or rule on another by force.

Source: Vital Speeches of the Day, February 15, 1973; City News Publishing Company, Southold, New York. By permission of the publisher.

We shall continue, in this era of negotiation, to work for the limitation of nuclear arms and to reduce the danger of confrontation between the great powers.

We shall do our share in defending peace and freedom in the world. But we shall expect others to do their share.

The time has passed when America will make every other nation's conflict our own, or make every other nation's future our responsibility, or presume to tell the people of other nations how to manage their own affairs.

Just as we respect the right of each nation to determine its own future, we also recognize the responsibility of each nation to secure its own future.

Just as America's role is indispensable in preserving the world's peace, so is each nation's role indispensable in preserving its own peace.

Together with the rest of the world, let us resolve to move forward from the beginnings we have made. Let us continue to bring down the walls of hostility which have divided the world for too long, and to build in their place bridges of understanding—so that despite profound differences between systems of government, the people of the world can be friends.

Let us build a structure of peace in the world in which the weak are as safe as the strong, in which each respects the right of the other to live by a different system, in which those who would influence others will do so by the strength of their ideas and not by the force of their arms.

Let us accept that high responsibility not as a burden, but gladly—gladly because the chance to build such a peace is the noblest endeavor in which a nation can engage; gladly also because only if we act greatly in meeting our responsibilities abroad will we remain a great Nation, and only if we remain a great Nation will we act greatly in meeting our challenges at home.

We have the chance today to do more than ever before in our history to make life better in America—to ensure better education, better health, better housing, better transportation, a cleaner environment—to restore respect for law, to make our communities more livable—and to ensure the God-given right of every American to full and equal opportunity.

Because the range of our needs is so great, because the reach of our opportunities is so great, let us be bold in our determination to meet those needs in new ways.

Just as building a structure of peace abroad has required turning away from old policies that have failed, so building a new era of progress at home requires turning away from old policies that have failed.

Abroad, the shift from old policies to new has not been a retreat from our responsibilities, but a better way to peace.

And at home, the shift from old policies to new will not be a retreat from our responsibilities, but a better way to progress.

Abroad and at home, the key to those new responsibilities lies in

the placing and the division of responsibility. We have lived too long
with the consequences of attempting to gather all power and responsibility in Washington.

Abroad and at home, the time has come to turn away from the
condescending policies of paternalism—of "Washington knows
best."

A person can be expected to act responsibly only if he has responsibility. This is human nature. So let us encourage individuals at
home·and nations abroad to do more for themselves, to decide more
for themselves. Let us locate responsibility in more places. And let us
measure what we will do for others by what they will do for
themselves.

That is why today I offer no promise of a purely governmental
solution for every problem. We have lived too long with that false
promise. In trusting too much in government, we have asked of it
more than it can deliver. This leads only to inflated expectations, to
reduced individual effort, and to a disappointment and frustration
that erode confidence both in what government can do and in what
people can do.

Government must learn to take less from people so that people
can do more for themselves.

Let us remember that America was built not by government, but
by people—not by welfare, but by work—not by shirking responsibility, but by seeking responsibility.

In our own lives, let each of us ask—not just what will government do for me, but what can I do for myself?

In the challenges we face together, let each of us ask—not just
how can government help, but how can I help?

Your National Government has a great and vital role to play.
And I pledge to you that where this Government should act, we will
act boldly and we will lead boldly. But just as important is the role
that each and every one of us must play, as an individual and as a
member of his own community.

From this day forward, let each of us make a solemn commitment
in his own heart: to bear his responsibility, to do his part, to live his
ideals—so that together, we can see the dawn of a new age of
progress for America, and together, as we celebrate our 200th anniversary as a nation, we can do so proud in the fulfillment of our
promise to ourselves and to the world.

As America's longest and most difficult war comes to an end, let
us again learn to debate our differences with civility and decency.
And let each of us reach out for that one precious quality government cannot provide—a new level of respect for the rights and
feelings of one another, a new level of respect for the individual
human dignity which is the cherished birthright of every American.

Above all else, the time has come for us to renew our faith in
ourselves and in America.

In recent years, that faith has been challenged.

Our children have been taught to be ashamed of their country,
ashamed of their parents, ashamed of America's record at home and
its role in the world.

At every turn we have been beset by those who find everything wrong with America and little that is right. But I am confident that this will not be the judgment of history on these remarkable times in which we are privileged to live.

America's record in this century has been unparalleled in the world's history for its responsibility, for its generosity, for its creativity, and for its progress.

Let us be proud that our system has produced and provided more freedom and more abundance, more widely shared, than any system in the history of the world.

Let us be proud that in each of the four wars in which we have been engaged in this century, including the one we are now bringing to an end, we have fought not for our selfish advantage, but to help others resist aggression.

And let us be proud that by our bold, new initiatives, by our steadfastness for peace with honor, we have made a breakthrough toward creating in the world what the world has not known before—a structure of peace that can last, not merely for our time, but for generations to come.

We are embarking here today on an era that presents challenges as great as those any nation, or any generation, has ever faced.

We shall answer to God, to history, and to our conscience for the way in which we use these years.

As I stand in this place, so hallowed by history, I think of others who have stood here before me. I think of the dreams they had for America and I think of how each recognized that he needed help far beyond himself in order to make those dreams come true.

Today I ask your prayers that in the years ahead I may have God's help in making decisions that are right for America and I pray for your help so that together we may be worthy of our challenge.

Let us pledge together to make these next 4 years the best 4 years in America's history, so that on its 200th birthday America will be as young and as vital as when it began, and as bright a beacon of hope for all the world.

Let us go forward from here confident in hope, strong in our faith in one another, sustained by our faith in God who created us, and striving always to serve His purpose.

Ending The War And Restoring Peace

VIETNAM

By RICHARD M. NIXON, *President of the United States*

Address to the Nation on National TV and Radio,

Washington, D. C., January 23, 1973

GOOD EVENING. I have asked for this radio and television time tonight for the purpose of announcing that we today have concluded an agreement to end the war and bring peace with honor in Vietnam and in Southeast Asia.

The following statement is being issued at this moment in Washington and Hanoi:

At 12:30 Paris time today, January 23, 1973, the Agreement on Ending the War and Restoring Peace in Vietnam was initialed by Dr. Henry Kissinger on behalf of the United States, and Special Adviser Le Duc Tho on behalf of the Democratic Republic of Vietnam.

The agreement will be formally signed by the parties participating in the Paris Conference on Vietnam on January 27, 1973, at the International Conference Center in Paris.

The cease-fire will take effect at 2400 Greenwich Mean Time, January 27, 1973. The United States and the Democratic Republic of Vietnam express the hope that this agreement will insure stable peace in Vietnam and contribute to the preservation of lasting peace in Indochina and Southeast Asia.

That concludes the formal statement.

Throughout the years of negotiations, we have insisted on peace with honor. In my addresses to the Nation from this room of January 25 and May 8, I set forth the goals that we considered essential for peace with honor.

In the settlement that has now been agreed to, all the conditions that I laid down then have been met. A cease-fire, internationally supervised, will begin at 7 p.m., this Saturday, January 27, Washington time. Within 60 days from this Saturday, all Americans held prisoners of war throughout Indochina will be released. There will be the fullest possible accounting for all of those who are missing in action.

During the same 60-day period, all American forces will be withdrawn from South Vietnam.

Source: Vital Speeches of the Day, February 15, 1973; City News Publishing Company, Southold, New York. By permission of the publisher.

The people of South Vietnam have been guaranteed the right to determine their own future, without outside interference.

By joint agreement, the full text of the agreement and the protocols to carry it out, will be issued tomorrow.

Throughout these negotiations we have been in the closest consultation with President Thieu and other respresentatives of the Republic of Vietnam. This settlement meets the goals and has the full support of President Thieu and the Government of the Republic of Vietnam, as well as that of our other allies who are affected.

The United States will continue to recognize the Government of the Republic of Vietnam as the sole legitimate government of South Vietnam.

We shall continue to aid South Vietnam within the terms of the agreement and we shall support efforts by the people of South Vietnam to settle their problems peacefully among themselves.

We must recognize that ending the war is only the first step toward building the peace. All parties must now see to it that this is a peace that lasts, and also a peace that heals, and a peace that not only ends the war in Southeast Asia, but contributes to the prospects of peace in the whole world.

This will mean that the terms of the agreement must be scrupulously adhered to. We shall do everything the agreement requires of us and we shall expect the other parties to do everything it requires of them. We shall also expect other interested nations to help insure that the agreement is carried out and peace is maintained.

As this long and very difficult war ends, I would like to address a few special words to each of those who have been parties in the conflict.

First, to the people and Government of South Vietnam: By your courage, by your sacrifice, you have won the precious right to determine your own future and you have developed the strength to defend that right. We look forward to working with you in the future, friends in peace as we have been allies in war.

To the leaders of North Vietnam: As we have ended the war through negotiations, let us now build a peace of reconciliation. For our part, we are prepared to make a major effort to help achieve that goal. But just as reciprocity was needed to end the war, so, too, will it be needed to build and strengthen the peace.

To the other major powers that have been involved even indirectly: Now is the time for mutual restraint so that the peace we have achieved can last.

And finally, to all of you who are listening, the American people: Your steadfastness in supporting our insistence on peace with honor has made peace with honor possible. I know that you would not have wanted that peace jeopardized. With our secret negotiations at the sensitive stage they were in during this recent period, for me to have discussed publicly our efforts to secure peace would not only have violated our understanding with North Vietnam, it would have

seriously harmed and possibly destroyed the chances for peace.
Therefore, I know that you now can understand why, during these
past several weeks, I have not made any public statements about
those efforts.

The important thing was not to talk about peace, but to get peace
and to get the right kind of peace. This we have done.

Now that we have achieved an honorable agreement, let us be
proud that America did not settle for a peace that would have
betrayed our allies, that would have abandoned our prisoners of war,
or that would have ended the war for us but would have continued
the war for the 50 million people of Indochina. Let us be proud of
the 2½ million young Americans who served in Vietnam, who served with honor and distinction •   •   •   •

The Indochina Conflict

THE BUDGET CRISIS

By RICHARD M. NIXON, *President of the United States*

Delivered to the nation over radio, March 29, 1973

FOUR YEARS and two months ago, when I first came into this office as President, by far the most difficult problem confronting the nation was the seemingly endless war in Vietnam. Five hundred and fifty thousand Americans were in Vietnam. As many as 300 a week were being killed in action. Hundreds were held as prisoners of war in North Vietnam. And no progress was being made at the peace negotiations.

I immediately initiated a program to end the war and win an honorable peace. Eleven times over the past four years I have reported to the nation from this room on the progress we have made toward that goal.

And tonight, the day we have all worked and prayed for has finally come.

For the first time in 12 years, no American military forces are in Vietnam. All of our American P.O.W.'s are on their way home.

The 17 million people of South Vietnam have the right to choose their own government without outside interference., And, because of our program of Vietnamization, they have the strength to defend that right.

We have prevented the imposition of a Communist government by force on South Vietnam.

There are still some problem areas: the provision of the agreement requiring an accounting for all missing in action in Indochina; the provision with regard to Laos; the provision prohibiting infiltration from North Vietnam into South Vietnam have not been complied with.

We have and will continue to comply with the agreement.

We shall insist that North Vietnam comply with the agreement and the leaders of North Vietnam should have no doubt as to the consequences if they fail to comply with the agreement.

But despite these difficulties we can be proud tonight of the fact that we have achieved our goal of obtaining an agreement which provides peace with honor in Vietnam.

And on this day let us honor those who made this achie ...ient possible, those who sacrificed their lives, those who were disabled, those who made everyone of us proud to be an American as they returned from years of Communist imprisonment, and every one of

Source: Vital Speeches of the Day, April 15, 1973; City News Publishing Company, Southold, New York. By permission of the publisher.

the two-and-a-half million Americans who served honorably in our
nation's longest war.

Never have men served with greater devotion abroad with less apparent support at home.

Let us provide these men with the veterans' benefits and the job
opportunities they have earned, and let us honor them with the
respect they deserve.

And I say again tonight, let us not dishonor those who served
their country by granting amnesty to those who deserted America.

Tonight I want to express the appreciation of the nation to others
who helped make this day possible.

I refer to you, the great majority of Americans, listening to me
tonight, who despite an unprecedented barrage of criticism from a
small but vocal minority, stood firm for peace with honor.

I know it was not easy for you to do so. We have been through
some difficult times together. I recall the time in November, 1969,
when hundreds of thousands of demonstrators marched on the
White House.

The time in April, 1970, when I found it necessary to order attacks on Communist bases in Cambodia. The time in May, 1972,
when I ordered the mining of Haiphong and air strikes on military
targets in North Vietnam in order to stop a massive Communist
offensive in South Vietnam.

And then — and this was perhaps the hardest decision I have
made as President — on Dec. 18, 1972, when our hopes for peace
were so high, and when the North Vietnamese stone-walled us at
the conference table — I found it necessary to order more air strikes
on military targets in North Vietnam in order to break the deadlock.

On each of these occasions, the voices of opposition we heard in
Washington were so loud they at times seemed to be the majority.
But across America, the overwhelming majority stood firm against
those who advocated peace at any price — even if the price would
have been defeat and humiliation for the United States.

And because you stood firm, stood firm for doing what was right,
Colonel McKnight was able to say for his fellow P.O.W.'s when he
returned home a few days ago, "Thank you for bringing us home on
our feet instead of on our knees."

Let us turn now to some of our problems at home.

Tonight, I ask your support in another battle, but we can be
thankful this is not a battle in war abroad but a battle we must win if
we are to build a new prosperity without war and without inflation
at home.

What I refer to is the battle of the budget — not just the battle
over the Federal budget, but even more important, the battle of your
budget — the family budget of every home in America.

One of the most terrible costs of war is inflation. The cost of
living has skyrocketed during and after every war America has been
engaged in.

We recognized this danger four years ago. We've taken strong
action to deal with it. As a result of our policies we have cut the rate
of inflation in half from the high point it reached in 1969 and
1970.

And today, our rate of inflation in the United States is the lowest of any industrial nation in the world.

But these positive statistics are small comfort to a family trying to make both ends meet. And they are no comfort at all to the housewife who sees meat prices soaring every time she goes to the market.

The major weak spot in our fight against inflation is in the area of meat prices.

I have taken action to increase imports from abroad and production at home. This will increase the supply of meat and it will help bring prices down later this year. But what we need is action that will stop the rise in meat prices now.

And that is why I have today ordered the Cost of Living Council to impose a ceiling on prices of beef, pork and lamb. The ceiling will remain in effect as long as it is necessary to do the job. Meat prices must not go higher and with the help of the housewife and the farmer they can and they should go down.

This ceiling will help in our battle against inflation. But it is not a permanent solution. We must act on all fronts. And here is where the Federal budget comes in.

I have submitted to Congress for the next fiscal year the largest budget in our history — $268-billion. The amount I have requested in this budget for domestic programs in such fields as health, housing, education, aid to the elderly, the handicapped, the poor, is twice as big as the amount I asked for these items four years ago.

However, some members of Congress believe the budget in these areas should be even higher. Now if I were to approve the increases in my budget that have been proposed in the Congress, it would mean a 15 per cent increase in your taxes, or an increase in prices for every American. And that is why I shall veto the bills which would break the Federal budget which I have submitted.

If I do not veto these bills, increased prices or taxes would break the family budgets of millions of Americans, including, possibly, your own.

This is not a battle between Congress and the President. It is your battle. It is your money, your prices, your taxes I am trying to save.

Twenty-five years ago, as a freshman Congressman, I first came into this office. I met Harry Truman, who was then President of the United States.

I remember he had a sign on the desk. It read: "The buck stops here." Now that meant, of course, that a President can't pass the buck to anyone else when a tough decision has to be made.

It also means that your buck stops here.

If I do not now ask to stop the spending increases which Congress sends to this desk, you will have to pay the bill.

I admit there is an honest difference of opinion on the matter of the Federal budget. If you are willing to pay the higher taxes or prices that will result if we increase Federal spending over my budget — as some in Congress have proposed — you should ask your Senators and your Congress to override my veto.

But, if you want to stop the rise in taxes and prices, I have a suggestion to make.

I remember when I was a Congressman and a Senator I always seemed to hear from those who wanted government to spend more. I seldom heard from the people who had to pay the bills — the taxpayer. And if your Congressman or Senator has the courage to vote against more Government spending so that you won't have to pay higher prices or taxes, let him know that you support him.

Winning the battle to hold down the Federal budget is essential if we are to achieve our goal of a new prosperity. Prosperity without war and without inflation.

I ask you tonight for your support in helping to win this vitally important battle.

Let me turn finally tonight to another great challenge we face.

As we end America's longest war, let us resolve that we shall not lose the peace.

During the past year we've made great progress toward our goal of a generation of peace for America and the world. The war in Vietnam has been ended.

After 20 years of hostility and confrontation we have opened a constructive new relationship with the Peoples Republic of China where one-fourth of all the people in the world live.

We negotiated last year with the Soviet Union a number of important agreements, including an agreement which takes a major step in limiting nuclear arms.

Now there are some who say that in view of all this progress toward peace, why not cut our defense budget?

Well, let's look at the facts. Our defense budget today takes the lowest percentage of our gross national product that it has in 20 years. There's nothing I would like better than to be able to reduce it further. But we must never forget that we would not have made the progress toward lasting peace that we have made in this past year unless we had had the military strength that commanded respect.

This year we have begun new negotiations with the Soviet Union for further limitations on nuclear arms. And we shall be participating later in the year in negotiations for mutual reduction of forces in Europe.

If prior to these negotiations we in the United States unilaterally reduce our defense budget or reduce our forces in Europe, any chance for successful negotiations for mutual reduction of forces or limitation of arms will be destroyed.

There is one unbreakable rule of international diplomacy. You can't get something in a negotiation unless you have something to give.

If we cut our defenses before negotiations begin, any incentive for other nations to cut theirs will go right out the window.

If the United States reduces its defenses and others do not, it will increase the danger of war.

It is only a mutual reduction of forces which will reduce the danger of war.

And that is why we must maintain our strength until we get agreements under which other nations will join us in reducing the burden of armament.

What is at stake is whether the United States shall become the second strongest nation in the world.

If that day ever comes, the chance for building a new structure of peace in the world would be irreparably damaged and free nations everywhere would be living in mortal danger.

A strong United States is not a threat to peace. It is the free world's indispensable guardian of peace and freedom. I ask for your support tonight for keeping the strength which enabled us to make great progress toward world peace in the past year and which is indispensable as we continue our bold new initiatives for peace in the years ahead.

As we consider some of our problems tonight, let us never forget how fortunate we are to live in America at this time in our history.

We have ended the longest and most difficult war in our history in a way that maintains the trust of our allies and the respect of our adversaries.

We are the strongest and most prosperous nation in the world. Because of our strength, America has the magnificent opportunity to play the leading role of bringing down the walls of hostility which divide the people of the world, in reducing the burden of armaments in the world, of building a structure of lasting peace in the world.

And because of our wealth, we have the means to move forward at home on exciting new programs, programs for progress which will provide better environment, education, housing and health care for all Americans, and which will enable us to be more generous to the poor, the elderly, the disabled and the disadvantaged than any nation in the history of the world.

These are goals worthy of a great people. Let us therefore put aside those honest differences about war which had divided us and dedicate ourselves to meet the great challenges of peace which can unite us.

As we do, let us not overlook a third element. An element more important even than military might or economic power because it is essential for greatness in a nation. The pages of history are strewn with the wreckage of nations which fell by the wayside, at the height of their strength and wealth, because their people became weak, soft and self-indulgent and lost the character and the spirit which had led to their greatness.

As I speak to you tonight I am confident that will not happen to America, and my confidence has been increased by the fact that a war which cost America so much in lives, money and division at home has as it ended provided an opportunity for millions of Americans to see again the character and the spirit which made America a great nation.

A few days ago in this room I talked to a man who had spent almost eight years in a Communist prison camp in North Vietnam. For over four years he was in solitary confinement. In that four-year period he never saw and never talked to another human being except his Communist captors. He lived on two meals a day, usually just a piece of bread, a bowl of soup. All he was given to read was Communist propaganda. All he could listen to was the Communist propaganda on radio.

I asked him how he was able to survive and come home standing tall and proud, saluting the American flag.

He paused a long time before he answered.

And then he said, "It is difficult for me to answer. I am not very good at words. All I can say is that it was faith. Faith in God and faith in my country."

If men who suffered so much for America can have such faith, let us who have received so much from America renew our faith — our faith in God, our faith in our country and our faith in ourselves.

If we meet the great challenges of peace that lie ahead with this kind of faith, then one day it will be written: this was America's finest hour.

Thank you. Good evening.

The Watergate Affair

THE INTEGRITY OF THE WHITEHOUSE

By RICHARD M. NIXON, *President of the United States*

Broadcast from Washington, D. C., April 30, 1973

G OOD EVENING. I want to talk to you tonight from my heart on a subject of deep concern to every American. In recent months members of my Administration and officials of the Committee for the Re-election of the President — including some of my closest friends and most trusted aides — have been charged with involvement in what has come to be known as the Watergate affair.

These include charges of illegal activity during and preceding the 1972 Presidential election and charges that responsible officials participated in efforts to cover up that illegal activity.

The inevitable result of these charges has been to raise serious questions about the integrity of the White House itself. Tonight I wish to address those questions.

Last June 17 while I was in Florida trying to get a few days' rest after my visit to Moscow, I first learned from news reports of the Watergate break-in. I was appalled at this senseless, illegal action, and I was shocked to learn that employes of the re-election committee were apparently among those guilty. I immediately ordered an investigation by appropriate Government authorities.

On Sept. 15, as you will recall, indictments were brought against seven defendants in the case.

As the investigation went forward, I repeatedly asked those conducting the investigation whether there was any reason to believe that members of my Administration were in any way involved. I received repeated assurances that there were not. Because of these continuing reassurances, because I believed the reports I was getting, because I had faith in the persons from whom I was getting them, I discounted the stories in the press that appeared to implicate members of my Administration or other officials of the campaign committee.

Until March of this year, I remained convinced that the denials were true and that the charges of involvement by members of the White House staff were false.

The comments I made during this period, the comments made by my press secretary in my behalf, were based on the information provided to us at the time we made those comments.

Source: Vital Speeches of the Day, May 15, 1973;
City News Publishing Company, Southold, New
York. By permission of the publisher.

However, new information then came to me which persuaded me that there was a real possibility that some of these charges were true and suggesting further that there had been an effort to conceal the facts both from the public — from you — and from me.

As a result, on March 21 I personally assumed the responsibility for coordinating intensive new inquiries into the matter and I personally ordered those conducting the investigations to get all the facts and to report them directly to me right here in this office.

I again ordered that all persons in the Government or at the re-election committee should cooperate fully with the F.B.I., the prosecutors and the grand jury.

I also ordered that anyone who refused to cooperate in telling the truth would be asked to resign from Government service.

And with ground rules adopted that would preserve the basic constitutional separation of powers between the Congress and the Presidency, I directed that members of the White House staff should appear and testify voluntarily under oath before the Senate committee which was investigating Watergate.

I was determined that we should get to the bottom of the matter, and that the truth should be fully brought out no matter who was involved.

At the same time, I was determined not to take precipitive action and to avoid if at all possible any action that would appear to reflect on innocent people.

I wanted to be fair, but I knew that in the final analysis the integrity of this office — public faith in the integrity of this office — would have to take priority over all personal considerations. Today, in one of the most difficult decisions of my Presidency, I accepted the resignations of two of my closest associates in the White House, Bob Haldeman and John Ehrlichman, two of the finest public servants it has been my privilege to know. I want to stress that in accepting these resignations I mean to leave no implication whatever of personal wrongdoing on their part, and I leave no implication tonight of implication on the part of others who have been charged in this matter. But in matters as sensitive as guarding the integrity of our democratic process, it is essential not only that rigorous legal and ethical standards be observed, but also that the public, you, have total confidence that they are both being observed and enforced by those in authority, and particularly by the President of the United States. They agreed with me that this move was necessary in order to restore that confidence, because Attorney General Kleindienst, though a distinguished public servant, my personal friend for 20 years, with no personal involvement whatever in this matter, has been a close personal and professional associate of some of those who are involved in this case, he and I both felt that it was also necessary to name a new Attorney General.

The counsel to the President, John Dean, has also resigned.

As the new Attorney General, I have today named Elliott Richardson, a man of unimpeachable integrity and rigorously high principle. I have directed him to do everything necessary to insure that the Department of Justice has the confidence and the trust of every law-abiding person in this country. I have given him absolute authority to make all decisions bearing upon the prosecution of the Watergate case and related matters. I have instructed him that if he should consider it appropriate he has the authority to name a special supervising prosecutor for matters arising out of the case.

Whatever may appear to have been the case before, whatever improper activities may yet be discovered in connection with this whole sordid affair, I want the American people, I want you, to know beyond the shadow of a doubt that during my term as President justice will be pursued fairly, fully and impartially, no matter who is involved.

This office is a sacred trust, and I am determined to be worthy of that trust!

Looking back at the history of this case, two questions arise:

How could it have happened — who is to blame?

Political commentators have correctly observed that during my 27 years in politics, I've always previously insisted on running my own campaigns for office.

In both domestic and foreign policy, 1972 was a year of crucially important decisions, of intense negotiations, of vital new directions, particularly in working toward the goal which has been my overriding concern throughout my political career — the goal of bringing peace to America, peace to the world.

And that is why I decided as the 1972 campaign approached that the Presidency should come first and politics second. To the maximum extent possible, therefore, I sought to delegate campaign operations, to remove the day-to-day campaign decisions from the President's office and from the White House.

I also, as you recall, severely limited the number of my own campaign appearances.

Who then is to blame for what happened in this case?

For specific criminal actions by specific individuals those who committed those actions must of course bear the liability and pay the penalty. For the fact that alleged improper actions took place within the White House or within my campaign organization, the easiest course would be for me to blame those to whom I delegated the responsibility to run the campaign. But that would be a cowardly thing to do.

I will not place the blame on subordinates, on people whose zeal exceeded their judgment and who may have done wrong in a cause they deeply believed to be right. In any organization the man at the top must bear the responsibility.

That responsibility, therefore, belongs here in this office. I accept it.

And I pledge to you tonight from this office that I will do everything in my power to insure that the guilty are brought to justice and that such abuses are purged from our political processes in the years to come long after I have left this office.

Some people, quite properly appalled at the abuses that occurred, will say that Watergate demonstrates the bankruptcy of the American political system. I believe precisely the opposite is true.

Watergate represented a series of illegal acts and bad judgments by a number of individuals. It was the system that has brought the facts to light and that will bring those guilty to justice.

A system that in this case has included a determined grand jury, honest prosecutors, a courageous judge — John Sirica, and a vigorous free press.

It is essential that we place our faith in that system, and especially in the Judicial System.

It is essential that we let the judicial process go forward, respecting those safeguards that are established to protect the innocent as well as to convict the guilty.

It is essential that in reacting to the excesses of others, we not fall into excesses ourselves.

It is also essential that we not be so distracted by events such as this that we neglect the vital work before us, before this nation, before America at a time of critical importance to America and the world.

Since March, when I first learned that the Watergate affair might in fact be far more serious than I had been led to believe, it has claimed far too much of my time and my attention. Whatever may now transpire in the case, whatever the actions of the grand jury, whatever the outcome of any eventual trials, I must now turn my full intention — and I shall do so — once again to the larger duties of this office.

I owe it to this great office that I hold, and I owe it to you, to my country.

I know that, as Attorney General, Elliot Richardson will be both fair and he will be fearless in pursuing this case wherever it leads. I am confident that with him in charge justice will be done.

There is vital work to be done toward our goal of a lasting structure of peace in the world — work that cannot wait, work that I must do.

Tomorrow, for example, Chancellor Brandt of West Germany will visit the White House for talks that are a vital element of the Year of Europe, as 1973 has been called.

We are already preparing for the next Soviet-American summit meeting later this year.

This is also a year in which we are seeking to negotiate a mutual and balanced reduction of armed forces in Europe which will reduce our defense budget and allow us to have funds for other purposes at home so desperately needed.

It is the year when the United States and Soviet negotiators will seek to work out the second and even more important round of our talks on limiting nuclear arms, and of reducing the danger of a nuclear war that would destroy civilization as we know it.

It is a year in which we confront the difficult tasks of maintaining peace in Southeast Asia and in the potentially explosive Middle East.

There's also vital work to be done right here in America to insure prosperity — and that means a good job for everyone who wants to work; to control inflation that I know worries every housewife, everyone who tries to balance the family budget in America. To set in motion new and better ways of insuring progress toward a better life for all Americans.

When I think of this office, of what it means, I think of all the things that I want to accomplish for this nation, of all the things I want to accomplish for you.

On Christmas Eve, during my terrible personal ordeal of the renewed bombing of North Vietnam which, after 12 years of war, finally helped to bring America peace with honor, I sat down just before midnight. I wrote out some of my goals for my second term as President. Let me read them to you.

To make this country be more than ever a land of opportunity — of equal opportunity, full opportunity — for every American; to provide jobs for all who can work and generous help for those who cannot; to establish a climate of decency and civility in which each person respects the feelings and the dignity in the God-given rights of his neighbor; to make this a land in which each person can dare to dream, can live his dreams not in fear but in hope, proud of his community, proud of his country, proud of what America has meant to himself, and to the world.

These are great goals. I believe we can, we must work for them, we can achieve them.

But we cannot achieve these goals unless we dedicate ourselves to another goal. We must maintain the integrity of the White House.

And that integrity must be real, not transparent.

There can be no whitewash at the White House.

We must reform our political process, ridding it not only of the violations of the law but also of the ugly mob violence and other inexcusable campaign tactics that have been too often practiced and too readily accepted in the past including those that may have been a response by one-sided to the excesses or expected excesses of the other side.

Two wrongs do not make a right.

I've been in public life for more than a quarter of a century. Like any other calling, politics has good people and bad people and let me tell you the great majority in politics, in the Congress, in the Federal Government, in the state government are good people.

I know that it can be very easy under the intensive pressures of a campaign for even well-intentioned people to fall into shady tactics, to rationalize this on the grounds that what is at stake is of such importance to the nation that the end justifies the means.

And both of our great parties have been guilty of such tactics.

In recent years, however, the campaign excesses that have occurred on all sides have provided a sobering demonstration of how far this false doctrine can take us.

The lesson is clear. America in its political campaigns must not again fall into the trap of letting the end, however great that end is, justify the means.

I urge the leaders of both political parties, I urge citizens — all of you everywhere — to join in working toward a new set of standards, new rules and procedures to insure that future elections will be as nearly free of such abuses as they possibly can be made. This is my goal. I ask you to join in making it America's goal.

When I was inaugurated for a second term this past January 20, I gave each member of my Cabinet and each member of my senior White House staff a special four-year calendar with each day marked to show the number of days remaining to the Administration.

In the inscription on each calendar I wrote these words:

"The Presidential term which begins today consists of 1,461 days, no more, no less. Each can be a day of strengthening and renewal for America. Each can add depth and dimension to the American experience.

"If we strive together, if we make the most of the challenge and the opportunity that these days offer us, they can stand out as great days for America and great moments in the history of the world."

I looked at my own calendar this morning up at Camp David as I was working on this speech. It showed exactly 1,361 days remaining in my term.

I want these to be the best days in America's history because I love America. I deeply believe that America is the hope of the world, and I know that in the quality and wisdom of the leadership America gives lies the only hope for millions of people all over the world that they can live their lives in peace and freedom.

We must be worthy of that hope in every sense of the word.

Tonight, I ask for your prayers to help me in everything that I do throughout the days of my Presidency to be worthy of their hopes and of yours.

God bless America. And God bless each and every one of you.

The Watergate Charges

PROTECTING THE NATIONAL SECURITY

By RICHARD M. NIXON, *President of the United States*

Delivered on Nationwide Television, August 15, 1973

NOW THAT MOST of the major witnesses in the Watergate phase of the Senate committee hearings on campaign practices have been heard, the time has come for me to speak out about the charges made and to provide a perspective on the issue for the American people.

For over four months Watergate has dominated the news media. During the past three months the three major networks have devoted an average of over 22 hours of television time each week to this subject. The Senate committee has heard over two million words of testimony.

This investigation began as an effort to discover the facts about the break-in and bugging at the Democratic national headquarters and other campaign abuses.

But the weeks have gone by, it has become clear that both the hearings themselves and some of the commentaries on them have become increasingly absorbed in an effort to implicate the President personally in the illegal activities that took place.

Because the abuses occurred during my Administration, and in the campaign for my re-election I accept full responsibility for them. I regret that these events took place. And I do not question the right of a Senate committee to investigate charges made against the President to the extent that this is relevant to legislative duties.

However, it is my Constitutional responsibility to defend the integrity of this great office against false charges. I also believe that it is important to address the overriding question of what we as a nation can learn from this experience, and what we should now do. I intend to discuss both of these subjects tonight.

The record of the Senate hearings is lengthy. The facts are complicated, the evidence conflicting. It would not be right for me to try to sort out the evidence, to rebut specific witnesses, or to pronounce my own judgments about their credibility. That is for the committee and for the courts.

I shall not attempt to deal tonight with the various charges in detail. Rather, I shall attempt to put the events in perspective from the standpoint of the Presidency.

On May 22d, before the major witnesses had testified, I issued a detailed statement ·addressing the charges that had been made against the President.

Source: Vital Speeches of the Day, September 1, 1973; City News Publishing Company, Southold, New York. By permission of the publisher.

I have today issued another written statement, which addresses the charges that have been made since then as they relate to my own conduct. and which describes the efforts that I made to discover the facts about the matter.

On May 22. I stated in very specific terms — and I state again to every one of you listening tonight — these facts:•I had no prior knowledge of the Watergate break-in; I neither took part in nor knew about any of the subsequent cover-up activities; I neither authorized nor encouraged subordinates to engage in illegal or improper campaign tactics.

That was and that is the simple truth. In all of the millions of words of testimony, there is not the slightest suggestion that I had any knowledge of the planning for the Watergate break-in. As for the cover-up, my statement has been challenged by only one of the 35 witnesses who appeared — a witness who offered no evidence beyond his own impressions, and whose testimony has been contradicted by every other witness in a position to know the facts.

Tonight, let me explain to you what I did about Watergate after the break-in occurred, so that you can better understand the fact that I also had no knowledge of the so-called cover-up.

From the time when the break-in occurred, I pressed repeatedly to know the facts, and particularly whether there was any involvement of anyone at the White House. I considered two things essential:

First, that the investigation should be thorough and above-board: and second, that if there were any higher involvement, we should get the facts out first. As I said at my August 29 press conference last year "What really hurts in matters of this sort is not the fact that they occur, because overzealous people in campaigns do things that are wrong. What really hurts is if you try to cover it up." I believed that then, and certainly the experience of this last year has proved that to be true.

I knew that the Justice Department and the F.B.I. were conducting intensive investigations — as I had insisted that they should. The White House counsel, John Dean, was assigned to monitor these investigations, and particularly to check into any possible White House involvement. Throughout the summer of 1972, I continued to press the question, and I continued to get the same answer: I was told again and again that there was no indication that any persons were involved other than the seven who were known to have planned and carried out the operation, and who were subsequently indicted and convicted.

On Sept. 12 at a meeting that I held with the Cabinet. the senior White House staff and a number of legislative leaders, Attorney General Kleindienst reported on the investigation. He told us it had been the most extensive investigation since the assassination of President Kennedy, and that it has established that only those seven were involved.

On Sept. 15. the day the seven were indicted, I met with John Dean. the White House counsel. He gave me no reason whatever to believe that any others were guilty; I assumed that the indictments of only the seven by the grand jury confirmed the reports he had been giving to that effect throughout the summer.

On Feb. 16, I met with Acting Director Gray prior to submitting his name to the Senate for confirmation as permanent director of the F.B.I. I stressed to him that he would be questioned closely about the F.B.I.'s conduct of the Watergate investigation. I asked him if he still had full confidence in it. He replied that he did; that he was proud of its thoroughness and that he could defend it with enthusiasm before the committee.

Because I trusted the agencies conducting the investigations, because I believed the reports I was getting, I did not believe the newspaper accounts that suggested a cover-up. I was convinced there was no cover-up, because I was convinced that no one had anything to cover up.

It was not until March 21 of this year — that I received new information from the White House counsel that led me to conclude that the reports I had been getting for over nine months were not true. On that day, I launched an intensive effort of my own to get the facts and to get the facts out. Whatever the facts might be, I wanted the White House to be the first to make them public.

At first I entrusted the task of getting me the facts to Mr. Dean. When, after spending a week at Camp David, he failed to produce the written report I had asked for, I turned to John Ehrlichman and to the Attorney General — while also making independent inquiries of my own. By mid-April I had received Mr. Ehrlichman's report, and also one from the Attorney General based on new information uncovered by the Justice Department.

These reports made it clear to me that the situation was far more serious than I had imagined. It at once became evident to me that the responsibility for the investigation in the case should be given to the Criminal Division of the Justice Department. I turned over all the information I had to the head of that department, Assistant Attorney General Henry Petersen, a career Government employe with an impeccable nonpartisan record, and I instructed him to pursue the matter thoroughly. I ordered all members of the Administration to testify fully before the grand jury.

And with my concurrence, on May 18 Attorney General Richardson appointed a special prosecutor to handle the matter, and the case is now before the grand jury.

Far from trying to hide the facts, my effort throughout has been to discover the facts — and to lay those facts before the appropriate law-enforcement authorities so that justice could be done and the guilty dealt with.

I relied on the best law-enforcement agencies in the country to find and report the truth. I believed they had done so — just as they believed they had done so.

Many have urged that in order to help prove the truth of what I have said, I should turn over to the special prosecutor and the Senate committee recordings of conversations that I held in my office or my telephone.

However, a much more important principle is involved in this question than what the tapes might prove about Watergate.

Each day a President of the United States is required to make difficult decisions on grave issues. It is absolutely necessary, if the President is to be able to do his job as the country expects, that he be able to talk openly and candidly with his advisers about issues and individuals. This kind of frank discussion is only possible when those who take part in it know that what they say is in strictest confidence.

The Presidency is not the only office that requires confidentiality. A member of Congress must be able to talk in confidence with his assistants. Judges must be able to confer in confidence with their law clerks and with each other. For very good reasons, no branch of government has ever compelled disclosure of confidential conversations between officers of other branches of government and their advisers about government business.

This need for confidence is not confined to Government officials. The law has long recognized that there are kinds of conversations that are entitled to be kept confidential, even at the cost of doing without critical evidence in a legal proceeding. This rule applies, for example, to conversations between a lawyer and a client, between a priest and a penitent, and between a husband and a wife. In each case it is thought so important that the parties be able to talk freely to each other that for hundreds of years the law has said that these conversations are "privileged" and that their disclosure cannot be compelled in a court.

It is even more important that the confidentiality of conversations between a President and his advisers be protected. This is no mere luxury, to be dispensed with whenever a particular issue raises sufficient uproar. It is absolutely essential to the conduct of the Presidency, in this and in all future Administrations.

If I were to make public these tapes, containing as they do blunt and candid remarks on many different subjects, the confidentiality of the Office of the President would always be suspect from now on. It would make no difference whether it was to serve the interests of a court, of a Senate committee or the President himself — the same damage would be done to the principle, and that damage would be irreparable. Persons talking with the President would never again be sure that recordings or notes of what they said would not suddenly be made public. No one would want to advance tentative ideas that might later seem unsound. No diplomat would want to speak candidly in those sensitive negotiations which could bring peace or avoid war. No Senator or Congressman would want to talk frankly about the Congressional horse-trading that might get a vital bill passed. No one would want to speak bluntly about public figures, here and abroad.

That is why I shall continue to oppose efforts which would set a precedent that would cripple all future Presidents by inhibiting conversations between them and those they look to for advice. This principle of confidentiality of Presidential conversations is at stake in the question of these tapes. I must, and I shall oppose any efforts to destroy this principle, which is so vital to the conduct of this great office.

Turning now to the basic issues which have been raised by Watergate, I recognize that merely answering the charges that have been made against the President is not enough. The word "Watergate" has come to represent a much broader set of concerns.

To most of us, "Watergate" has come to mean not just a burglary and bugging of party headquarters, but a whole series of acts that either represent or appear to represent an abuse of trust. It has come to stand for excessive partianship, for "enemy lists," for efforts to use the great institutions of Government for partisan political purposes.

For many Americans, the term "Watergate" also has come to include a number of national security matters that have been brought into the investigation, such as those involved in my efforts to stop massive leaks of vital diplomatic and military secrets, and to counter the wave of bombings and burnings and other violent assaults of just a few years ago.

Let me speak first of the political abuses.

I know from long experience, that a political campaign is always a hard, and a tough contest. A candidate for high office has an obligation to his party, to his supporters, and to the cause he represents. He must always put forth his best efforts to win. But he also has an obligation to the country to conduct that contest within the law and within the limits of decency.

No political campaign ever justifies obstructing justice, or harassing individuals, or compromising those great agencies of government that should and must be above politics. To the extent that these things were done in the 1972 campaign, they were serious abuses. And I deplore them.

Practices of that kind do not represent what I believe Government should be, or what I believe politics should be. In a free society, the institutions of government belong to the people. They must never be used against the people.

And in the future, my Administration will be more vigilant in ensuring that such abuses do not take place, and that officials at every level understand that they are not to take place.

And I reject the cynical view that politics is inevitably or even usually a dirty business. Let us not allow what a few overzealous people did in Watergate to tar the reputation of the millions of dedicated Americans of both parties who fought hard but clean for the candidates of their choice in 1972. By their unselfish efforts, these people make our system work and they keep America free.

I pledge to you tonight that I will do all that I can to ensure that one of the results of Watergate is a new level of political decency and integrity in America — in which what has been wrong in our politics no longer corrupts or demeans what is right in our politics.

Let me turn now to the difficult questions that arise in protecting the national security.

It is important to recognize that these are difficult questions and that reasonable and patriotic men and women may differ on how they should be answered.

Only last year, the Supreme Court said that implicit in the President's constitutional duty is "the power to protect our Government against those who would subvert or overthrow it by unlawful means." How to carry out this duty is often a delicate question to which there is no easy answer.

For example, every President since World War II has believed that in internal security matters the President has the power to authorize wiretaps without first obtaining a search warrant.

An act of Congress in 1968 had seemed to recognize such power. Last year the Supreme Court held to the contrary. And my Administration is of course now complying with that Supreme Court decision. But until the Supreme Court spoke, I had been acting, as did my predecessors — President Truman, President Eisenhower, President Kennedy, President Johnson — in a reasonable belief that in certain circumstances the Constitution permitted and sometimes even required such measures to protect the national security in the public interest.

Although it is the President's duty to protect the security of the country, we of course must be extremely careful in the way we go about this — for if we lose our liberties we will have little use for security. Instances have now come to light in which a zeal for security did go too far and did interfere impermissibly with individual liberty.

It is essential that such mistakes not be repeated. But it is also essential that we do not overreact to particular mistakes by tying the President's hands in a way that would risk sacrificing our security, and with it our liberties.

I shall continue to meet my constitutional responsibility to protect the security of this nation so that Americans may enjoy their freedom. But I shall and can do so by constitutional means, in ways that will not threaten that freedom.

As we look at Watergate in a longer perspective, we can see that its abuses resulted from the assumption by those involved that their case placed them beyond the reach of those rules that apply to other persons and that hold a free society together.

That attitude can never be tolerated in our country. However, it did not suddenly develop in the year 1972. It became fashionable in the nineteen-sixties, as individuals and groups increasingly asserted the right to take the law into their own hands, insisting that their purposes represented a higher morality. Then, their attitude was praised in the press and even from some of our pulpits as evidence of a new idealism. Those of us who insisted on the old restraints, who warned of the overriding importance of operating within the law and by the rules, were accused of being reactionaries.

That same attitude brought a rising spiral of violence and fear of riots and arson and bombings, all in the name of peace and in the name of justice. Political discussion turned into savage debate. Free speech was brutally supressed as hecklers shouted down or even physically assaulted those with whom they disagreed. Serious people raised serious questions about whether we could survive as a free democracy.

The notion that the end justifies the means proved contagious. Thus it is not surprising, even though it is deplorable, that some persons in 1972 adopted the morality that they themselves had rightly condemned and committed acts that have no place in our political system.

Those acts cannot be defended. Those who were guilty of abuses must be punished. But ultimately the answer does not lie merely in the jailing of a few overzealous persons who mistakenly thought their cause justified their violations of the law.

Rather, it lies in a commitment by all of us to show a renewed respect for the mutual restraints that are the mark of a free and civilized society. It requires that we learn once again to work together, if not united in all of our purposes, then at least united in respect for the system by which our conflicts are peacefully resolved and our liberties maintained.

If there are laws we disagree with, let us work to change them — but let us obey them until they are changed. If we have disagreements over Government policies, let us work those out in a decent and civilized way, within the law, and with respect for our differences.

We must recognize that one excess begets another, and that the extremes of violence and discord in the 1960s contributed to the extremes of Watergate.

Both are wrong. Both should be condemned. No individual, no group and no political party has a corner on the market on morality in America.

If we learn the important lessons of Watergate, if we do what is necessary to prevent such abuses in the future — on both sides — we can emerge from this experience a better and a stronger nation.

Let me turn now to an issue that is important above all else, and that is critically affecting your life today and will affect your life and your children's in the years to come.

After 12 weeks and 2 million words of televised testimony, we have reached a point at which a continued, backward-looking obsession with Watergate is causing this nation to neglect matters of far greater importance to all of the American people.

We must not stay so mired in Watergate that we fail to respond to challenges of surpassing importance to America and the world. We cannot let an obsession with the past destroy our hopes for the future.

Legislation vital to your health and well-being sits unattended on the Congressional calendar. Confidence at home and abroad in our economy, our currency and our foreign policy is being sapped by uncertainty. Critical negotiations are taking place on strategic weapons, on troop levels in Europe that can affect the security of this nation and the peace of the world long after Watergate is forgotten. Vital events are taking place in Southeast Asia which could lead to a tragedy for the cause of peace.

These are matters that cannot wait. They cry out for action now.
And either we, your elected representatives here in Washington
ought to get on with the jobs that need to be done — for you — or
every one of you ought to be demanding to know why.

The time has come to turn Watergate over to the courts, where
the questions of guilt or innocence belong. The time has come for
the rest of us to get on with the urgent business of our nation.

Last November, the American people were given the clearest
choice of this century. Your votes were a mandate, which I accepted,
to complete the initiatives we began in my first term and to fulfill
the promises I made for my second term.

This Administration was elected to control inflation, to reduce the
power and size of government, to cut the cost of government so that
you can cut the cost of living, to preserve and defend those fundamental values that have made America great, to keep the nation's
military strength second to none, to achieve peace with honor in
Southeast Asia and to bring home our prisoners of war, and to build
a new prosperity, without inflation and without war, to create a
structure of peace in the world that would endure long after we are
gone.

These are great goals. They are worthy of a great people. And I
would not be true to your trust if I let myself be turned aside from
achieving those goals.

If you share my belief in these goals — if you want the mandate
you gave this Administration to be carried out — then I ask for your
help to insure that those who would exploit Watergate in order to
keep us from doing what we were elected to do will not succeed.

I ask tonight for your understanding, so that as a nation we can
learn the lessons of Watergate, and gain from that experience.

I ask for your help in reaffirming our dedication to the principles
of decency, honor and respect for the institutions that have sustained
our progress through these past two centuries.

And I ask for your support, in getting on once again with meeting
your problems, improving your life and building your future.

With your help, with God's help, we will achieve these great
goals for America.

State Of The Union Address

1974

By RICHARD M. NIXON, *President of the United States*

Delivered before Congress, Washington, D. C., January 30, 1974

MR. SPEAKER, Mr. President, my colleagues in the Congress, our distinguished guests, my fellow Americans. We meet here tonight at a time of great challenge and great opportunities for America. We meet at a time when we face great problems at home and abroad that will test the strength of our fiber as a nation.

But we also meet at a time when that fiber has been tested and it has proved strong.

America is a great and good land. And we are a great and good land because we are a strong, free, creative people. And because America is the single greatest force for peace anywhere in the world.

Today, as always in our history, we can base our confidence in what the American people will achieve in the future on the record of what the American people have achieved in the past.

Tonight, for the first time in 12 years a President of the United States can report to the Congress on the state of a union at peace with every nation of the world.

Because of this, in the 22,000-word message on the State of the Union that I have just handed to the Speaker of the House and the President of the Senate, I have been able to deal primarily with the problems of peace.

With what we can do here at home in America for the American people, rather than with the problems of war.

The measures I have outlined in this message set an agenda for truly significant progress for this nation and the world in 1974.

Before we chart where we are going let us see how far we have come. It was five years ago on the steps of this Capitol that I took the oath of office as your President. In those five years because of the initiatives undertaken by this Administration the world has changed, America has changed. As a result of those changes America is safer today, more prosperous today with greater opportunities for more of its people than ever before in our history.

Five years ago, America was at war in Southeast Asia, we were locked in confrontation with the Soviet Union, we were in hostile isolation from a quarter of the world's people who lived in mainland China. Five years ago our cities were burning and besieged. Five

Source: Vital Speeches of the Day, February 15, 1974;
          City News Publishing Company, Southold, New
          York. By permission of the publisher.

years ago our college campuses were a battleground. Five years ago crime was increasing at a rate that struck fear across the nation. Five years ago the spiraling rise in drug addiction was threatening human and social tragedy of massive proportion, and there was no program to deal with it.

Five years ago as young Americans had done for a generation before that, America's youth still lived under the shadow of the military draft.

Five years ago there was no national program to preserve our environment. Day by day our air was getting dirtier our water was getting more foul. And five years ago, American agriculture was practically a depressed industry with 100,000 farm families abandoning the farm every year.

As we look at America today, we find ourselves challenged by new problems. But we also find a record of progress to confound the professional criers of doom and prophets of despair.

We met the challenges we faced five years ago, and we will be equally confident of meeting those that we face today.

Let us see for a moment how we have met them. After more than 10 years of military involvement, all of our troops have returned from Southeast Asia, and they have returned with honor.

And we can be proud of the fact that our courageous prisoners of war, for whom a dinner was held in Washington tonight, that they came home with their heads high, on their feet and not on their knees.

In our relations with the Soviet Union, we have turned away from a policy of confrontation to one of negotiation. For the first time since World War II, the world's two strongest powers are working together toward peace in the world.

With the People's Republic of China after a generation of hostile isolation, we have begun a period of peaceful exchange and expanding trade.

Peace has returned to our cities, to our campuses. The 17-year rise in crime has been stopped. We can confidently say today that we are finally beginning to win the war against crime.

Right here in this nation's capital, which a few years ago was threatening to become the crime capital of the world, the rate in crime has been cut in half.

A massive campaign against drug abuse has been organized, and the rate of new heroin addiction, the most vicious threat of all, is decreasing rather than increasing.

For the first time in a generation, no young Americans are being drafted into the armed services of the United States.

And for the first time ever we have organized a massive national effort to protect the environment. Our air is getting cleaner, our water is getting purer, and our agriculture, which was depressed, is prospering.

Farm income is up 70 per cent. Farm production is setting all-time records, and the billions of dollars the taxpayers were paying in subsidies has been cut to nearly zero.

Over all, Americans are living more abundantly than ever before, today. More than 2.5 million new jobs were created in the past year alone. That is the biggest percentage increase in nearly 20 years.

People are earning more. What they earn buys more, more than ever before in history.

In the past five years the average American's real spendable income — that is what you really can buy with your income, even after allowing for taxes and inflation — has increased by 16 per cent.

Despite this record of achievement, as we turn to the year ahead, we hear once again the familiar voice of the perennial prophets of gloom telling us now that because of the need to fight inflation, because of the energy shortage, America may be headed for a recession.

Well, let me speak to that issue head on. There will be no recession in the United States of America.

Primarily due to our energy crisis our economy is passing through a difficult period, but I pledge to you tonight that the full powers of this Government will be used to keep America's economy producing and to protect the jobs of America's workers.

We are engaged in a long and hard fight against inflation. There have been and there will be in the future ups and downs in that fight. But if this Congress cooperates in our efforts to hold down the cost of Government, we shall win our fight to hold down the cost of living for the American people.

As we look back over our history, the years that stand out as the ones who signal achievement are those in which the Administration and the Congress — whether of one party or the other — working together, had the wisdom and the foresight to select those particular initiatives for which the nation was ready and the moment was right, and in which they seized the moment and acted.

Looking at the year 1974 which lies before us there are 10 key areas in which landmark accomplishments are possible this year in America.

If we make these our national agenda, this is what we will achieve in 1974:

We will break the back of the energy crisis.

We will lay the foundation for our future capacity to meet America's energy needs from America's own resources.

And we will take another giant stride toward lasting peace in the world, not only by continuing our policy of negotiation rather than confrontation where the great powers are concerned, but also by helping toward the achievement of a just and lasting settlement in the Middle East.

We will check the rise in prices without administering the harsh medicine of recession, and we will move the economy into a steady period of growth at a sustainable level.

We will establish a new system that makes high quality health care available to every American in a dignified manner and at a price he can afford.

We will make our states and localities more responsive to the needs of their own citizens. We will make a crucial breakthrough toward better transportation in our towns and in our cities across America. We will reform our systems of Federal aid to education to provide it when it is needed, where it is needed, so that it will do the most for those who need it the most.

We will make an historic beginning on the task of defining and protecting the right of personal privacy for every American.

And we will start on a new road toward reform of a welfare system that bleeds the taxpayer, corrodes the community and demeans those it is intended to assist.

And together with the other nations of the world, we will establish the economic framework within which Americans will share more fully in an expanding world-wide trade and prosperity in the years ahead, with more open access to both markets and supplies.

In all of the 186 State of the Union messages delivered from this place in our history, this is the first in which the one priority, the first priority, is energy.

Let me begin by reporting a new development which I know will be welcome news to every American. As you know, we have committed ourselves to an active role in helping to achieve a just and durable peace in the Middle East on the basis of full implementation of Security Council Resolutions 242 and 338. The first step in the process is the disengagement of Egyptian and Israel forces, which is now taking place.

Because of this hopeful development, I can announce tonight that I have been assured through my personal contacts with friendly leaders in the Middle Eastern area that an urgent meeting will be called in the immediate future to discuss the lifting of the oil embargo.

Now this — this is an encouraging sign. However, it should be clearly understood by our friends in the Middle East that the United States will not be coerced on this issue.

Regardless of the outcome of this meeting, the cooperation of the American people in our energy conservation program has already gone a long way toward achieving a goal to which I am deeply dedicated.

Let us do everything we can to avoid gasoline rationing in the United States of America.

Last week I sent to the Congress the comprehensive special message setting forth our energy situation recommending the legislative measures which are necessary to a program for meeting our needs. If the embargo is lifted, this will ease the crisis. But it will not mean an end to the energy shortage in America.

Voluntary conservation will continue to be necessary. And let me take this occasion to pay tribute once again to the splendid spirit of cooperation the American people have shown which has made possible our success in meeting this emergency up to this time.

The new legislation I have requested will also remain necessary. Therefore, I urge again that the energy measures that I have proposed be made the first priority of this session of the Congress.

These measures will require the oil companies and other energy producers to provide the public with the necessary information on their supplies. They will prevent the injustice of windfall profits for a few as a result of the sacrifices of the millions of Americans.

And they will give us the organization, the incentives, the authorities needed to deal with the short-term emergency and the move toward meeting our long-term needs.

Just as 1970 was the year in which we began a full-scale effort to protect the environment, 1974 must be the year in which we organize a full-scale effort to provide for our energy needs not only in this decade but through the 21st century.

As we move toward the celebration two years from now of the 200th anniversary of this nation's independence let us press vigorously on toward the goal that I announced last November for Project Independence.

Let this be our national goal. At the end of this decade, in the year 1980, the United States will not be dependent on any other country for the energy we need to provide our jobs, to heat our homes and to keep our transportation moving.

To indicate the size of the government commitment to spur energy research and development, we plan to spend $10-billion in Federal funds over the next five years. That is an enormous amount. But during the same five years, private enterprise will be investing as much as $200-billion, and in 10 years $500-billion to develop the new resources, the new technology, the new capacity America will require for its energy needs in the 1980's.

That's just a measure of the magnitude of the project we are undertaking. But America performs best when called to its biggest tasks. It can truly be said that only in America could a task so tremendous be achieved so quickly, and achieved not by regimentation but through the effort and ingenuity of a free people working in a free system.

Turning now to the rest of the agenda for 1974, the time is at hand this year to bring comprehensive high-quality health care within the reach of every American. I shall propose a sweeping new program that will assure comprehensive health insurance protection to millions of Americans who cannot now obtain it or afford it with vastly improved protection against catastrophic illnesses. This will be a plan that maintains the high standards of quality in America's health care and it will not require additional taxes.

Now I recognize that other plans have been put forward that would cost $80-billion and that would put our whole health care system under the heavy hand of the Federal Government.

This is the wrong approach. This has been tried abroad, and it's failed. It is not the way we do things here in America.

This kind of plan would threaten the quality of care provided by our whole health care system.

The right way is one that builds on the strengths of the present system and one that does not destroy those strengths.

One based on partnership not paternalism. Most important of all, let us keep this as the guiding principle of our health programs:

Government has a great role to play, but we must always make sure that our doctors will be working for their patients and not for the Federal Government.

Many of you will recall that in my State of the Union address three years ago I commented that most Americans today are simply fed up with government at all levels, and I recommended a sweeping set of proposals to revitalize state and local government, to make them more responsive to the people they serve.

I can report to you today that as a result of revenue sharing, passed by the Congress, and other measures, we have made progress toward that goal. After 40 years of moving power from the states and the communities to Washington, D.C., we have begun moving power back from Washington to the states and communities, and, most important, to the people of America.

In this session of the Congress, I believe we are near the breakthrough point on efforts which I have suggested, proposals to let people themselves make their own decisions for their own communities, and, in particular, on those to provide broad new flexibility in Federal aid for community development, for economic development, for education.

And I look forward to working with the Congress, with members of both parties, in resolving whatever remaining differences we have in this legislation so that we can make available nearly $5.5-billion to our states and localities to use not for what a Federal bureaucrat may want but for what their own people in those communities want. The decision should be theirs.

I think all of us recognize that the energy crisis has given new urgency to the need to improve public transportation, not only in our cities but in rural areas as well.

The program I have proposed this year will give communities not only more money but also more freedom to balance their own transportation needs.

It will mark the strongest Federal commitment ever to the improvement of mass transit as an essential element of the improvement of life in our towns and cities.

One goal on which all Americans agree is that our children should have the very best education this great nation can provide. In a special message last week, I recommended a number of important new measures that can make 1974 a year of truly significant advances for our schools and for the children they serve.

If the Congress will act on these proposals, more flexible funding will enable each Federal dollar to meet better the particular need of each particular school district. Advance funding will give school authorities a chance to make each year's plans knowing ahead of time what Federal funds they are going to receive. Special targeting will give special help to the truly disadvantaged among our people.

College students faced with rising costs for their education will be able to draw on an expanded program of loans and grants. These advances are a needed investment in America's most precious resource — our next generation. And I urge the Congress to act on this legislation in 1974.

One measure of a truly free society is the vigor with which it protects the liberties of its individual citizens. As technology has advanced in America, it has increasingly encroached on one of those liberties what I term the right of personal privacy. Modern information systems, data banks, credit records, mailing list abuses, electronic snooping, the collection of personal data for one purpose that may be used for another — all these have left millions of Americans deeply concerned for the privacy they cherish.

And the time has come, therefore, for a major initiative to define the nature and extent of the basic rights of privacy and to erect new safeguards to insure that those rights are respected.

I shall launch such an effort this year at the highest levels of the Administration, and I look forward again to working with this Congress and establishing a new set of standards that respect the legitimate needs of society but that also recognize personal privacy as a cardinal principle of American liberty.

Many of those in this chamber tonight will recall that it was three years ago that I termed the nation's welfare system a monstrous consuming outrage, an outrage against the community, against the taxpayer, and particularly against the children that it is supposed to help. That system is still an outrage. By improving its administration we have been able to reduce some of the abuses.

As a result, last year for the first time in 18 years there has been a halt in the growth of the welfare caseload. But as a system, our welfare program still needs reform as urgently today as it did when I first proposed in 1969 that we completely replace it with a different system.

In these final three years of my Administration, I urge the Congress to join me in mounting a major new effort to replace the discredited present welfare system with one that works, one that is fair to those who need help or cannot help themselves, fair to the community and fair to the taxpayer.

And let us have as our goal that there will be no Government program which makes it more profitable to go on welfare than to go to work.

I recognize that from the debates that have taken place within the Congress over the past three years on this program that we cannot expect enactment overnight of a new reform. But I do propose that the Congress and the Administration together make this the year in which we discuss, debate and shape such a reform so that it can be enacted as quickly as possible.

America's own prosperity in the years ahead depends on our sharing fully and equitably in an expanding world prosperity. Historic negotiations will take place this year that will enable us to insure fair treatment in international markets for American workers, American farmers, American investors and American consumers.

It is vital that the authorities contained in the trade bill I submitted to Congress be enacted, so that the United States can negotiate flexibly and vigorously on behalf of American interests. These negotiations can usher in a new era of international trade that not only increases the prosperity of all nations but also strengthens the peace among all nations.

In the past five years we have made more progress toward a lasting structure of peace in the world than in any comparable time in the nation's history.

We could not have made that progress if we had not maintained the military strength of America. Thomas Jefferson once observed that the price of liberty is eternal vigilence. By the same token and for the same reason in today's world, the price of peace is a strong defense as far as the United States is concerned.

In the past five years we have steadily reduced the burden of national defense as a share of the budget, bringing it down 44 per cent in 1969 to 29 per cent in the current year.

We have cut our military manpower over the past five years, by more than a third, from three and a half million to 2.2 million.

In the coming year, however, increased expenditures will be needed. They will be needed to assure the continued readiness of our military forces, to preserve present force levels in the face of rising costs and to give us the military strength we must have if our security is to be maintained and if our initiatives for peace are to succeed.

The question is not whether we can afford to maintain the necessary strength of our defense; the question is whether we can afford not to maintain it, and the answer to that question is no. We must never allow America to become the second strongest nation in the world.

I do not say this with any sense of belligerence, because I recognize a fact that is recognized around the world: America's military strength has always been maintained to keep the peace — never to break it. It has always been used to defend freedom, never to destroy it. The world's peace, as well as our own, depends on our remaining as strong as we need to be, as long as we need to be.

In this year, 1974, we will be negotiating with the Soviet Union to place further limits on strategic nuclear arms. Together with our allies we will be negotiating with the nations of the Warsaw Pact on mutual and balanced reduction of forces in Europe. And we will continue our efforts to promote peaceful economic development in Latin America, in Africa, in Asia. We will press for full compliance with the peace accords that brought an end to American fighting in Indochina, including particularly a provision that promised the fullest possible accounting for those Americans who are missing in action.

And having in mind the energy crisis to which I have referred earlier we will be working with the other nations of the world toward agreement on means by which oil supplies can be assured at reasonable prices on a stable basis and a fair way to the consuming and producing nations alike.

All of these are steps toward a future in which the world's peace and prosperity, and ours as well as a result, are made more secure.

Throughout the five years that I have served as your President I have had one overriding aim, and that was to establish a new structure of peace in the world that can free future generations of the scourge of war. I can understand that others may have different priorities. This has been and this will remain my first priority and the chief legacy I hope to leave from the eight years of my Presidency.

This does not mean that we shall not have other priorities because as we strengthen the peace we must also continue each year a steady strengthening of our society here at home.

Our conscience requires it. Our interests require it. And we must insist upon it.

As we create more jobs, as we build a better health care system, as we improve our education, as we develop new sources of energy, as we provide more abundantly for the elderly and the poor, as we strengthen the system of private enterprise that produces our prosperity, as we do all of this and even more, we solidify those essential bonds that hold us together as a nation.

Even more importantly, we advanced in what the final analysis Government in America is all about. What it is all about is more freedom, more security, a better life for each one of the 211-million people that live in this land.

We cannot afford to neglect progress at home while pursuing peace abroad, but neither can we afford to neglect peace abroad while pursuing progress at home. With a stable peace all is possible, but without peace nothing is possible.

In the written message that I have just delivered to the Speaker and to the President of the Senate, I commented that one of the continuing challenges facing us in the legislative process is that of the timing and pacing of our initiatives, selecting each year among many worthy projects those that are right for action at that time. What is true in terms of our domestic initiatives is true also in the world.

This period we now are in in the world, and I say this as one who has seen so much of the world not only in these past five years but going back over many years. We are in a period which presents a juncture of historic forces unique in this century. They provide an opportunity we may never have again to create a structure of peace solid enough to last a lifetime and more. Not just peace in our time, but peace in our children's time as well.

It is on the way we respond to this opportunity more than anything else that history will judge whether we in America have met our responsibility, and I am confident we will meet that great historic responsibility which is ours today.

It was 27 years ago that John F. Kennedy and I sat in this chamber as freshmen Congressmen, hearing our first State of the Union Address delivered by Harry Truman.

I know from my talks with him as members of the Labor Committee on which we both served, neither of us then even dreamed that either one or both might eventually be standing in this place that I now stand in now and that he once stood in before me.

It may well be that one of the freshmen members of the 93d Congress, one of you out there will deliver his own State of the Union Message 27 years from now in ,the year 2001. Well, whichever one it is, I want you to be able to look back with pride and to say that your first years here were great years and to recall that you were here in this 93d Congress when America ended its longest war and began its longest peace.

Mr. Speaker, and Mr. President and my distinguished colleagues and our guests, I would like to add a personal word with regard to an issue that has been of great concern to all Americans over the past year.

I refer, of course, to the investigations of the so-called Watergate affair.

As you know, I have provided to the special prosecutor voluntarily a great deal of material.

I believe that I have provided all the material that he needs to conclude his investigations and to proceed to prosecute the guilty and to clear the innocent.

I believe the time has come to bring that investigation and the other investigations of this matter to an end. One year of Watergate is enough.

And the time has come, my colleagues, for not only the executive, the President, but the members of Congress, for all of us to join together in devoting our full energies to these great issues that I have discussed tonight which involve the welfare of all the American people in so many different ways as well as the peace of the world.

I recognize that the House Judiciary Committee has a special responsibility in this area, and I want to indicate on this occasion that I will cooperate with the Judiciary Committee in its investigation.

I will cooperate so that it can conclude its investigation, make its decision and I will cooperate in any way that I consider consistent with my responsibilities for the office of the Presidency of the United States.

There is only one limitation: I will follow the precedent that has been followed by and defended by every President from George Washington to Lyndon B. Johnson of never doing anything that weakens the office of the President of the United States or impairs the ability of the President of the future to make the great decisions that are so essential to this nation and the world.

Another point I should like to make very briefly. Like every member of the House and Senate assembled here tonight, I was elected to the office that I hold. And like every member of the House and Senate, when I was elected to that office I knew that I was elected for the purpose of doing a job, and doing it as well as I possibly can.

And I want you to know that I have no intention whatever of ever walking away from the job that the people elected me to do for the people of the United States!

Now needless to say, it would be an understatement if I were not to admit that the year 1973 was not a very easy year for me personally or for my family. And as I've already indicated, the year 1974 presents very great and serious problems as very great and serious opportunities are also presented.

But my colleagues, this I believe: With the help of God who has blessed this land so richly, with the cooperation of the Congress and with the support of the American people, we can and we will make the year 1974 a year of unprecedented progress toward our goal, of building a structure of lasting peace in the world and a new prosperity without war in the United States of America.

Presidential Tapes And Materials

THE PRESIDENT AND WATERGATE

By RICHARD M. NIXON, *President of the United States*

The President's Answer to the Subpoena from the House Judiciary Committee, delivered over National Television, April 29, 1974

GOOD EVENING: I have asked for this time tonight in order to announce my answer to the House Judiciary Committee's subpoena for additional Watergate tapes, and to tell you something about the actions I shall be taking tomorrow — about what I hope they will mean to you and about the very difficult choices that were presented to me.

These actions will at last, once and for all, show that what I knew and what I did with regard to the Watergate break-in and coverup were just as I have described them to you from the very beginning.

I have spent many hours during the past few weeks thinking about what I would say to the American people if I were to reach the decision I shall announce tonight. And so, my words have not been lightly chosen; I can assure you they are deeply felt.

It was almost 2 years ago, in June 1972, that five men broke into the Democratic National Committee headquarters in Washington. It turned out that they were connected with my reelection committee, and the Watergate break-in became a major issue in the campaign.

The full resources of the FBI and the Justice Department were used to investigate the incident thoroughly. I instructed my staff and campaign aides to cooperate fully with the investigation. The FBI conducted nearly 1,500 interviews. For 9 months — until March 1973 — I was assured by those charged with conducting and monitoring the investigations that no one in the White House was involved.

Nevertheless, for more than a year, there have been allegations and insinuations that I knew about the planning of the Watergate break-in and that I was involved in an extensive plot to cover it up. The House Judiciary Committee is now investigating these charges.

On March 6, I ordered all materials that I had previously furnished to the Special Prosecutor turned over to the committee. These included tape recordings of 19 Presidential conversations and more than 700 documents from private White House files.

On April 11, the Judiciary Committee issued a subpoena for 42 additional tapes of conversations which it contended were necessary

Source: Vital Speeches of the Day, June 1, 1974;
         City News Publishing Company, Southold, New
         York. By permission of the publisher.

for its investigation. I agreed to respond to that subpoena by tomorrow.

In these folders that you see over here on my left are more than 1,200 pages of transcripts of private conversations I participated in between September 15, 1972, and April 27 of 1973, with my principal aides and associates with regard to Watergate. They include all the relevant portions of all of the subpoenaed conversations that were recorded, that is, all portions that relate to the question of what I knew about Watergate or the coverup and what I did about it.

They also include transcripts of other conversations which were not subpoenaed, but which have a significant bearing on the question of Presidential actions with regard to Watergate. These will be delivered to the committee tomorrow.

In these transcripts, portions not relevant to my knowledge or actions with regard to Watergate are not included, but everything that is relevant is included — the rough as well as the smooth, the strategy sessions, the exploration of alternatives, the weighing of human and political costs.

As far as what the President personally knew and did with regard to Watergate and the coverup is concerned, these materials — together with those already made available — will tell it all.

I shall invite Chairman Rodino and the committee's ranking minority member, Congressman Hutchinson of Michigan, to come to the White House and listen to the actual, full tapes of these conversations, so that they can determine for themselves beyond question that the transcripts are accurate and that everything on the tapes relevant to my knowledge and my actions on Watergate is included. If there should be any disagreement over whether omitted material is relevant, I shall meet with them personally in an effort to settle the matter. I believe this arrangement is fair, and I think it is appropriate.

For many days now, I have spent many hours of my own time personally reviewing these materials, and personally deciding questions of relevancy. I believe it is appropriate that the committee's review should also be made by its own senior elected officials, and not by staff employees.

The task of Chairman Rodino and Congressman Hutchinson will be made simpler than was mine by the fact that the work of preparing the transcripts has been completed. All they will need to do is to satisfy themselves of their authenticity and their completeness.

Ever since the existence of the White House taping system was first made known last summer, I have tried vigorously to guard the privacy of the tapes. I have been well aware that my effort to protect the confidentiality of Presidential conversations has heightened the sense of mystery about Watergate and, in fact, has caused increased suspicions of the President. Many people assume that the tapes must incriminate the President, or that otherwise, he would not insist on their privacy.

But the problem I confronted was this: Unless a President can protect the privacy of the advice he gets, he cannot get the advice he needs.

This principle is recognized in the constitutional doctrine of executive privilege, which has been defended and maintained by every President since Washington and which has been recognized by the courts whenever tested as inherent in the Presidency. I consider it to be my constitutional responsibility to defend this principle.

Three factors have now combined to persuade me that a major unprecedented exception to that principle is now necessary.

First, in the present circumstances, the House of Representatives must be able to reach an informed judgment about the President's role in Watergate.

Second, I am making a major exception to the principle of confidentiality because I believe such action is now necessary in order to restore the principle itself, by clearing the air of the central question that has brought such pressures upon it — and also to provide the evidence which will allow this matter to be brought to a prompt conclusion.

Third, in the context of the current impeachment climate, I believe all the American people, as well as their Representatives in Congress, are entitled to have not only the facts but also the evidence that demonstrates those facts.

I want there to be no question remaining about the fact that the President has nothing to hide in this matter.

The impeachment of a President is a remedy of last resort; it is the most solemn act of our entire constitutional process. Now, regardless of whether or not it succeeded, the action of the House in voting a formal accusation requiring trial by the Senate would put the Nation through a wrenching ordeal it has endured only once in its lifetime, a century ago, and never since America nas become a world power with global responsibilities.

The impact of such an ordeal would be felt throughout the world, and it would have its effect on the lives of all Americans for many years to come.

Because this is an issue that profoundly affects all the American people, in addition to turning over these transcripts to the House Judiciary Committee, I have directed that they should all be made public — all of these that you see here.

To complete the record, I shall also release to the public transcripts of all those portions of the tapes already turned over to the Special Prosecutor and to the committee that relate to Presidential actions or knowledge of the Watergate affair.

During the past year, the wildest accusations have been given banner headlines and ready credence, as well. Rumor, gossip, innuendo, accounts from unnamed sources of what a prospective witness might testify to have filled the morning newspapers and then are repeated on the evening newscasts day after day.

Time and again, a familiar pattern repeated itself. A charge would be reported the first day as what it was — just an allegation. But it would then be referred back to the next day and thereafter as if it were true.

The distinction between fact and speculation grew blurred. Eventually, all seeped into the public consciousness as a vague general impression of massive wrongdoing, implicating everybody, gaining credibility by its endless repetition.

The basic question at issue today is whether the President personally acted improperly in the Watergate matter. Month after month of rumor, insinuation, and charges by just one Watergate witness — John Dean — suggested that the President did act improperly.

This sparked the demands for an impeachment inquiry. This is the question that must be answered. And this is the question that will be answered by these transcripts that I have ordered published tomorrow.

These transcripts cover hour upon hour of discussions that I held with Mr. Haldeman, John Ehrlichman, John Dean, John Mitchell, former Attorney General Kleindienst, Assistant Attorney General Petersen, and others with regard to Watergate.

They were discussions in which I was probing to find out what had happened, who was responsible, what were the various degrees of responsibilities, what were the legal culpabilities, what were the political ramifications, and what actions were necessary and appropriate on the part of the President.

I realize the transcripts will provide grist for many sensational stories in the press. Parts will seem to be contradictory with one another, and parts will be in conflict with some of the testimony given in the Senate Watergate committee hearings.

I have been reluctant to release these tapes not just because they will embarrass me and those with whom I have talked — which they will — and not just because they will become the subject of speculation and even ridicule — which they will — and not just because certain parts of them will be seized upon by political and journalistic opponents — which they will.

I have been reluctant because in these and in all the other conversations in this office, people have spoken their minds freely, never dreaming that specific sentences or even parts of sentences would be picked out as the subjects of national attention and controversy.

I have been reluctant because the principle of confidentiality is absolutely essential to the conduct of the Presidency. In reading the raw transcripts of these conversations, I believe it will be more readily apparent why that principle is essential and must be maintained in the future. These conversations are unusual in their subject matter, but the same kind of uninhibited discussion — and it is that — the same brutal candor, is necessary in discussing how to bring warring factions to the peace table or how to move necessary legislation through the Congress.

Names are named in these transcripts. Therefore, it is important to remember that much that appears in them is no more than hearsay or speculation, exchanged as I was trying to find out what really had happened, while my principal aides were reporting to me on rumors and reports that they had heard, while we discussed the various, often conflicting stories that different persons were telling.

As the transcripts will demonstrate, my concerns during this period covered a wide range. The first and obvious one was to find out just exactly what had happened and who was involved.

A second concern was for the people who had been, or might become, involved in Watergate. Some were close advisers, valued friends, others whom I had trusted. And I was also concerned about the human impact on others, especially some of the young people and their families who had come to Washington to work in my Administration, whose lives might be suddenly ruined by something they had done in an excess of loyalty or in the mistaken belief that it would serve the interests of, the President.

And then I was quite frankly concerned about the political implications. This represented potentially a devastating blow to the Administration and to its programs, one which I knew would be exploited for all it was worth by hostile elements in the Congress as well as in the media. I wanted to do what was right, but I wanted to do it in a way that would cause the least unnecessary damage in a highly charged political atmosphere to the Administration.

And fourth, as a lawyer, I felt very strongly that I had to conduct myself in a way that would not prejudice the rights of potential defendants.

And fifth, I was striving to sort out a complex tangle, not only of facts but also questions of legal and moral responsibility. I wanted, above all, to be fair. I wanted to draw distinctions, where those were appropriate, between persons who were active and willing participants on the one hand, and on the other, those who might have gotten inadvertently caught up in the web and be technically indictable but morally innocent.

Despite the confusions and contradictions, what does come through clearly is this:

John Dean charged in sworn Senate testimony that I was "fully aware of the coverup" at the time of our first meeting on September 15, 1972. These transcripts show clearly that I first learned of it when Mr. Dean himself told me about it in this office on March 21 — some 6 months later.

Incidentally, these transcripts — covering hours upon hours of conversations — should place in somewhat better perspective the controversy over the 18½ minute gap in the tape of a conversation I had with Mr. Haldeman back in June of 1972.

Now, how it was caused is still a mystery to me and I think to many of the experts, as well. But I am absolutely certain, however, of one thing: that it was not caused intentionally by my secretary, Rose Mary Woods, or any of my White House assistants. And certainly if the theory were true that during those 18½ minutes Mr. Haldeman and I cooked up some sort of a Watergate coverup scheme, as so many have been quick to surmise, it hardly seems likely that in all of our subsequent conversations — many of them are here — which neither of us ever expected would see the light of day, there is nothing remotely indicating such a scheme; indeed, quite the contrary.

From the beginning, I have said that in many places on the tapes there were ambiguities — statements and comments that different people with different perspectives might interpret in drastically different ways — but although the words may be ambiguous, though the discussions may have explored many alternatives, the record of my actions is totally clear now, and I still believe it was totally correct then.

A prime example is one of the most controversial discussions, that with Mr. Dean on March 21 — the one in which he first told me of the coverup, with Mr. Haldeman joining us midway through the conversation.

His revelations to me on March 21 were a sharp surprise, even though the report he gave to me was far from complete, especially since he did not reveal at that time the extent of his own criminal involvement.

I was particularly concerned by his report that one of the Watergate defendants, Howard Hunt, was threatening blackmail unless he and his lawyer were immediately given $120,000 for legal fees and family support, and that he was attempting to blackmail the White House, not by threatening exposure on the Watergate matter, but by threatening to reveal activities that would expose extremely sensitive, highly secret national security matters that he had worked on before Watergate.

I probed, questioned, tried to learn all Mr. Dean knew about who was involved, what was involved. I asked more than 150 questions of Mr. Dean in the course of that conversation.

He said to me, and I quote from the transcripts directly: "I can just tell from our conversation that these are things that you have no knowledge of."

It was only considerably later that I learned how much there was that he did not tell me then — for example, that he himself had authorized promises of clemency, that he had personally handled money for the Watergate defendants, and that he had suborned perjury of a witness.

I knew that I needed more facts. I knew that I needed the judgments of more people. I knew the facts about the Watergate coverup would have to be made public, but I had to find out more about what they were before I could decide how they could best be made public.

I returned several times to the immediate problem posed by Mr. Hunt's blackmail threat, which to me was not a Watergate problem, but one which I regarded, rightly or wrongly, as a potential national security problem of very serious proportions. I considered long and hard whether it might in fact be better to let the payment go forward, at least temporarily, in the hope that this national security matter would not be exposed in the course of uncovering the Watergate coverup.

I believed then, and I believe today, that I had a responsibility as President to consider every option, including this one, where production of sensitive national security matters was at issue — protection of such matters. In the course of considering it and of "just thinking out loud," as I put it at one point, I several times suggested that meeting Hunt's demands might be necessary.

But then I also traced through where that would lead. The money could be raised. But money demands would lead inescapably to clemency demands, and clemency could not be granted. I said, and I quote directly from the tape: "It is wrong, that's for sure." I pointed out, and I quote again from the tape: "But in the end we are going to be bled to death. And in the end it is all going to come out anyway. Then you get the worst of both worlds. We are going to lose, and people are going to — "

And Mr. Haldeman interrupts me and says: "And look like dopes!"

And I responded, "And in effect look like a coverup. So that we cannot do."

Now I recognize that this tape of March 21 is one which different meanings could be read in by different people. But by the end of the meeting, as the tape shows, my decision was to convene a new grand jury and to send everyone before the grand jury with instructions to testify.

Whatever the potential for misinterpretation there may be as a result of the different options that were discussed at different times during the meeting, my conclusion at the end of the meeting was clear. And my actions and reactions as demonstrated on the tapes that follow that date show clearly that I did not intend the further payment to Hunt or anyone else be made. These are some of the actions that I took in the weeks that followed in my effort to find the truth, to carry out my responsibilities to enforce the law.

As a tape of our meeting on March 22, the next day, indicates, I directed Mr. Dean to go to Camp David with instructions to put together a written report. I learned 5 days later, on March 26, that he was unable to complete it. And so on March 27 I assigned John Ehrlichman to try to find out what had happened, who was at fault, and in what ways and to what degree.

One of the transcripts I am making public is a call that Mr. Ehrlichman made to the Attorney General on March 28, in which he asked the Attorney General to report to me, the President, directly, any information he might find indicating possible involvement of John Mitchell or by anyone in the White House. I had Mr. Haldeman separately pursue other, independent lines of inquiry.

Throughout, I was trying to reach determinations on matters of both substance and procedure on what the facts were and what was the best way to move the case forward. I concluded that I wanted everyone to go before the grand jury and testify freely and fully. This decision, as you will recall, was publicly announced on March 30, 1973. I waived executive privilege in order to permit everybody to testify. I specifically waived executive privilege with regard to conversations with the President, and I waived the attorney-client privilege with John Dean in order to permit him to testify fully and, I hope, truthfully.

Finally, on April 14 — 3 weeks after I learned of the coverup from Mr. Dean — Mr. Ehrlichman reported to me on the results of his investigation. As he acknowledged, much of what he had gathered was hearsay, but he had gathered enough to make it clear that the next step was to make his findings completely available to the Attorney General, which I instructed him to do.

And the next day, Sunday, April 15, Attorney General Klein-dienst asked to see me, and he reported new information which had come to his attention on this matter. And although he was in no way whatever involved in Watergate, because of his close personal ties, not only to John Mitchell but to other potential people who might be involved, he quite properly removed himself from the case.

We agreed that Assistant Attorney General Henry Petersen, the head of the Criminal Division, a Democrat and career prosecutor, should be placed in complete charge of the investigation.

Later that day I met with Mr. Petersen. I continued to meet with him, to talk with him, to consult with him, to offer him the full cooperation of the White House, as you will see from these transcripts, even to the point of retaining John Dean on the White House Staff for an extra 2 weeks after he admitted his criminal involvement because Mr. Petersen thought that would make it easier for the prosecutor to get his cooperation in breaking the case if it should become necessary to grant Mr. Dean's demand for immunity.

On April 15, when I heard that one of the obstacles to breaking the case was Gordon Liddy's refusal to talk, I telephoned Mr. Petersen and directed that he should make clear not only to Mr. Liddy but to everyone that — and now I quote directly from the tape of that telephone call — "As far as the President is concerned, everybody in this case is to talk and to tell the truth." I told him if necessary I would personally meet with Mr. Liddy's lawyer to assure him that I wanted Liddy to talk and to tell the truth.

From the time Mr. Petersen took charge, the case was solidly within the criminal justice system, pursued personally by the Nation's top professional prosecutor with the active, personal assistance of the President of the United States.

I made clear there was to be no coverup.

Let me quote just a few lines from the transcripts — you can read them to verify them — so that you can hear for yourself the orders I was giving in this period.

Speaking to Haldeman and Ehrlichman, I said: " ... It is ridiculous to talk about clemency. They all knew that."

Speaking to Ehrlichman, I said: "We all have to do the right thing ... We just cannot have this kind of a business ... "

Speaking to Haldeman and Ehrlichman, I said: "The boil had to be pricked ... We have to prick the boil and take the heat. Now that's what we are doing here."

Speaking to Henry Petersen, I said: "I want you to be sure to understand that you know we are going to get to the bottom of this thing."

Speaking to John Dean, I said: "Tell the truth. That is the thing I have told everybody around here."

And then speaking to Haldeman: "And you tell Magruder, now Jeb, this evidence is coming in, you ought to go to the grand jury. Purge yourself if you're perjured and tell this whole story."

I am confident that the American people will see these transcripts for what they are, fragmentary records from a time more than a year ago that now seems very distant, the records of a President and of a man suddenly being confronted and having to cope with information which, if true, would have the most far-reaching consequences not only for his personal reputation but, more important, for his hopes, his plans, his goals for the people who had elected him as their leader.

If read with an open and a fair mind and read together with the record of the actions I took, these transcripts will show that what I have stated from the beginning to be the truth has been the truth: that I personally had no knowledge of the break-in before it occurred, that I had no knowledge of the coverup until I was informed of it by John Dean on March 21, that I never offered clemency for the defendants, and that after March 21 my actions were directed toward finding the facts and seeing that justice was done, fairly and according to the law.

The facts are there. The conversations are there. The record of actions is there.

To anyone who reads his way through this mass of materials I have provided, it will be totally abundantly clear that as far as the President's role with regard to Watergate is concerned, the entire story is there.

As you will see, now that you also will have this mass of evidence I have provided, I have tried to cooperate with the House Judiciary Committee. And I repeat tonight the offer that I have made previously: to answer written interrogatories under oath and if there are then issues still unresolved to meet personally with the Chairman of the committee and with Congressman Hutchinson to answer their questions under oath.

As the committee conducts its inquiry, I also consider it only essential and fair that my counsel, Mr. St. Clair, should be present to cross-examine witnesses and introduce evidence in an effort to establish the truth.

I am confident that for the overwhelming majority of those who study the evidence that I shall release tomorrow — those who are willing to look at it fully, fairly, and objectively — the evidence will be persuasive and, I hope, conclusive.

We live in a time of very great challenge and great opportunity for America.

We live at a time when peace may become possible in the Middle East for the first time in a generation.

We are at last in the process of fulfilling the hope of mankind for a limitation on nuclear arms — a process that will continue when I meet with the Soviet leaders in Moscow in a few weeks.

We are well on the way toward building a peace that can last, not just for this but for other generations as well.

And here at home, there is vital work to be done in moving to control inflation, to develop our energy resources, to strengthen our economy so that Americans can enjoy what they have not had since 1956: full prosperity without war and without inflation.

Every day absorbed by Watergate is a day lost from the work that

must be done — by your President and by your Congress — work
that must be done in dealing with the great problems that affect
your prosperity, affect your security, that could affect your lives.

The materials I make public tomorrow will provide all the additional evidence needed to get Watergate behind us and to get it
behind us now.

Never before in the history of the Presidency have records that
are so private been made so public.

In giving you these records — blemishes and all — I am placing
my trust in the basic fairness of the American people.

I know in my own heart that through the long, painful, and difficult process revealed in these transcripts, I was trying in that period
to discover what was right and to do what was right.

I hope and I trust that when you have seen the evidence in its en-
tirety, you will see the truth of that statement.

As for myself, I intend to go forward, to the best of my ability
with the work that you elected me to do. I shall do so in a spirit
perhaps best summed up a century ago by another President when
he was being subjected to unmerciful attack. Abraham Lincoln said:

"I do the very best I know how — the very best I can; and I
mean to keep doing so until the end. If the end brings me out all
right, what is said against me won't amount to anything. If the end
brings me out wrong, ten angels swearing I was right would make
no difference."

Thank you and good evening.

Presidential Resignation

LET HE WHO IS WITHOUT SIN CAST THE FIRST STONE

By RICHARD M. NIXON, *President of the United States*

Delivered from the White House, Washington, D. C., August 8, 1974

GOOD EVENING. This is the 37th time I have spoken to you from this office in which so many decisions have been made that shape the history of this nation.

Each time I have done so to discuss with you some matters that I believe affected the national interest. And all the decisions I have made in my public life I have always tried to do what was best for the nation.

Throughout the long and difficult period of Watergate, I have felt it was my duty to persevere; to make every possible effort to complete the term of office to which you elected me.

In the past few days, however, it has become evident to me that I no longer have a strong enough political base in the Congress to justify continuing that effort.

As long as there was such a base, I felt strongly that it was necessary to see the constitutional process through to its conclusion; that to do otherwise would be unfaithful to the spirit of that deliberately difficult process, and a dangerously destabilizing precedent for the future.

But with the disappearance of that base, I now believe that the constitutional purpose has been served. And there is no longer a need for the process to be prolonged.

I would have preferred to carry through to the finish whatever the personal agony it would have involved, and my family unanimously urged me to do so.

But the interests of the nation must always come before any personal considerations. From the discussions I have had with Congressional and other leaders I have concluded that because of the Watergate matter I might not have the support of the Congress that I would consider necessary to back the very difficult decisions and carry out the duties of this office in the way the interests of the nation will require.

I have never been a quitter.

To leave office before my term is completed is opposed to every instinct in my body. But as President I must put the interests of America first.

America needs a full-time President and a full-time Congress, particularly at this time with problems we face at home and abroad.

Source: *Vital Speeches of the Day*, August 15, 1974;
         City News Publishing Company, Southold, New
         York. By permission of the publisher.

To continue to fight through the months ahead for my personal vindication would almost totally absorb the time and attention of both the President and the Congress in a period when our entire focus should be on the great issues of peace abroad and prosperity without inflation at home.

Therefore, I shall resign the Presidency affective at noon tomorrow.

Vice President Ford will be sworn in as President at that hour in this office.

As I recall the high hopes for America with which we began this second term, I feel a great sadness that I will not be here in this office working on your behalf to achieve those hopes in the next two and a half years.

But in turning over direction of the Government to Vice President Ford I know, as I told the nation when I nominated him for that office 10 months ago, that the leadership of America will be in good hands.

In passing this office to the Vice President I also do so with the profound sense of the weight of responsibility that will fall on his shoulders tomorrow, and therefore of the understanding, the patience, the cooperation he will need from all Americans.

As he assumes that responsibility he will deserve the help and the support of all of us. As we look to the future, the first essential is to begin healing the wounds of this nation. To put the bitterness and divisions of the recent past behind us and to rediscover those shared ideals that lie at the heart of our strength and unity as a great and as a free people.

By taking this action, I hope that I will have hastened the start of that process of healing which is so desperately needed in America.

I regret deeply any injuries that may have been done in the course of the events that led to this decision. I would say only that if some of my judgments were wrong — and some were wrong — they were made in what I believed at the time to be the best interests of the nation.

To those who have stood with me during these past difficult months, to my family, my friends, the many others who've joined in supporting my cause because they believed it was right, I will be eternally grateful for your support.

And to those who have not felt able to give me your support, let me say I leave with no bitterness toward those who have opposed me, because all of us in the final analysis have been concerned with the good of the country however our judgments might differ.

So let us all now join together in affirming that common commitment and in helping our new President succeed for the benefit of all Americans.

I shall leave this office with regret at not completing my term but with gratitude for the privilege of serving as your President for the past five and a half years.

These years have been a momentous time in the history of our nation and the world. They have been a time of achievement in which we can all be proud — achievements that represent the shared ef-

forts of the administration, the Congress and the people. But the
challenges ahead are equally great.

And they, too, will require the support and the efforts of a
Congress and the people, working in cooperation with the new Administration.

We have ended America's longest war. But in the work of secur-
ing a lasting peace in the world, the goals ahead are even more far-
reaching and more difficult. We must complete a structure of peace,
so that it will be said of this generation — our generation of
Americans — by the people of all nations, not only that we ended
one war but that we prevented future wars.

We have unlocked the doors that for a quarter of a century stood
between the United States and the People's Republic of China. We
must now insure that the one-quarter of the world's people who live
in the People's Republic of China will be and remain, not our
enemies, but our friends.

In the Middle East, 100 million people in the Arab countries,
many of whom have considered us their enemies for nearly 20 years,
now look on us as their friends. We must continue to build on that
friendship so that peace can settle at last over the Middle East and so
that the cradle of civilization will not become its grave.

Together with the Soviet Union we have made the crucial
breakthroughs that have begun the process of limiting nuclear arms.
But, we must set as our goal, not just limiting, but reducing and
finally destroying these terrible weapons so that they cannot destroy
civilization.

And so that the threat of nuclear war will no longer hang over the
world and the people, we have opened a new relation with the Soviet
Union. We must continue to develop and expand that new
relationship so that the two strongest nations of the world will live
together in cooperation rather than confrontation.

Around the world — in Asia, in Africa, in Latin America, in the
Middle East — there are millions of people who live in terrible
poverty, even starvation. We must keep as our goal turning away
from production for war and expanding production for peace so that
people everywhere on this earth can at last look forward, in their
children's time if not in our time, to having the necessities for a decent life.

Here in America we are fortunate that most of our people have
not only the blessings of liberty but also the means to live full and
good, and by the world's standards even abundant lives.

We must press on, however, toward a goal not only of more and
better jobs but of full opportunity for every man, and of what we are
striving so hard right now to achieve — prosperity without inflation.

For more than a quarter of a century in public life, I have shared
in the turbulent history of this evening.

I have fought for what I believe in. I have tried, to the best of my
ability, to discharge those duties and meet those responsibilities that
were entrusted to me.

Sometimes I have succeeded. And sometimes I have failed. But always I have taken heart from what Theodore Roosevelt said about the man in the arena whose face is marred by dust and sweat and blood, who strives valiantly, who errs and comes short again and again because there is not effort without error and shortcoming, but who does actually strive to do the deed, who knows the great devotion, who spends himself in a worthy cause, who at the best knows in the end the triumphs of high achievements and with the worst if he fails, at least fails while daring greatly.

I pledge to you tonight that as long as I have a breath of life in my body I shall continue in that spirit. I shall continue to work for the great causes to which I have been dedicated throughout my years as a Congressman, a Senator, Vice President and President, the cause of peace — not just for America but among all nations — prosperity, justice and opportunity for all of our people.

There is one cause above all to which I have been devoted and to which I shall always be devoted for as long as I live.

When I first took the oath of office as President five and a half years ago, I made this sacred commitment; to consecrate my office, my energies and all the wisdom I can summon to the cause of peace among nations.

As a result of these efforts, I am confident that the world is a safer place today, not only for the people of America but for the people of all nations, and that all of our children have a better chance than before of living in peace rather than dying in war.

This, more than anything, is what I hoped to achieve when I sought the Presidency. This, more than anything, is what I hope will be my legacy to you, to our country, as I leave the Presidency.

To have served in this office is to have felt a very personal sense of kinship with each and every American. In leaving it, I do so with this prayer: May God's grace be with you in all the days ahead.

BIBLIOGRAPHICAL AIDS

To prepare a reputable bibliography on Richard Nixon at this time is an impossible task. A good biography may not be forthcoming for years in the future, as evidence and revelations continually pour forth. Almost each of the key figures seems to be preparing his version in some form.

Mr. Nixon, himself, has made preparations for his side of the story. He has already (late 1974) acquired the veteran and expert political writer Franklin R. Gannon to help him in his task. But their difficulties are compounded because the President's papers have been denied to him by Congress.

Congress itself has already published accounts of its hearings. The complete "tell-tale" tapes so far have not been released - except in selected items.

Finally, only history will reveal the "success" side of Richard Nixon: detenté with China and Russia, the Cambodian incursion and the whole Vietnam story, a Middle East peace with reasonable costs of oil, an economic picture without inflation, unemployment, and with a responsible welfare program. Furthermore, will Watergate bring a political future which will be held in confidence by the American people? And will recent events bring about significant changes in the "Imperial Presidency"? Surely most books on government will need an almost complete rewriting, especially those dealing with presidential power. Finally, of course, there is Richard Nixon himself - his future, and his "rating" among the presidents.

NIXON'S WRITINGS

It should be noted that to this list should be added the pre-Presidential papers which Nixon donated to the National Archives, and which are not yet available to scholars.

Also, the presidential papers (including tapes) to which access has been sealed by court orders pending litigation and legislation.

Congressional Quarterly. Nixon: The Years of his Presidency. Washington: Congressional Quarterly, 1970. Yearly compilation of his major messages, statements, conferences. At the present time the volumes cover the first five years of Nixon's presidency: 1969-

Nixon, Richard M. Six Crises. New York, 1962. The book he was so proud of and was constantly recommending to his aides for their edification. Deals with the

Hiss case, the Fund, Ike's heart attack, his reception in Caracas, his "kitchen debate" with Khrushchev, and the Kennedy Campaign in 1960.

Presidential Documents: A Weekly Compilation of Presidential Documents. Washington: G.P.O., 1966- .
Published every Monday by the office of the Federal
Register National Archives and Records Service, General Services Administration. Washington, D.C.
20408.
Contains statements, messages and other Presidential
material released by the White House the preceding
week. Also lists appointments and nominations.
Nixon's Administrations are covered in Vols. 5-10.

NIXON: BIOGRAPHIES, CAMPAIGNS,
DOMESTIC POLICIES, FOREIGN POLICIES

Allen, Gary. Richard Nixon: The Man Behind The Mask.
Belmont, Massachusetts: Western Islands, 1971.

Alsop, Stewart. Nixon and Rockefeller: A Double Portrait. Garden City: Doubleday, 1960. Emphasizes
Nixon as a politician.

Brandon, Henry. The Retreat of American Power. Garden
City, New York: Doubleday, 1973. An excellent ac-
count of the foreign policy of President Nixon and
Kissinger in their first four years together.

Burke, Vincent. Nixon's Good Deed. New York: Columbia
University Press, 1974. The complete story of the
Family Assistance Plan, how and why Nixon proposed
it, how and why it failed to be fulfilled. Contains
a chronology of the plan, and a good bibliography.

Chesen, Eli S. President Nixon's Psychiatric Profile; A
Psychodynamic-Genetic Interpretation. New York:
Wyden, 1973. An imagined psychiatric examination,
not very satisfactory without interviewing the subject.

Costello, William. The Facts About Nixon. New York:
Viking, 1960. While not very friendly, a valuable,
almost a tell-tale account of the real Nixon in his
earlier career.

Drury, Allen. Courage and Hesitation: Inside the Nixon
Administration. Garden City, New York: Doubleday,

1972. Essentially a picture book, but with some
interesting comments about the man, his family, and
his staff.

Evans, Rowland, Jr., and Novak, Robert D. Nixon in the
White House: The Frustration of Power. New York:
Random House, 1971. An excellent account of Nixon's
first two years in the presidency.

Ferlinghetti, Lawrence. Tyrannus Nix?. New York: New
Directions, 1969.

Fitzgerald, Frances. Fire in the Lake. Boston: Little,
Brown, 1972. Probably the best account of Vietnam,
for an understanding of its culture and the impact
of the American presence. There are many other good
books on Vietnam. Check a good recent book on American foreign policy.

Gardner, Floyd C. The Great Nixon Turnabout; America's
New Policy in the Post-Liberal Era. (How a cold
warrior climbed clean out of his skin). Essays and
articles. New York: New Viewpoints, 1973.

Gartner, Alan, et al. What Nixon is Doing to Us. New
York: Harper and Row, 1973.

Graubard, Stephen. Kissinger; Portrait of a Mind. New
York: Norton, 1973. The title truly describes the
book. A biography which does credit to Kissinger
remains to be written.

Harris, Mark. Mark the Glove Boy; or, The Last Days of
Richard Nixon. Philadelphia: Curtis, 1972.

Hess, Stephen and Mazo, Earl. Nixon: A Political Portrait. New York, 1968. Harper. A rewriting and
updating of Mazo's 1959 book.

Hiss, Alger. In the Court of Public Opinion. New York,
1957. Hiss presents his view - and the reader can
still remain baffled.

Hoffman, Paul. The New Nixon. New York: Tower, 1970.
A Public Affairs book.

Hoyt, Edwin P. The Nixons: An American Family. New
York: Random, 1972. Almost entirely genealogical
in its scope.

Keogy, James. President Nixon and the Press. New York:
Funk and Wagnalls, 1972. Takes the Nixon side in

the issue of fair presentation by the media.

Kornitzer, Bela. The Real Nixon: An Intimate Biography.
New York, 1960. Too intimate to be of real value.

Landan, David. Kissinger: The Uses of Power. Boston:
Houghton Mifflin, 1972. Neither a good biography
nor a convincing account of Kissinger's foreign
policy.

McGinniss, Joe. The Selling of the President, 1968.
New York: Trident Press, 1969. Interesting account
of the Nixon use of the media, with a (then) rare
portrait of a person who is normal, temperish and
often profane.

Mazlish, Bruce. In Search of Nixon. New York: Basic
Books, 1972. A psychohistorical inquiry, with the
couch too short. Nixon's own Six Crises is a better
analysis.

Mazo, Earl. Richard Nixon: A Political and Personal
Portrait. New York: Harper, 1959. Updated by
Hess and Mazo in 1968.

Morrison, Rodney J. Expectations and Inflation: Nixon,
Politics, and Economics. Lexington, Massachusetts:
D.C. Heath, 1973.

Murphy, Reg. The Southern Strategy. New York: Scrib-
ner, 1971.

Osborne, John. The Nixon Watch. New York: Liverright,
1970. Articles from the New Republic.

_____. The Second Year of the Nixon Watch. New York:
Liverright, 1971.

_____. The Third Year of the Nixon Watch. New York:
Liverright, 1972.

_____. The Fourth Year of the Nixon Watch. New York:
Liverright, 1973.

Ott, David. Nixon, McGovern and the Federal Budget.
Washington: American Enterprise, 1972.

Panetta, Leon E. Bring Us Together; The Nixon Team and
the Civil Rights Retreat. Philadelphia: Lippin-
cott, 1971

Roth, Philip. Our Gang (Starring Tricky and His Friends).

New York, Random, 1971.

Safine, William. Eye on Nixon. New York: Hawthorn, 1972.

Safire, William. Before the Fall: An Inside View of the Pre-Watergate White House. Garden City, New York: Doubleday, 1975.

Silk, Leonard. Nixonomics. New York: Random House, 1972. "How the Dismal Science of Free Enterprise became the Black Art of Controls," related in a witty form.

Spalding, Henry D. The Nixon Nobody Knows. Middle Village, New York: Jonathan David, 1972. Campaign literature trying to show a warm and human man, misunderstood by his critics.

Vidal, Gore. An Evening with Richard Nixon. New York: Random House, 1972. Sometimes amusing, but more usually tasteless.

Voorhis, Horace Jeremiah. The Strange Case of Richard Milhous Nixon. New York: Ericksson, 1972. Nixon's first victim strikes back almost 40 years later.

Whalen, Richard J. Catch the Falling Flag; A Republican's Challenge to His Party. Boston: Houghton Mifflin, 1972. A conservative criticizes Nixon.

White, Theodore H. The Making of the President - 1960. New York, 1961. Superb account of the Kennedy - Nixon campaign.

_____. The Making of the President - 1968. New York, 1969. White, good as usual.

_____. The Making of the President - 1972. New York, 1973. While White is in his usual top form on the campaign itself, he has been handicapped by writing too soon before the Watergate revelations.

Wills, Garry. Nixon Agonistes: The Crisis of the Self-Made Man. New York: Mentor, 1970. Views him critically as "the last liberal." Stimulating, although often tendentious study.

Witcover, Jules. The Resurrection of Richard Nixon. New York: G.P. Putnam, 1970. A fascinating report by a veteran political reporter of the strategy behind the resurgence of a Nixon, defeated for the

governorship of California in 1962 to the successful presidential campaign of 1968.

Woodstone, Arthur. Nixon's Head. New York: St. Martins,
    1972. Even at this early date, the study shows
    Nixon as an unstable neurotic who is a menace to
    himself and the world.

PERIODICALS

    Just a list of the articles written about Richard
Nixon would fill several volumes. The student is advised
to consult Reader's Guide to Periodical Literature and
The Social Sciences and Humanities Index. The New York
Times index would, of course, be invaluable. Vital
Speeches, also indexed, would contribute, besides Nixon's
major addresses, speeches by many of his associates.

WATERGATE
(naturally will need constant updating)

American Civil Liberties Union. Why President Nixon
    Should Be Impeached. Washington: Public Affairs
    Press, 1973. Brief account (53p).

Barrett, Marvin. Moments of Truth. New York: T.T. Cro-
    well, 1975.

Berger, Raoul. Impeachment: The Constitutional Prob-
    lems. Cambridge, Massachusetts: Harvard University
    Press, 1973.

Berstein, Carl and Woodward, Bob. All the President's
    Men. New York: Simon and Schuster, 1974. Fasci-
    nating story by the two Washington Post reporters
    who uncovered the Watergate conspiracy. Reads like
    a "Who Done It" with the reporters resorting to tac-
    tics almost as despicable as the conspirators. And
    who is "Deep Throat" - their chief informant, ap-
    parently in a high position in the White House?

Berstein, Carl, et al. The Presidential Transcripts.
    New York: Delacarte, 1974.

Black, Charles Lund. Impeachment; A Handbook. New Haven,
    Connecticut: Yale University Press, 1974.

Chester, Lewis, et al. Watergate, The Full Inside Story.
    New York: Ballantine Books, 1973. By the London
    Sunday Times Team.

Congressional Quarterly. Impeachment and the U.S. Con-
    gress. Diamond, Robert A., Ed. Washington, 1974.

_____. Watergate: Chronology of a Crisis. Compiled
    by B. Dickinson, Jr. Washington, 1973.

Debrovir, William A., et al. The Offenses of Richard M.
    Nixon: A Guide for the People of the United States
    of America. New York: Quadrangle, 1974.

Ehrlich, Walter. Presidential Impeachment; An American
    Dilemma. St. Charles, Missouri: Forum Press, 1974.

Evans, Les and Myers, Les. Watergate and the Myth of
    American Democracy. New York: Path. Press, 1974.

Jenness, Linda and Pulley, Andrew, eds. Watergate: The
    View from the Left. New York: Path. Press, 1973.

McCrystal, Cal, et al. Watergate. Westminister, Mary-
    land: Ballantine, 1973.

Magruder, Jeb Stuart. An American Life; One Man's Road
    to Watergate. New York: Atheneum, 1974. One of
    the first inside stories by one of the conspirators.
    Interesting in its portrayal of the pecking order
    in the Committee for the Reelection of the President.

Mankiewicz, Frank. Perfectly Clear; Nixon from Whittier
    to Watergate. New York: Quadrangle, 1973. Nothing
    much new on Watergate but sheds some light on Nix-
    on's earlier misdeeds.

_____. U.S. v. Richard M. Nixon. New York: Quadran-
    gle, 1975.

Mosher, Frederick C. Watergate. New York: Basic Books,
    1974.

Myers, Allen, et al. The Watergate Conspiracy: What It
    Reveals About American Capitalistic Society. New
    York: Path. Press, 1973.

Myerson, Michael. Watergate: Crime in the Suites. New
    York: International, 1973.

New York Times. "The End of a Presidency." New York,
    1974.

_____. The Watergate Hearings: Break-in and Cover-up. (Proceedings of the Senate Select Committee on Presidential Campaign Activities). New York: Bantam, 1973.

Nilolaieff, George A., comp. The President and the Constitution. New York: H.W. Wilson, 1974.

Nixon, Richard M. The White House Transcripts. New York: Bantam, 1974. As submitted to the House Judiciary Committee. Contains chronology.

Rather, Dan and Gates, Gary P. The Palace Guard. New Yorker: Harper and Row, 1974. Two top CBS newsmen, with humor, take cracks at the White House Staff - especially Ehrlichman and Haldeman. Interesting reading.

Ripon Society. Jaws of Victory; the Game-Plan Politics of 1972, the Crisis of the Republican Party, and the Future of the Constitution. Boston: Little, Brown, 1974.

Saffell, D. Watergate: Its Effects on the American Political System. Cambridge, Massachusetts: Winthrop, 1974.

Sussman, Barry. The Great Coverup: Nixon and the Scandal. New York: Crowell, 1974.

Szulc, Tad. Compulsive Spy: The Strange Career of E. Howard Hunt. New York: Viking, 1973.

Tretick, Stanley and Shunnon, William V. They Could Not Trust the King. New York: MacMillan, 1974.

United States Congress. House. Impeachment; Selected Materials. From the Committee on the Judiciary. Washington: G.P.O., 1973.

United States Congress. Senate. Select Committee on Presidential Campaign Activities. Final Report. Washington: G.P.O., 1974.

Washington Post Staff. The Fall of a President. New York, 1974.

White, Theodore H. Breach of Faith: The Fall of Richard Nixon. New York: Atheneum, 1975. Especially interesting because it was written particularly for Reader's Digest, whose editors had always been stalwart Nixon supporters. But the title shows White's position.

Winter, Ralph K., Jr. Watergate and the Law: Political Campaigns and Presidential Power. Washington: American Enterprise, 1974.

Wise, David. The Politics of Lying: Government Deception, Secrecy, and Power. New York: Random, 1973. Mostly about the Nixon administration, but includes examples of previous presidents.

Wise, Helen D. What Do We Tell Our Children? Watergate and the Future of Our Country. New York: Braziller, 1974.

Woodstone, Arthur. Nixon's Head. New York: St. Martin, 1973.

NAME INDEX

Abrams, Creighton, 55
Acheson, Dean, 4
Adams, Earl, 9
Agnew, Spiro T., 14, 15, 16,
   17, 24, 26, 27, 28, 29,
   30, 32, 39, 46, 47, 49,
   57, 61, 68, 69
Albert, Carl, 43, 69
Aldrin, Edwin, Jr., 23
Allen, James E., Jr., 36,
   39
Allende, Salvador (Gossens),
   79
Al-Sadat, Anwar, 40
Anderson, Jack, 52
Anne, Princess (G.B.), 37
Armstrong, Neil, 23
Ash, Roy L., 59

Barber, Anthony, 50
Barker, Bernard, 77
Berrigan, The Rev. Philip F.,
   43
Black, Hugo L., 48
Black, Shirley Temple, 47
Blackmun, Harry A., 34, 35
Blount, Winton M., 15, 43
Boggs, Hale, 44, 53, 57
Boldt, George H., 49
Bork, Robert, 70
Brandt, Willy, 46, 51, 65
Brennan, Peter J., 59
Brezhnev, Leonid, 54, 66, 77
Brinegar, Claude S., 59
Brown, Edmund G. (Pat), 10
Bruce, David K. E., 37, 47,
   62
Buchanan, Patrick J., 12, 80
Buckley, James L., 41, 74
Burch, Dean, 81
Burger, Warren E., 20, 21,
   22, 79
Burns, Arthur F., 26, 31
Bush, George, 42
Butterfield, Alexander, 67
Butz, Earl L., 49, 57, 59
Buzhardt, Fred, 80
Byrd, Harry F., 9
Byrne, W. Matt, 65

Caldera, Rafael, 21
Calley, William L., Jr., 44

Carswell, G. Harrold, 30,
   33
Chafee, John H., 20
Chambers, Whittaker, 3, 4
Chapin, Dwight L., 16, 75
Charles, Prince (G.B.), 37
Chotiner, Murray, 2, 10, 30
Chou En-Lai, 47, 52, 53
Clifford, Clark, 22
Colby, William E., 79
Collins, Michael, 23
Colson, Charles, 27, 47,
   55, 60, 74, 77
Connally, John B., 42, 49
   78
Cook, G. Bradford, 62
Cox, Archibald, 65, 69, 70
Cox, Edward Finch, 46
Cox, Patricia "Trish"
   (Nixon), daughter, 2, 46

Dash, Samuel, 81
Davis, Benjamin O., Jr., 39
Dayan, Moshe, 16
Dean, John W., III, 17, 37,
   55, 57, 62, 63, 64, 65,
   66, 78
Dent, Frederick B., 59
Dewey, Thomas E., 5
Dirksen, Everett M., 25
Dole, Robert J., 43
Douglas, Helen Gahagan, 4
Douglas, William O., 34, 42
Drinan, The Rev. Robert F.,
   68

Eagleton, Thomas, 56
Ehrlichman, John D., 10, 14,
   16, 17, 18, 27, 36, 47,
   55, 64, 65, 66, 69, 74,
   77, 78
Eisenhower, David, 13, 16
Eisenhower, Dwight D., 4,
   5, 6, 7, 8, 9, 10, 12,
   14, 16, 18
Eisenhower, John, 17
Eisenhower, Julie (Nixon),
   daughter, 3, 13, 16
Eisler, Gerhart, 3
Ellsberg, Daniel, 47, 51,
   65
Ellsworth, Robert, 12

Ervin, Sam J., Jr., 61

Fielding, Dr. Lewis, 47, 48
Finch, Robert H., 10, 16, 22,
  30, 36
Fitzhugh, Gilbert W., 38
Ford, Gerald R., 34, 53, 69,
  72, 76, 78, 79, 80, 81
Fortas, Abe, 15, 20, 24, 30
Furness, Betty, 19

Gates, Thomas, 32
Genovese, Eugene D., 12
Gesell, Gerhard A., 71
Goldwater, Barry M., 11, 12,
  78
Goodell, Charles E., 25, 39,
  41
Gore, Albert A., 41
Graham, The Rev. Billy, 30
Gray, L. Patrick, III, 54,
  61, 63
Grayson, C. Jackson, 49
Griffin, Robert P., 25
Gromyko, Andrei, 40

Haig, Alexander M., Jr., 20,
  65
Haldeman, H. R. (Bob), 10,
  14, 16, 27, 30, 37, 55,
  62, 64, 65, 66, 71, 74,
  78
Hardin, Clifford M., 16, 49
Harlan, John M., 48
Harriman, W. Averell, 16
Hatfield, Mark, 39
Haynsworth, Clement F., Jr.,
  24, 26, 28
Heath, Edward, 50
Helms, Richard M., 61
Hershey, Lewis B., 26, 32
Herter, Christian, 3, 6
Hickel, Walter J., 15, 17,
  34, 42
Hillings, Patrick J., 10
Hirohito, Emperor, 48, 54
  68
Hiss, Alger, 3, 4, 10
Ho Chi Minh, 24
Hodgson, James D., 36, 59
Hoover, J. Edgar, 20, 38, 44,
  53, 54, 66

Humphrey, Hubert H., 11,
  14, 15, 53, 54
Hunt, Dorothy, 59
Hunt, E. Howard, 46, 47,
  48, 54, 57, 59, 60, 64,
  65, 71
Hussein, King, 19
Huston, Tom Charles, 37

Irwin, John N., 18
Ismail, Hafez, 62

Jaffe, Jerome H., 46
Jaworski, Leon, 70, 75, 76,
  80
Johnson, Lyndon B., 8, 9,
  11, 12, 13, 15, 38, 61,
  66

Kalmbach, Herbert W., 55,
  56, 77
Kelley, Clarence M., 66
Kennedy, David M., 15, 42
Kennedy, Edward M., 23
Kennedy, John F., 8, 9, 11,
  66
Kennedy, Robert F., 13, 14,
  19
Khrushchev, Nikita, 8
Kiesinger, Kurt Georg, 24
King, The Rev. Martin Luther,
  Jr., 13
Kissinger, Henry A., 16, 17,
  20, 22, 43, 47, 49, 53,
  54, 56, 57, 58, 59, 60,
  61, 62, 69, 70, 71, 74,
  76, 78, 79
Klein, Herbert G., 10, 14,
  16, 66
Kleindienst, Richard G., 17,
  52, 53, 59, 64, 65, 76
Knauer, Virginia Harrington
  Wright, 19
Knowland, William, 2
Knowles, John H., 22
Kopechne, Mary Jo, 23
Korff, Rabbi Baruch, 76
Koster, Samuel W., 32
Kosygin, Aleksei N., 31
Krogh, Egil, Jr., 17, 47,
  65, 69
Ky, Nguyen Kao, 45

Laird, Melvin R., 15, 18,
   24, 31, 32, 59, 66
Le May, Curtis E., 15
Liddy, G. Gordon, 47, 48,
   54, 55, 57, 60, 63, 65,
   69, 77
Lockhart, William B., 38
Lodge, Henry Cabot, 9, 16,
   28
Lon Nol, 33, 34, 73
Love, John A., 67, 72
Lynn, James T., 59

MacArthur, Douglas, 4
MacGregor, Clark, 56, 58
Magruder, Jeb Stuart, 64, 76
Mansfield, Mike, 43, 53
Manson, Charles, 38
Mao Tse-Tung, 52
Marcantonio, Vito, 4
Mardian, Robert, 74
Marland, Sidney P., Jr., 39
Martin, William McChesney,
   Jr., 26, 31
Martinez, Eugenio R., 77
McCarthy, Eugene J., 13
McCarthy, Joseph, 4, 6
McCloskey, Paul Norton, Jr.,
   47
McCord, James W., Jr., 49,
   54, 60, 63
McGovern, George, 35, 43, 52,
   53, 54, 55, 56, 58,
McIntire, The Rev. Carl, 45
McLaughlin, The Rev. John,
   81
Meany, George, 53
Meir, Golda, 39
Miller, William E., 11
Mitchell, John N., 12, 15,
   52, 55, 56, 65, 66, 67,
   74, 75
Mitchell, Martha, 55
Moorer, Thomas H., 34
Morgan, Edward L., 17, 18, 81
Morton, Rogers, 42, 43, 59
Moynihan, Daniel P., 27, 42
Mundt, Karl, 3
Muskie, Edmund S., 14, 51,
   52, 53

Nagako, Empress, 48

Nixon, Don, brother, 10
Nixon, Frank, father, 1
Nixon, Hannah, (Milhous),
   mother, 1
Nixon, Thelma Catherine "Pat"
   (Ryan), wife, 1, 7, 51, 52

Ordaz, Dias, 39
Oswald, Lee Harvey, 11

Pahlavi, Shah Mohammad, 67
Parkinson, Kenneth W., 74
Patman, Wright, 24
Petersen, Henry E., 65, 80
Peterson, Peter G., 51, 59,
   64
Podgorny, Nikolai, 28
Pompidou, Georges, 32, 50,
   66
Pompidou, Mme., 32
Porter, Herbert L., 73
Porter, William J., 47
Powell, Lewis F., Jr., 49,
   50
Proxmire, William, 11

Reagan, Ronald, 13, 14
Rebozo, Charles G. (Bebe),
   13, 24
Rehnquist, William H., 49,
   50
Rhodes, John, 78
Richardson, Elliot L., 35,
   59, 65, 66, 70
Richey, Charles R., 80
Rockefeller, Nelson A., 8,
   13, 14, 20, 21, 22, 25,
   27, 72, 79, 81
Rodino, Peter W., Jr., 75,
   76
Rogers, William P., 15, 17,
   20, 31, 35, 36, 46, 61,
   69
Romney, George, 12, 13, 16,
   59
Roosevelt, Franklin D., 3
Ruckelshaus, William, 64, 70
Ruth, Henry S., Jr., 80

Sadat, Anwar, 71
Sargent, Francis W., 33
Sato, Eisaku, 28, 40, 51

Saxbe, William B., 70, 72
Schiller, Karl, 50
Schlesinger, James R., 61, 67
Scott, Hugh, 25, 53, 62, 75, 78
Scranton, William, 36
Segretti, Donald H., 48, 70, 75
Shell, Joseph, 10
Shriver, Sargent, 56
Shultz, George P., 16, 25, 36, 59, 61, 75
Sihanouk, Norodom, 33
Simon, William E., 72, 74, 75
Sirhan, Sirhan B., 14, 19
Sirica, John J., 60, 63, 69, 70, 71, 73, 74, 76, 80, 81
Sloan, Hugh W., Jr., 16
Smith, Howard K., 10, 43
Sparkman, John J., 5, 7
Spater, George A., 67
Stans, Maurice H., 16, 51, 55, 65, 71, 75
St. Clair, James D., 75, 78
Stassen, Harold E., 5, 6
Stennis, John, 70
Stevenson, Adlai E., 5, 7
Sturgis, Frank, 54
Suharto, President, 35

Taft, Robert A., 4
Tanaka, Kaknei, 57, 68
Tarr, Curtis W., 32
Tate, Sharon, 38
Taylor, Zachary, 16

Thieu, Nguyen Van, 21, 25, 30, 58, 63
Tho, Le Duc, 56, 59, 60, 61, 70
Thurmond, Strom, 14
Thuy, Xuan, 27
Tito, Marshal, 49
Trinh, Nguyen Duy, 61
Trudeau, Pierre, 53
Truman, Harry S., 3, 4
Tydings, Joseph D., 41

Ulasewicz, Anthony T., 55

Vesco, Robert L., 53, 65
Volpe, John A., 16, 59
Voorhis, Jerry, 2

Waldheim, Kurt, 56
Wallace, George C., 15, 52, 54
Warren, Earl, 4, 6, 15, 16, 20, 22, 77
Weinberger, Caspar W., 36, 59
Weyand, Frederick C., 55
Wheeler, Earle G., 34, 67
Whitlam, (Edward) Gough, 67
Wilson, Harold, 31
Woods, Rose Mary, 10, 71

Yost, Charles W., 42
Young, David, 47, 69

Zetterberg, Stephen, 4
Ziegler, Ronald L., 10, 14, 64, 66